Dramatherapy a

Dramatherapy and Social Theatre: Necessary Dialogues considers the nature of drama, theatre and dramatherapy, examining how dramatherapy has evolved over the past decade and how the relationship between dramatherapy and social theatre has developed as a result of this.

In this book Sue Jennings brings together international dramatherapists and theatre practitioners to challenge, clarify, describe and debate some of the theoretical and practical issues in dramatherapy and social theatre. Contributors cover topics including:

- dramatherapy in communities;
- ground rules and definitions;
- cross-cultural perspectives;
- dramatherapy with adoptive and foster families;
- research with professional actors.

Dramatherapy and Social Theatre is illustrated throughout with case vignettes providing examples of how theatre and therapeutic processes can be brought together. It will be valuable reading for both professionals and students involved in dramatherapy and theatre studies.

Sue Jennings is a Dramatherapist, Play Therapist, Performer and Story-teller in the UK, Malaysia, Romania and Kazakhstan. Her life-long work has been pioneering dramatherapy training and practice. Sue is an Honorary Fellow of Roehampton University, London and Visiting Professor at Tel Hai College, Israel. Sue has published many books on dramatherapy.

Dramatherapy and Social Theatre

Necessary dialogues

Edited by Sue Jennings

Routledge
Taylor & Francis Group

LONDON AND NEW YORK

First published 2009 by Routledge
27 Church Road, Hove, East Sussex BN3 2FA

Simultaneously published in the USA and Canada
by Routledge
270 Madison Avenue, New York, NY 10016

*Routledge is an imprint of the Taylor & Francis Group, an Informa
business*

Typeset in Times by Garfield Morgan, Swansea, West Glamorgan
Printed and bound in Great Britain by TJ International Ltd, Padstow,
Cornwall
Paperback cover design by Andy Ward

This publication has been produced with paper manufactured to strict
environmental standards and with pulp derived from sustainable
forests.

British Library Cataloguing in Publication Data
A catalogue record for this book is available from the British Library

Library of Congress Cataloging-in-Publication Data
Jennings, Sue, 1938–
    Dramatherapy and social theatre : necessary dialogues / edited by
Sue Jennings.
        p. cm.
    Includes bibliographical references and index.
    ISBN 978-0-415-42206-2 (hardback) – ISBN 978-0-415-42207-9
(pbk.) 1. Drama–Therapeutic use. 2. Theater and society. I. Title.
    RC489.P7J448 2009
    616.89'1523–dc22

                                                                2008050368

ISBN: 978-0-415-42206-2 (hbk)
ISBN: 978-0-415-42207-9 (pbk)

Contents

List of contributors

Sandy Akerman is the co-founder and Artistic Director of Headbangers Theatre Company. She lectures in Applied Drama at Exeter University and was an honorary research fellow on the RAP project and is drama consultant on the Healthy Lifestyles project facilitated by Peninsula Medical School, Exeter. She specialises in interactive issue-based theatre work for young people and has been a practitioner and lecturer since 1992.
headbangers@btinternet.com

Marina Barham is a Palestinian woman, who has been working in the field of theatre since 1996. Barham has an MA degree from Warwick University, UK, a BA degree from Bethlehem University, Palestine. Barham is a co-founder of two theatre companies in the south of Palestine; Inad Theater and Al-Harah Theater. She has been actively working in the field of development and theatre for over 18 years. Ms Barham believes that theatre is a powerful tool of resistance and empowerment.
alharahtheater@yahoo.com

Claudio Bernardi is Professor of Drama at the Catholic University of Milan, and he is one of the most important scholars of social theatre. He wrote *Il teatro sociale. L'arte tra disagio e cura*, Carocci, Roma, 2004, and has edited together with Guglielmo Schininà and Monica Dragone, *War Theatres and Action for Peace. Community-based Dramaturgy and the Conflict Scene*, Euresis, Milano, 2002.
claudio.bernardi@unicatt.it

Terrence Wendell Brathwaite works in the NHS as a cross-cultural dance movement therapist, using integrative and eclectic dance/movements within the psychotherapeutic relationship, to facilitate health and healing in mentally, physically and emotionally challenged outpatients. Since migrating from Trinidad in 1991, he has pioneered cross-cultural dance movement therapy in the UK, and more recently in Kazakhstan as an international consultant to the British Council. He is third generation Laban, having been a student (1970–79) of Professor Alexander

MacDougall (formerly of the Joos Ballet Company) who was trained by Rudolf von Laban himself. A former choreographer and principal concert dancer with the world-renowned Trinidad Ballet Company, whose tour sponsors included Messrs Sol Hurok (America's biggest and most prestigious concert agents), Terry performed on stage and television internationally for 10 years, retiring in 1980 after the company's 'crowning glory' presentation at the United Nations Headquarters General Assembly Hall in New York, USA. Over the past 14 years he has served as Head of the Dance Movement Therapy Department and Research Committee at the Birmingham Centre for Arts Therapies (BCAT), while maintaining a tenured senior lectureship (Global Commercial & Industrial Law) status at Coventry University, UK.
T7122@aol.com

John Casson has been a dramatherapist for 23 years and a psychodrama psychotherapist for 16. His groundbreaking research with people who hear voices is recounted in his book: *Drama, Psychotherapy and Psychosis: Dramatherapy and Psychodrama with People Who Hear Voices* (Routledge, 2004). He is a puppeteer and playwright: his play *Voices and Visions* based on his research was given its premier performances (directed by Helen Parry) in Manchester in 2006. He is in private practice as a therapist and supervisor and is a senior trainer in the Northern School of Psychodrama. He is the inventor of the Communicube (see www.communicube.co.uk). For further information see www.creativepsychotherapy.info
drjohncasson@googlemail.com

Aanand Chabukswar has been working with a range of groups within India for a decade doing social theatre and dramatherapy. He works with the WCCL Foundation – an NGO pioneering the action research and training of ABT (arts-based therapy) in India. He has made culture-specific applications of ABT, and has written and taught in workshops across India, Europe and SE Asia. He also teaches applied theatre at the University of Pune.
aanandc@vsnl.net

David Evans, founder and Artistic Director of IMULE Theatre-for-development, was formerly Honorary Research Fellow at the Department of Child Health, Peninsula Medical School, Universities of Exeter and Plymouth. He has convened the Practices and Perspectives module of the Applied Drama course at the University of Exeter Drama Department. Over the last 15 years he has worked experimentally with cross-cultural theatre, and applications of theatre in educational and health contexts. He is currently development and training manager of the Health Behaviour Group charity.
David.L.Evans@exeter.ac.uk

Roger Grainger is a dramatherapist and psychotherapist who also works as an actor and Anglican priest. He has written widely in all these areas, and his books about rites of passage, liturgy and drama gained him a Doctorate of Divinity from London University. More recently, he produced a synthesis of dramatherapy research for a doctorate at Leeds Metropolitan University.

Rev. Dr Roger Grainger, 7 Park Grove, Horbury, Wakefield, Yorks, WE4 6EE

Andy Hickson is Director of Actionwork. He is a theatre director, and has had shows performed at the Globe, Sadlers Wells, Norwich Playhouse and many venues abroad. Andy specialises in using creative action methods to explore violence and other issues. Andy is also a film-maker and was a runner-up in the 2008 Motorola film competition. Writing credits include *Creative Action Methods in Groupwork*, which has been translated into Polish and Japanese, and *The Groupwork Manual* (both published by Speechmark), as well as numerous articles and chapters. More details of Andy's work can be found at www.actionwork.com.

Sue Jennings is an international pioneer of dramatherapy and play therapy. She has published over 20 books that provide practical working models of dramatic action in clinical, community and educational practice. She has also developed her own theories of dramatic development and the concept of 'dramatic intelligence' and Neuro-Dramatic-Play. She lives and works in Romania with her partner Peter, where she trains teachers and clinicians in social theatre and therapeutic play. Her work takes her to Kazakhstan and Malaysia where she is developing new ideas for working creatively with children and adults with autism. She believes her work rests on a continuum between social theatre and dramatherapy.

drsuejennings@hotmail.com

Tom Magill is a former alcoholic ex-prisoner who transformed his life through drama and now works with homeless people, prisoners and ex-prisoners passing on his experiences. He has taught theatre studies at the Department of Media and Performing Arts, University of Ulster, and at Trinity College Dublin. He has also been a visiting lecturer at the University of Ibadan in Nigeria, the University of Duisburg in Germany, and New York University in the USA. Tom established the Educational Shakespeare Company in Belfast in 1999, where he has directed many films and documentaries with marginalised groups, including two short films that won Arthur Koestler prizes. He serves as Augusto Boal's representative in Northern Ireland and recently directed *MICKEY B*, a feature film adaptation of *Macbeth*, with long-term prisoners from HMP Maghaberry maximum-security prison.

tom_magill@yahoo.com

Jennifer Marquis-Muradaz has a master's degree in Motion Picture Producing from the University of Southern California and an undergraduate theatre degree from New York University, where she studied with Jan Cohen-Cruz, Mady Schutzman and Augusto Boal. Between 2005 and 2007 she produced seven films with offenders and ex-offenders, including a feature adaptation of *Macbeth* with serving prisoners inside Northern Ireland's Maghaberry Prison. Prior to this she co-founded the Cynosure Screenwriting Awards in Los Angeles, a screenplay awards programme for film scripts with female and minority protagonists. She also worked for Rattler Productions in New York, touring plays with interracial casts and themes around the USA. Jennifer has taught film at Mercy College and published several works on the intersection of religion, film and parenting.

Joan Moore is a freelance Health Professions Council registered dramatherapist, trained play therapist and adoption support provider (Ofsted registered) working with families in adoption and foster care, including expert witness assessments in legal proceedings. Joan specialises in therapeutic life story work, engaging parents and children in performance of the child's life story, working both in and out of metaphor and providing substitute parents with training and information on attachment related issues. Having trained in teaching, community and youth work, and social work, Joan previously worked in the fields of juvenile justice, child protection and permanence planning, has run therapeutic groups for parents with complex needs at an early intervention centre and delivers training for local authorities and related agencies. joanmoore@ntlworld.com

Kyoko Okumoto is a teacher in a mainstream Japanese school. Her work is strongly influenced by Dr Johan Galtung, Director of TRANSCEND. Her work currently is in social theatre and the peace process. okumoto@wilmina.ac.jp

Salvo Pitruzzella is a dramatherapist, psychodramatist and creative drama teacher from Palermo, Italy. He works as a dramatherapist with adolescents and adults in psychiatric units. Since 1998, he has been Director of the Dramatherapy course at the Arts Therapies Training Centre, Lecco, Italy (www.artiterapie.it). Author of *Introduction to Dramatherapy: Person and Threshold*, published in 2004 by Brunner-Routledge, he edited the first unabridged Italian translation of William Blake's poem *Vala, or The Four Zoas*, published in 2007, for the 250th anniversary of Blake's birth. He is currently engaged in writing a book on creativity in the arts therapies, in which a new model of the creative process, based on Blake's 'Fourfold Vision', is expounded. salvopitruzzella@fastnet.it

Lilia Raileanu works in the Republic of Moldova as a psychologist and social theatre practitioner. Active in the field of human rights and community development, she has worked with various vulnerable groups such as children and women at risk, unemployed people, refugees, survivors of human trafficking, LGBT (lesbian, gay, bisexual, transgender) people, and so on. For the first time in Moldova, she developed a forum and legislative theatre on homosexuality and discrimination issues and co-wrote a practical guide on participatory drama.
liliarai2002@yahoo.com

Guglielmo Schininà is a social theatre operator and trainer who specialises in working in war-torn situations, migration crisis, and cultural integration. He has worked with many different groups, including war victims, refugees, victims of trafficking, vulnerable migrants, Roma, people living in camps and collective centres, psychiatric clients, LGBT people, social workers, psychologists, actors. He is currently Psychosocial Program Manager for the Middle East for IOM (International Organization for Migration), president of the NGO Nemoprofeta, social and cultural integrations, and teaches on relevant Masters courses at the S. Anna University in Pisa, and at the University of Torino.
postpessimist@hotmail.com

Mady Schutzman is a writer, scholar, and theatre artist. For over 25 years, she has worked as a freelance practitioner and scholar of Augusto Boal's Theatre of the Oppressed (TO). She worked with Boal extensively in both Brazil and the USA and has conducted TO workshops throughout the US and Canada with a wide variety of people, most recently employees of a Homeland Security Training Center. She is co-editor with Jan Cohen-Cruz of two collections of essays about his work: *Playing Boal: Theatre, Therapy, Activism* (1994) and *A Boal Companion: Dialogues on Theatre and Cultural Politics* (2006). Schutzman is also author of *The Real Thing: Performance, Hysteria, and Advertising* (Wesleyan University Press, 1999) and has published essays in several journals including *The Drama Review*, *Women and Performance*, *Theatre Topics*, and *The Journal of Medical Humanities*. She teaches in the MFA Writing Program and the School of Critical Studies at California Institute of the Arts.
mschutzm@calarts.edu

Anna Seymour is a state-registered dramatherapist, supervisor, trainer, and academic. She has worked in the UK and internationally with individuals and groups of all ages. As a professional actor and director she was involved with more than 30 shows specialising in radical theatre for particular communities. She is visiting lecturer in Drama at the University of Sheffield and co-director of the training organisation, the Northern Trust for Dramatherapy. She was editor of the *British Association*

of Dramatherapists' journal for five years and has published numerous articles on theatre and therapy, most recently contributing to the second edition of Phil Jones' *Drama as Therapy, Theatre as Living*, Routledge, 2007.
anna.seymour@tiscali.co.uk

John Somers is an honorary fellow in the Department of Drama, Exeter University, UK. He is Founding Editor of the journal *Research in Drama Education* and Founding Director of the international conference, *Researching Drama and Theatre in Education*. He founded the Exeter MA in Applied Drama. He is Artistic Director of *Exstream Theatre Company*, which specialises in interactive theatre in non-theatre sites. He originates and directs original community plays, most recently *Foresight*, which involved over 200 community participants. His play *On the Edge* won prestigious awards for its contribution to a better understanding of mental health issues. He works extensively internationally, most recently in Finland, Estonia, Taiwan, Turkey, Poland and China. He won the *American Alliance of Theatre and Education* Special Recognition Award in 2003. Books include *Drama in the Curriculum* (1995), *Drama and Theatre in Education: Current Research* (1996) and *Drama as Social Intervention* (2006). He has published many articles.
J.W.Somers@exeter.co.uk

James Thompson is Professor of Applied and Social Theatre at the University of Manchester and a director of the Centre for Applied Theatre Research. He is currently the co-director of *In Place of War* – a major research project funded by the UK's Arts and Humanities Research Council. He was Guest Editor of the 2004 *TDR: The Journal of Performance Studies Social Theatre* edition (T183) and is author of *Applied Theatre: Bewilderment and Beyond* (Peter Lang, 2003) and *Digging Up Stories: Applied Theatre, Performance and War* (Manchester University Press, 2005). He has research interests in applied theatre, community-based performance and theatre in war zones (particularly the Democratic Republic of Congo, Rwanda and Sri Lanka) and has worked as a practitioner in Brazil, Burkina Faso, Sri Lanka, the UK and the USA.
James.Thompson@manchester.ac.uk

Dr John H. Tripp is a recently retired paediatrician. He is a senior lecturer at the Department of Child Health, Peninsula Medical School Universities of Exeter and Plymouth and Director of the RAP (respect and protect) project. With an international reputation as a researcher in behaviourally effective interventions for adolescent sexual health, John is the founder and chief executive of the Health Behaviour Group charity.
J.H.Tripp@exeter.ac.uk

Elektra Tselikas is a sociologist and dramatherapist living between Austria and Greece. After a varied and rich international career in teaching, research, therapeutic and theatrical practice, she has recently retired to enjoy the beautiful colours of the Mediterranean. She now redirects her attention towards the power of colour and light, focusing on the importance of colour as a vital ingredient of our life. Elektra Tselikas is the author of *Supervision and Dramatherapy* (Jessica Kingsley Publishers) and of several articles and books in English, German and Greek. Elektra.tselikas@gmail.com

Lucilia Valente, PhD, CPsychol, is an associate professor in the Theatre Department of the University of Évora and President of the Portuguese Association of Integrative Dramatherapy. She obtained her first degree in Education through Art at the Conservatoire of Lisbon. Between 1986 and 1991 she was a full-time student at the University of Wales, in the UK, researching Dramatherapy theory and practice. From 1992 to 1996 she was Head of the Creative Arts Department at the University of Minho, where in 1993 she created a postgraduate programme on Integrated Arts for school teachers, which she directed until 1996. In 1994 she founded, and was the first President of, the Portuguese Movement of Artistic Intervention and Education through Art. In 1996 she moved to the University of Évora and was the first director of the Theatre Studies course. Currently she is the director of a training programme, Drama in Education. She is responsible for the research project Arts and Community at CIEP (Research Centre of Education and Psychology).

Alenka Vidrih studied at the Actor's Studio in Paris and the National Academy of Arts in Llubliana, winning the Sever's national award for best actor. After working for five years at the National Theatre, she left to develop her own work in social and community theatre, with an increasing application in clinical areas. Her work integrates educational and social theatre approaches to practice, and she now works with unemployed people, managers in business, teachers and artists, as well as lecturing on the postgraduate course in Art Therapy at the University of Llubliana.
zavod-alenkavidrih@siol.com

Introduction

I first became interested in the subject of this book after the 2002 conference, 'War Theatres and Actions for Peace. Community-Based Dramaturgy and the Conflict's Scene' in Milan. There were many presenters there who were working in war-torn or conflict settings from many parts of the world. I was the only dramatherapist and the only person who made use of practical work to illustrate pertinent points.

I was not used to it being 'all talk', although it was held at a university, and the more applied side was brought in through films and visual presentations. It seemed to me a contradiction that we were talking about a very practical subject, and that we believed in the essential nature of theatre as a medium of resolution and change, yet we were not prepared to participate and look at our own outcomes!

There was a lot of lively debate outside the conference itself, and we talked long into the night. One session took place in an old socialist commune where we ended up by accident, when searching for a pub with a garden! Leaders in the field including myself, Richard Schechner, Guglielmo Schninà and James Thompson debated the whole subject of 'Social Theatre'. Schechner proposed that it should become a term that encompassed all uses of theatre that were not commercial theatre, and that it should include dramatherapy and psychodrama.

I am not too sure whether 'umbrellas' are necessarily helpful at this stage. Social and applied theatre practitioners, although they share with dramatherapists the fact that they work with people and communities with special needs, nevertheless differ in their practice in many aspects. These topics are discussed more fully in the chapters by Anna Seymour (Chapter 2) and Guglielmo Schninà (Chapter 3). Dramatherapists have to abide by a strict code of ethics, and it is mandatory in their work that they have regular supervision of their practice.

My doubts are also concerning the place of 'theatre art' in relation to social theatre. I am known for my belief in the theatre art being at the core of the dramatherapeutic process, (see also Chapter 7 by John Casson). My understanding of social and applied theatre is that it works directly with the community, the issues and the conflicts, and that theatre is devised around these specific situations. However, I need to take a greater distance through the healing power of metaphor and symbol, through myth and legend within which people can find their own story within the greater story.

The debate continued on that night in Milan and it was proposed that there should be a special edition of the *Drama Review* on this very topic. Sadly, in the end there was no therapy contribution in that edition (2004: 48). Nevertheless there are some important debates that readers interested in the topic can pursue.

Of course it often comes back to a question of definition, and many chapters attempt to deal with 'What is social theatre?' Just as theatre itself eludes finite description, maybe the same is for social theatre. We have many terms in this book: applied theatre, social theatre, theatre of empowerment, theatre for peace studies, theatre in education. Perhaps the definitive debate will continue to rumble on!

New topics have been raised through this book, such as 'post-traumatic stress disorder' (see Chapter 3 by Schininà and Chapter 4 by Thompson). It is too generalized a term to be useful, and it is often misused as a diagnosis. Too many assumptions are made on the nature of trauma.

Several writers discuss the subject of 'performance theory' in relation to social theatre and dramatherapy. Is performance theatre? Is theatre performance? How do we define the performance of roles in everyday life? This discussion continues.

The most important theme of this book is that dramatherapists and theatre practitioners of many kinds have come together to challenge, clarify, describe and debate some of the issues of theory and practice. I have tried to reflect as much contrast as possible in my choice of contributors and as wide a geographical spread among people willing to contribute. I was disappointed that Professor Mooli Lahad and Nira Kaplansky were unable to write up their very recent research in time, and that two US contributors just disappeared! Everyone else's presence is here in 22 chapters of rich experience from the USA, the UK, Moldova, Japan, Sicily, Italy, Slovenia, India and Palestine. The gender balance is roughly half and half, and the age balance runs from 30 years to 70 years.

I thought long and hard about the division into sections, and at one time wondered whether to put everyone's chapter in alphabetical order! However in Part I I have grouped the five people who are debating ground rules and definitions of dramatherapy and social theatre. Tselikas (Chapter 1) goes beyond the current debate and proposes a consideration of 'brain mappings' in order to more fully understand the processes of theatre from the point of view of neuroscience. In Part II there is a wide variation in relation to performance and texts, and Part III focuses more on cross-cultural perspectives in relation to political influences and change. Part IV is a group of experienced practitioners in dramatherapy, and social and applied theatre demonstrating their practice and research.

Finally I chose to use two specific pieces as prologue and epilogue. My own journey through theatre art performances acts as an overall introduction at the level of practical and personal experience. Because it integrates many aspects of the debate to follow, it seemed right to place it as the starting point. For the epilogue I chose Roger Grainger's chapter on his research with professional actors. It feels appropriate to allow the journey to come back to theatre again.

I regret any hurt caused to people who are not represented this time. I hope you will find the journey as challenging and as fruitful as I have found it.

Sue Jennings
Transylvania and Somerset
April 2008

Prologue

'Escape unto myself: Personal experience and public performance'

Sue Jennings

Introduction

It is a popular truism that 'theatre is a form of escape', an escape from the rigours or stresses of everyday life or studies or work. Is it an escape from something or to something?

The late Bernard Miles (Miles and Trewin 1981), having listed all the actors and performers that he considered great, went on to say:

> all doctors, nurses and psychiatrists in their own humble or arrogant ways, transporting us into worlds beyond our everyday selves, either by escape from reality (and what harm is there in that?) or by escape into a deeper reality; either helping us to forget, or if we can bear it, to remember.

In this chapter I address the theme of the transformation of personal experience into performance art. I illustrate this process with examples from my own life as a dramatherapist and performer. However I take a different stance from the one that is usually followed in autobiographical theatre, playback theatre and similar approaches. Many of the dramatherapy training courses have a final module where the students create a perform-ance either based on their own life experience or on their journey through the course. Simply it follows a three-stage process: 'express the personal – create the distance – transform into theatre art'.

However I believe there are other processes at work. I have always maintained that there are intuitive connections with roles and texts for individuals and groups, and that these connections make an impact on people's own lives. It is not a conscious working out of experiences, rather it is a surprise encounter that enables insight and understanding at a deeper level of the self. This gives the possibility of movement and change.

Just as small children choose food and nurture that is healthy and older children select stories and modes of playing that make sense of their worlds, so young people and adults have the capacity to choose material that 'speaks to them' or perhaps 'speaks for them'. And I emphasise that it applies both to individual people and to groups.

This idea has far-reaching implications for our understanding of theatre and therapy and could influence the practice and training for both drama-therapists and social theatre practitioners in the future.

The context

In the year 1990 I had reached a major stage of my life. I was in charge of the counselling and support of the infertility service 'The Rowan Clinic' at the Royal London Hospital. I appointed a multi-cultural team of staff. We offered both individual and group work, and sessions for couples and we had high pregnancy rates. I was also lecturing in dramatherapy and social anthropology to medical students, and teaching experiential dramatherapy to anthropology Master's students at the University of London (SOAS). I had a private practice for clients and supervisees and was regularly invited overseas to run workshops and give keynote speeches. I had a staff flat at the hospital and a little house in Stratford-upon-Avon. My own develop-ment of and with dramatherapy had come a long way from the volunteer work in children's homes 30 years ago. Everything took on an idyllic feel when I surveyed the past, present and future.

I was on one of my overseas trips to Norway where I had been working with Åse Minde, leading art therapist and eating disorder specialist. Åse and I had developed joint models of teaching (later to be published in Jennings and Minde 1994), and we enjoyed the dialogue between art therapy and dramatherapy.

The first discovery of a breast lump results in the mixed reactions of 'maybe it is nothing – it's just tissue' to 'why didn't I notice this before – I have cancer'. I showed Åse the lump and we agreed that I should have it looked at as soon as I returned to London. One advantage of working in a hospital is that medical treatment is readily available and within a week I had been examined, two lumps were discovered, both were cancers. I decided on a second opinion and ended up in Harley Street with my daughter, in a private consulting practice that has deep-pile grey carpet and deep dusky pink walls, with the faint whiff of cigar smoke as you go up the stairs. We declined the offer of a whisky and it was a laugh/cry situation where the consultant used the dramatherapy technique of 'sculpting' to describe the difference between invasive and non-invasive tumours. He arranged pencils and paperweights and lined up an army to illustrate how the army of cancer soldiers makes an attack!

I went with the surgery with wonderful support from my children and close friends and ended up on tamoxifen for the next few years. The most difficult part to manage in hospital was the arrival of a 'cancer counsellor' who tried to force me to look at pictures of women with one breast embracing their husbands, and accused me of avoiding reality (I did not have a partner at the time). Asking her to leave made no avail so in sheer desperation I said, 'How dare you assume that I am heterosexual.' With a little dainty shriek she took her wicker basket of pamphlets and fled from the room.

Cancer on your case notes is life changing and I was reviewing everything I was doing and where I was going. Dramatherapy had had my primary attention for over 20 years and my work in theatre had become less of a priority – I was hungry for artistic expression. Why was I so disconnected from the theatre as a performer?

It was time to reactivate my theatrical career by rejoining Equity, finding myself an agent and putting my somewhat meagre cv about. I met in the street at Stratford a wonderful comic actor, Des Barrett whom I got to know at one of the Dramatherapy and Shakespeare Symposia. He asked me what I was doing and promptly invited me for a coffee to give me some advice. 'You have to learn to blag, Sue', he said, 'We all do it!' I started to remonstrate and he went on, 'Remember how I started? I boasted that I could be an actor and a friend challenged me to a bet! So I went to a few workshops and marketed myself well!!' Des has never looked back.

We went through my cv and he promptly enlarged on it in various ways, 'and think of the specialisms you know about; you have a working knowledge of prisons and hospitals, and you know about disturbed children – it will all build your career, and you will be a godsend to directors'. I went home a little heartened because I did wonder if I was on a fool's errand and that evening Joanna Lumley was being interviewed on Parkinson. He asked her about her early career in the theatre and she laughed so much and said, 'Well I learnt to blag you know – that's how most of us start!'

My dear friend actor Clare Higgins was very supportive and also amused. She said 'Here am I thinking of training as a counsellor and here are you going into theatre – we can both help each other!'

Not everyone was so supportive, and indeed many clinicians were very dismissive of my engaging with my own artistic process. Paradoxically most arts therapists – music, dance-movement and art – are expected to continue to engage with their own creativity. Somehow I wasn't being allowed to be considered in the same way. It reminded me of an earlier occasion when I was lecturing at a school of art and requested a space for an experimental improvisation group. I was promptly sent an invoice! There were the art staff and art therapists busy doing their own studio work but it was said that my situation 'was different'. 'I think I have read the situation correctly' was the lofty response I received! There were others who feared for my 'safety' – 'what if all goes pear-shaped? What about your status then?' they said. I was encouraged by the phone call from the Royal Shakespeare Theatre; Katie Mitchell was producing *Beckett* and needed some help with the aspects of 'madness' in the plays. It was a joy to work with Juliet Stephenson and Debra Gillett on their roles, and did a lot for my self-esteem.

Stage one

I decided to move everything forward by working on a one-woman show. I asked my writer sister if she could create a story about a sixteenth-century wise woman who was branded as a witch. I wanted the theme of Allyson taking control of her own destiny and drinking poison before she was hanged. Like many women at that time, Allyson was condemned to death because a new-born baby died. The reality was that the baby was already dead before she was called to deliver it, but the priest and the village gossips all ganged up against her. The text of the play carefully blends narrative and reverie, with the performer taking on the roles of Allyson from teenager to young adult to mature woman, her Aunt Joan (who also died as a 'witch'), young women of the village, the young priest, the old priest, and the magistrate. Quite an undertaking for a fledging performer! However every performance brought new ideas and thoughts, I found a new strength as I challenged my director and costume designer regarding the interpretation of the play. My long-term friend Audrey Hillyar, a retired costume maker from the National Theatre came to my rescue. She bought various pieces from the Royal Shakespeare Theatre's costume department (including a bloody tunic worn by a soldier in *Macbeth* and a long grubby shift worn by Richard II), and made some rag shoes for me and a head covering. Aasmund Vic, a special friend, found the right poison bottle from the National Theatre of Oslo and all my children pulled out the stops for this to work for me.

The premiere of Allyson was at a Danish conference on Arts Therapies and I received a standing ovation. Subsequently I toured the play to hospitals and fringe venues, a run at the Edinburgh Festival and then a sold-out performance at the Greenwich Studio Theatre Festival. People commented that the theme of the play is about a healer and midwife and the story of what happens to her when she is accused of getting it wrong, and they asked me if there were parallels with my own life.

Reflections

It wasn't until several years later that I could 'bear to remember' what the play is really about for me. I had left home in my late teens, and gone on tour as a dancer in musicals and revues. I had some opportunities in repertory theatre and schools' drama. When I was not working I stayed in London looking for new shows and ended up pregnant. The shock of it all actually delayed anything – what to do – who to tell – I was lost on a tide of emotion. My family were appalled and a termination seemed to me the only way through.

However everything had to remain so secret and the burden of guilt caused me to have long-term depression. There seemed no way forward and even a suggestion from a cousin that I should stay single and look after my parents in their old age as a way of making restitution! I had personal therapy of various kinds and only succeeded in shocking my therapists, and my attempts to seek redemption through religion led to stone walls. Allyson was indeed a healer and midwife – she was able to heal me through that repeated performance about the death of a child and enabled me to move forward.

Stage two

My theatrical career was slow to say the least and I was impatient for more work. I was inspired by the real-life story of Elizabeth Garrett Anderson, the first woman doctor. I did all the research myself and created a play based on her correspondence to another pioneer Emily Davidson, who founded Girton College, Cambridge – the first university college for women. I was amazed at this woman's tenacity and strength. She took rejection after rejection and kept going until she had been accepted into a medical school, only to be thrown out again by jealous male students. She finally qualified as a doctor and opened a hospital for women and children. She became the first female Dean of students. I was inspired! I had several photographs of her and was able to copy one of her dresses. How did women in Victorian clothes do anything? I love this show, which takes Elizabeth through her life, including being banned from the dissecting room while she was studying, and ends with her seeing off her daughter who had also trained as a doctor and was taking the first group of women doctors to the war front in France.

I met some of her descendants when I premiered the show in Jersey and Guernsey. Her great granddaughters asked me, 'How did you walk as she did? She was renowned for her particular walk!' They were kindness itself and gave me photos and notes from her life – it made such a difference to have actual objects that she had touched! Again I toured the play extensively not only to theatre but also to schools and museums. Some of the critics were less kind, especially when I performed the show at the Aldborough Festival that was in Elizabeth Garrett Anderson's home town. However, overall the show went well, and I enjoyed the passage through her life from young girl to medical campaigner for women to mother to older respected woman.

Reflections

If the play about Allyson gave me some personal courage, I realised that Elizabeth was giving me professional courage. How many times in my life had the doors been closed by men who were either threatened by successful women or believed that women should be at home and have 'little hobbies'. The pioneering of dramatherapy had meant that I needed to talk with doctors and psychiatrists, the majority of whom are still male. I needed to speak with directors of trusts and charities, prison governors and special school heads. How often the replies had been, 'yes it sounds very interesting but it is not what you call essential – drama is recreational – it is a luxury – people should have it as a reward – if disturbed people do drama it will make them more disturbed or mad or dangerous'.

Looking back now I wonder how I managed to withstand the oft-time abuse and cynicism. It came to a head when I had been asked to put together the *Handbook of Dramatherapy* (Cattanach *et al.* 1993) with a select group of author-dramatherapists. I was discussing the project with my then supervisor who looked quite askance at the idea. 'Oh dear Sue, I don't think so – it should be a book on psychotherapy – the handbook of psychotherapy – with a chapter about dramatherapy!'

Stage three

I was determined to do a Shakespeare. Having longed to be in plays of Shakespeare and feeling that the schools tours of my youth were a long time ago (leading roles of Nerissa, Jessica and Puck touring for a year) I decided that I must create something myself. *Romeo and Juliet* had always been an important play for me and I had been part of a prison project in the USA to work with the play in the notorious Rikers prison. The part of the nurse is, in my opinion, often underplayed. There is no mention of what happens to her at the end of the play (Shakespeare often does this!), yet together with the Friar she is very culpable. She goes along with Juliet and her teenage marriage to Romeo and then betrays her by suggesting she then goes with Paris since Romeo has got himself into trouble. There is a kind of naïve parenting on the one hand but also a wise woman in the making on the other. It is she that Juliet's mother turns to when she cannot even remember her daughter's age. I wrote the play interspersing it with Shakespeare text and left some questions to be explored at the end. I played the Nurse, Juliet, her father, the Friar and Romeo, as well as Mercutio in a rapid dialogue that took in the main themes of the play. An important scene for me is when the nurse knows Romeo is at the window and tried without success to call Juliet inside. The play had a run at a London fringe and then toured schools and small theatres. I was asked to do a special performance for women at Broadmoor Hospital. Margaret Orr, an amazing psychiatrist who I always said I wanted to look after me if I was mentally ill, said that the play raised issues about mothering and abandonment. She felt this was important for some of the female patients in the secure hospital. This performance was an electric moment as I just went with the text and trusted Shakespeare! Both patients and staff asked, 'but how do you look so young when you are playing Juliet?' The performance opened up areas of discussion with myself and the women about the Nurse's role as a mother substitute and the mistakes she made.

Reflections

It was the performance at Broadmoor that jolted my consciousness. Having been involved in the production of *Hamlet* with Mark Rylance and helping to organise the RSC coming to Broadmoor, I was all too aware of the impact of dramatic metaphor on offender patients. However you do not know this until you actually perform it yourself. What the play did was to jolt me into acknowledging my own failings as a mother, where I had neglected my own children and gone with sometimes naïve ideas that in retrospect were downright irresponsible! How does one make restitution as a parent? Often as a grandparent and by acknowledging with one's children one less than perfect parenting. These ideas filtered through slowly and it was really with the advent of grandmotherhood that I became more and more aware of these shortcomings. Shakespeare is the wisest counsellor that I know and has certainly provided me with some excellent personal therapy!

Stage four

The play of Elizabeth Garrett Anderson took an unexpected turn when I was asked to perform it on a regular basis at the Wellcome Trust. They had a Science for Life permanent exhibition for schools and I would perform three or four times per week. They asked me whether I would think about the life of Rosalind Franklin as a performance. Here was another woman pioneer scientist who contributed the data for the discovery of DNA, later published by male scientists after she had died of ovarian cancer. I created a piece based on her life with information garnered from her family and friends and recent writings about her life and work. I was now performing both these pieces and with Rosalind Franklin conducted some DNA experiments as I was talking. I was getting even more strength from the redoubtable women!

Reflections

Rosalind Franklin became a synthesis of personal and professional: reassurance that women do have brains and can discover new concepts but that men can steal them and turn them into their own. This is a theme that came to haunt me in later shows as we shall see.

Stage five

I was continuing acting with small parts in *The Bill* and *Casualty*, but the regularity of live performance still eluded me. I became good friends with a fellow actor, Joan Walker, and we decided to perform a two-person show thus doubling the cast! We had been thwarted from performing the Melanie Klein play: the rights were withdrawn because of a US production. We had an extraordinary reaction from Kleinian therapists, incandescent at our affrontery: to explore Klein in a workshop! We decided to find a playwrite to create a play called *Mrs Freud and Mrs Jung* – a vehicle for exploring these famous men through the views of their wives. It had an excellent run and tour with overall favourable reviews, and was runner-up in a fringe festival.

Reflections

I realised much later of course that the permission to challenge idols, especially psychoanalytic ones, gave me a feeling of complete release. I could stand up as myself and not just in the role of Mrs Freud and say, 'Do we really believe certain of Freud's theories? Have we examined them in relation to contemporary knowledge and not been critical?' I often had the response from therapists that I must be avoiding something or was too damaged to see it. This was before they knew that I had had long-term therapy on the couch, four times a week for five years; and how my children suffered with my early morning absence, let alone being deprived of financial security because I had mortgaged myself in order to pay for the therapy.

Stage six

My strong drive to do my next play took over all my thinking and waking hours. I wanted to continue the female theme and to tackle women's issues. I was moved by how women were put in institutions for having illegitimate babies. The Catholic Church has been highly criticised for taking away the babies from young girls who are pregnant and punishing the girls by forcing them to work in laundries. I developed a play, *The Spiral of Madness* about three generations of women who had a diagnosis of 'madness' on their case notes. Naomi was a young woman raped by a priest who was put into an institution and had her baby removed. She was given electric shock treatment and told 'not to be silly'. Her daughter Rhiannon was fostered and abused by the foster father and one of his sons. She has an eating disorder as a way of controlling her life and eventually runs away. Another girl, Sally, runs away from the home and finds Rhiannon. Sally is pregnant and it turns out she is HIV positive. Sally dies and Rhiannon brings up her child. After all these years she has had a letter from her mother that the foster home withheld.

This play had a run at a London Fringe and then toured fringe festivals and medical schools. A big event was the performance for the Royal College of Psychiatrists conference, where there was a lot of consternation. My dear friend Aanand was stage manager and struggled to create a safe place for this very difficult play to be performed. People wandered in and out or left in the middle of a difficult speech – I wonder what they would say to their patients if they behaved like that? However the ensuing discussion was fascinating. The female psychiatrists were asking in-depth questions about the process of the play and one said to me, 'Sue, it is quite remarkable – you have just enacted the story of one of my clients.' However the men were less sure and suggested the play was out of date and that people did not behave like that now! I did not need to respond – the women all shook their heads.

The ending of this show was extraordinary – health and safety did not permit us to take our lunches with us and eat on the journey – we had a deadline to meet at another venue! So we had to forgo lunch.

Reflections

This play was full of paradoxes for me. To go mad three times a night and to have ECT, as well as to play the role of narrator was very taxing both physically and emotionally, but Clare Higgins helped me with the direction. Many women found the story gave a resolution that addressed forgiveness. While I was focusing on the taxing demands on me as an actor – tears, rage, self-harming – I proceeded without any connections to my own fears about 'going mad'; and there was the theme of the lost baby again as well as abuse from men, including professional men. It was only when I was nudged by my lifelong soul mate, the late Gordon Wiseman, that the enormity of it all dawned on me! We were discussing where I might go next and he said, 'Suze, isn't it time to move on? To have fun? Be a bit naughty?'

In the early hours of the following morning I had a phone call from Gordie, 'I've just had a wonderful idea', he said, 'I think you should do *The Wife of Bath*.

Stage seven

He was absolutely right. I had come through so much in my journey through these plays and it was time to move on. I re-read the Wife of Bath's story and also how she is introduced at the beginning of *The Canterbury Tales*. What an amazing woman! Now looking for her fifth husband after her extraordinary bawdy and touching life experience. Ending up finding true love, even though she had a violent incident.

She was a lusty woman and a lover of life with her own brand of logic. She wore amazing clothes, rode a horse and took on the men in debate and repartee. She was the first person to talk about the difference between Mars and Venus and said she was endowed with a bit of each.

Sadly Gordie died before he could see the play come to fruition but he was very much a part of it, his spirit was with me as I wrote and rehearsed and adapted.

It was breathtaking – to be able to have so much fun on stage – to take people along with the humour and also to sing accompanied.

Reflections

It was strange looking back that I needed to have permission to enjoy myself! Again I was using theatre to work through life issues that were not in the forefront of my consciousness. The *Wife of Bath* allowed me to own my life with all its ups and downs, and to enjoy myself without feeling burdened, fearful and guilt ridden.

Closing thoughts

The journey through seven shows has obviously had a profound effect on my view of myself and my life. It has also enabled me to understand the topics of the plays in ways that I had never considered. So not only have I had the opportunity to encounter myself but to encounter life events that have meaning in the wider world. These revelations are very recent and it was only in 2007 that the full impact of these shows became manifest, during a fallow period for me when I deliberately took time out from being a performer. I think that I needed some distance from the stories in order to come closer to them, the ultimate paradox of theatre.

This journey is not yet complete I know, so all I can do is come to a pause and share the experience. It has been so momentous for me that some resolution has come about. Having been unpartnered for some 20 years, I have met the love of my life, Peter. Like the *Wife of Bath*, I have found my true love!

I can allow myself to love again after a theatre experience of profound depth. Truly I have been able 'to escape unto myself'.

References

Aston Smith, J. (1989) *Allyson Healer and Midwife: The Story of a Green Witch*, play script, Rowan Publications.

Cattanach, A., Chesner, A., Jennings, S., Meldrum, B. and Mitchell, S. (1993) *The Handbook of Dramatherapy*, London: Routledge.

Jennings, S. (1992) *My Dear Emily: The Story of Elizabeth Garrett Anderson*, unpublished play script.

Jennings, S. (1994) *The Nurse's Tale: Romeo and Juliet*, unpublished play script.

Jennings, S. (1996) *The Story of Rosalind Franklin*, play script sponsored by the Wellcome Trust.

Jennings, S. (1998) *A Spiral of Madness*, unpublished play script.

Jennings, S. (2000) *The Wife of Bath*, unpublished play script.

Jennings, S. and Minde, A. (1994) *Arts Therapy and Dramatherapy: Masks of the Soul*, London: Jessica Kingsley Publishers.

Miles, B. and Trewin, J.C. (1981) *Curtain Calls*, Guildford, Surrey: Lutterworth Press.

Part I

Dramatherapy and social theatre

A debate of ground rules and definitions

Introduction

This section is very much the exposition of the subjects that follow in the other sections. It lays out the main debate, some of it critically and much of it challenging to any of our assumptions about theatre, therapy and the *status quo*.

The opening chapter by Elektra Tselikas takes us through a journey from 'social to theatre to the individual and to the theatre again', offering us an overview of the connections and power of social theatre for social and individual transformation and integration. She draws on both theatre theory and neuroscience to present us with a new paradigm: perhaps there is no social domain within which we can explore relationships and dynamics, maybe we create the social out of our theatre practice.

Anna Seymour (Chapter 2) lays the basis for contemporary dramatherapy practice in the UK, and draws on the recent literature of social theatre. She challenges the idea of the collapse of boundaries between theatre and life, so that life and art all become types of performance. She emphasises that dramatherapists have clinical responsibility to their clients by maintaining the boundaries that operate at an artistic and clinical level; dramatherapists engage in a paradoxical process that is at the core of their practice. Seymour has concerns that what is essentially an analogy between theatre and life needs to be kept as an analogy. The 'theatre of war' is not theatre; it may seem *like* theatre but it *is* war!

Guglielmo Schininà (Chapter 3) describes an overview of his social theatre work in the Balkans, Middle East and Sicily, mainly in war-torn settings. He describes his interventions as 'psychosocial' and goes on to say that it is important to integrate healing, participation and education, rather than splitting them into separate concerns. However Schininà is concerned that practitioners are not addressing the work that needs to be done on the self, at a personal level, in order to train skilled social theatre practitioners. In a sense he echoes, from a social theatre point of view, the dramatherapy perspective described in the previous chapter. And like the chapter that follows, he has concerns about the over-frequent use of the word 'trauma'.

Schininà's policy of integrating some dramatherapy training into his programme means that the healing–participation–education perspective has a reality in practice.

James Thompson (Chapter 4) challenges both dramatherapists and social theatre practitioners in another sense. He has concerns about the imposition of values from western European cultures on to societies that have their own means of dealing with stress and tragedy. He describes how practitioners want to *make* people tell their stories rather than allow them the healing benefits of silence for example. Of course for clinicians this is where appropriate supervision would expect to address these issues. However, with my own experiences in Romania and Kazakhstan there appears to be no supervisory training in cross-cultural practice for dramatherapists (and play therapists) working in non-western settings. Thompson suggests that an often misplaced diagnosis of trauma can lead to an expectation that telling your story is the cure. However skilled non-psychotherapeutic practitioners would challenge that 'personal telling' is necessarily the most efficacious way to deal with trauma. Thompson's critique is a timely reminder to practitioners in both disciplines.

Finally in this section, Claudio Bernardi (Chapter 5) discusses the 'Dramaturgy of communities', placing it in a historical context. He discusses the traditional 'community' – the village, for example – where face-to-face interaction is possible. He contrasts that with global living, where a community is more to do with a common lifestyle, or people sharing a common purpose. He has created a complex social theatre intervention that includes both the 'vision' and the 'action' that are necessary to the dramaturgy of communities. He says that we need both the 'I' of the traditional society as well as the 'we' thinking in solitary communities.

The I and the we reminds me of the original work pioneered by the late Veronica Sherborne in her developmental movement. She emphasised that we learn about I and we by working against another body as well as working with another body. Dramatherapists more and more are realising that they can learn from theatre about the primacy of the body and that initially all roles are embodied (Jennings 2008).

Reference

Jennings, S. (2008) 'Embodied Roles and Dramatic Play', in S. Jennings, *Neuro-dramatic and Attachment Development*, London: Jessica Kingsley Publishers.

1 Social theatre

An exercise in trusting the art

Elektra Tselikas

Introduction

In this chapter, I concern myself with the connections of 'social' and 'theatre'. I investigate new ways of looking at the 'social' and explore possible consequences regarding the relationships of thinking 'socially' and acting 'dramatically' or 'theatrically'. Rather than trying to discuss existing definitions or to offer new ones, I present what seems to me a new mode of thinking the 'social' and connecting it to theatre practices. In that sense, the chapter has rather a theoretical orientation. I think that this is useful insofar as practice reports and accounts about empirical case studies abound, whereas theoretical attempts to grasp relationships and connections between theatre practices and the 'social' are rather few.

Before I go on to explore possible connections between the 'social' and theatre, it is necessary to present in a first section this new way of looking at the 'social'. This will allow us to establish a common base on what we mean when we speak of 'social' groups, 'social' actions and so forth, so we understand how they can be related to theatre practices. In this first section, I draw mainly on Bruno Latour's Actor Network Theory (ANT) (Latour 2005). In the second section I explore possible connections between the 'social' and theatre and I point to possible effects of these connections, hence letting theatre emerge as a powerful practice able to contribute substantially to what Latour calls reassembling the social. In the third section, I discuss recent results of brain research, based particularly on the work of Antonio Damasio (2003) regarding the neurobiological roots of feeling and their potential for transformation. These findings are important since ever more evidence is being presented about the roots of feelings in bodily experiences. I connect these findings to theatre practices and the resulting potential for living the 'social'. I hope to have gone full circle by the end of the chapter, from the 'social' to theatre, to the individual and to the theatre again, and to have helped the reader gain an overview of the connections and power of social theatre for social and individual transformation and integration.

Section 1

Of the 'social'

It is surprising to declare that there is no such thing as a 'social' context or a society providing the context in which everything is framed: 'there is no social dimension of any sort, not "social context", no distinct domain of reality to which the label "social" or "society" could be attributed' (Latour 2005, p. 4). Such a thesis contradicts everything that sociologists have been fond of until now, positing the existence of a specific sort of phenomenon called 'society', 'social order', 'social practice' or 'social structure', a frame possessing specific qualities able to explain, reinforce, express, maintain, reproduce, or subvert what are believed to be 'social' phenomena, phenomena that cannot be grasped or explained by other disciplines. According to such an under-standing, the social domain is a given; it does not only permeate other domains but also accounts for several dynamics – for example, relational or interactional – that take place in these domains. In such a mode of thinking, theatre – notably 'social theatre' – can be practised in order to express, transform, integrate or subvert such 'social' dynamics or contexts.

Now, let's see what if there is no given 'social' domain, indeed? What if there is no such thing as a society? If 'social' is not a glue that holds different elements together, but rather – according to this type of reasoning – is what is glued together by other types of connectors. In other words, social aggregates are not a given through which aspects of or dynamics in economics, linguistics, psychology, management and so on can be grasped, described or explained. Instead, social aggregates are rather resulting within the economic, linguistic, psychological or management sectors and should be described or explained by the specific associations provided by these sectors.

To the social theatre practitioner, these preoccupations will sound like hair-splitting debates, and maybe they are. Yet they have far-reaching consequences. One most important consequence is that if we conceive of the 'social' as a given entity we tend to see relationships, interactions and other 'social' expressions as given dynamics that result within the given 'social' entity. Hence, we concentrate our attention on these 'social' interactions before we concern ourselves with the types of connections between things that are not themselves 'social' and that exist within the mentioned domains, a much more fluid conception. Seeing the 'social' as a given entity with given dynamics is what social workers, counsellors, therapists and related professionals have been doing until now. They emphasize the importance of relations and interactions assuming that, if those are brought into harmony – for example through theatre practices – individuals and groups will function more appropriately.

In contrast to that, a view I would like to adopt here sees no given 'social' domain but only traces that are left by very specific movements that happen within particular types of connections between things that are not them-selves 'social'. The consequence of such a view is that it places the subject matter before the relationship. The 'social' emerges within contexts that are created through connections of elements that have no 'social' qualities in themselves. And hence, when intervening in such a context, we are concerned with tasks that aim at solving problems connected with the subject matter rather than with relationships. Through particular tasks, we create spaces that can become 'social'. And this is precisely what theatre does. This is where theatre can deploy each 'actor' (human and non-human) so as to create spaces that allow for the 'social' to emerge. This is, indeed, the power hidden in theatre practices, as we discuss in Section 2 of this chapter.

Before I elaborate on these connections between assuming and solving tasks and the creation of spaces that let the 'social' emerge, I would like to invite the reader to have a look at what a 'social' group is, or can be, according to the view adopted here. Since the 'social' domain is believed to be peopled by 'social' groups, and social theatre is in some way related to 'social' groups, it seems necessary to take a closer look at these particular phenomena.

Of social groups

As the 'social' does not exist of and by itself, groups exist only by the traces they leave. As Latour points out, mapping the controversies in the formation of groups is more interesting and far reaching for the researcher of the 'social' than describing established connections since 'group formations leave many more traces in their wake than already established connections which, by definition, might remain mute and invisible' (Latour 2005, p. 31). Hence, visibility is the crucial point here, and, in order for the traces left by group formations to be visible, some items will always be present: 'groups are made to talk; anti-groups are mapped; new resources are fetched so as to make their boundaries more durable; and professions with their highly specialized paraphernalia are mobilized' to report about the groups (Latour 2005, p. 31). In other words, groups cannot be defined like other given objects through an ostensive definition but only through a performative one. Groups are made by the various ways and manners in which they are said to exist. This performative element supports group members and groups to 'create' and present themselves, to exist and to be visible. According to Latour 'if you stop making and remaking groups you stop having groups' (ibid., p. 35). And in that same sense, groupings are not buildings in need of restoration but movements in need of continuations. If a dancer stops dancing, the dance is finished. The difference between an ostensive and a performative definition is that 'the object of a performative definition vanishes when it is no longer performed – or if it stays, then it means that other actors have taken over the relay' (ibid., p. 38). Now, we have here an important difference to a constructivist approach, according to which the 'social' world would be constructed through narratives, made up in our minds and then narrated in various ways. In a certain way, a constructivist approach negates the existence of an objective real world, whereas actor network theory postulates indeed the existence of such a world that is being assembled through the actions of human and non-human actors and actants – an actant being something, a way that makes actors do things. For example expressions such as 'carried over by routine', or 'victims of social structure', or 'explained by capitalism' refer to actants. All of these are comparable: they are different ways to make actors do things. The term 'actant' seems fruitful as it helps us avoid psychologizing concepts like 'motivations' and the like and hence keeps the elements we deal with on a very concrete level and a level that can be translated into actions. In this way, the existence of 'social' groups is being traced through the actions that contribute to their creation.

I think the relevance of an actor network approach is rather obvious if we want to investigate the relationships of theatre and the 'social', since the worlds created and emerging within theatre activities are concrete and real at least as long as the performance lasts. And, as we will see in Section 3 of this chapter, the 'social' world that is assembled through the deployment of actors and actants during theatre work leaves its traces on the individuals involved, even after the group has ceased to exist. Yet, before I proceed into discussing this in more detail, I would like to introduce two terms that will allow us to further understand the dynamics behind the creation of the 'social' and its relationship to theatre practices.

Of intermediaries and mediators

To recapitulate my exposition so far, 'social' in terms of actor network theory designates a type of momentary association that is characterized by the way it gathers together into new shapes. It is, thus, a movement, a displacement, a transformation, a translation, and enrolment that happens in the moment (Latour 2005, pp. 64–65). The 'social' is characterized by its fluidity. Now, if we conceive of the 'social' as a movement and we take a closer look at the elements that are being shuffled or reshuffled together so it can happen, we need to distinguish between elements that have the power to transform and others that do not possess that power. In the first case we would speak of mediators, and in the second of intermediaries. An intermediary transports meaning or force without transformation, whereas a mediator transforms, translates, modifies the meaning or the elements it is supposed to carry. I have mentioned above that all things in an association – human and non-human – can be actors or actants. If we add the differentiation between intermediaries and mediators to this description, we have tools that allow us to handle or recognize pretty complex situations. Suddenly, a piece of cloth is no longer just a piece of cloth; depending on its quality – texture, shine, colour, feel and so on; compare for example a piece of fine silk-cashmere knitwear and a synthetic jumper – it can act as a mediator in a scene and make a lot of difference to the way actors behave, express themselves, use the piece of cloth, relate to each other, and so on. Mediators strongly influence the way things are deployed in the creation of a 'social' context, whereas intermediaries may transport 'social' meaning but they do this just for illustrative purposes without further influencing what is happening. For example a cross on the wall may symbolize a religious context, it is not used in the action, but by just transporting the meaning 'religious place' it acts as an intermediary. If it is used in the scene making a difference to the actors' actions, then it becomes a mediator and contributes substantially to the making of the 'social' in that moment. In other words, intermediaries describe a state of affairs, while mediators dynamize it and are able to take it into endless directions. What counts is not the number or type of figures one adds to the association, but the range of mediators one is able to deploy for the association to happen. Again, what seems to be a hair-splitting debate has far-reaching consequences for the relationship between the 'social' and theatre. Whether we conceive of things – human and non-human actors and actants – as intermediaries or mediators will strongly influence the direction our 'social' and theatre practices take. Mediators are, indeed, those elements that allow the 'social' to emerge in its fluidity and transformability, still remaining sufficiently concrete that they can be translated into actions that make a difference. Yet, once again I must ask the reader for patience until we get into this in more detail in Section 2.

I have been mentioning 'actors' and 'actants', and now has come the moment to more closely look at what we mean by these terms.

Of actors, actants and actions

Interestingly enough the notion of 'actor' that is so easily used in the social sciences comes from the theatre. And in fact, when action is involved, 'it's never clear who and what is acting when we act since an actor on stage is never alone in acting' (Latour 2005, p. 46). Now, if we follow this line of reasoning we come to some conclusions that feel shocking in a world that is led by the ideology that agency is by free will, rational and so forth. Because our conclusion is that 'an actor is what is made to act by many others' (ibid., p. 46) and that 'other agencies over which we have no control make us do things' (ibid., p. 50). These other agencies do not have to be humans, they can be non-human objects or – as we have seen above – actants.

In that sense, what action implies is that an agent – human or non-human – is doing something that makes some difference to a state of affairs, transforming parts or the whole of the configuration. The word 'figuration' that is included in 'configuration' reminds us that also more abstract entities like cultural norms for example, which we call here 'figurations', can force or forbid actors to do things. All of these being deployed and acting as mediators result in a truly complex and multidimensional, yet at the same time quite concrete, association of elements that create a space within which the 'social' can emerge.

Connecting this notion of action with the mediators we have been mentioning, we come to a picture made up of concatenations of mediators where every point is fully acting, yet every action remains concrete, with no need to resort to abstract psychological interpretations to describe it. Action remains truthfully unpredictable, a surprise, a mediation, an event because the uncertainty about action is being acknowledged, as well as the fact that it is not clear at all, who is pulling the strings or moving the masks (see also Peter Brook 1987, pp. 217ff.).

It is rather obvious that there are certain connections between this view of the 'social' and theatre. This view offers a resource that allows us to perceive the emergence of the 'social', its mystery and magic, still keeping it concrete and visible, a gift for the director who would put it on stage. And it preserves us from reducing social theatre to 'creative interactions'.

Before we proceed to Section 2, one last point needs to be tackled. I have been speaking of humans and non-humans that can take part in the action. In theatre, as in fairy tales, we believe everything is possible, objects can have a soul, speak, act. Within sober actor-network-theory, objects, indeed, have agency. Let's see how.

Of objects

Summing up what we have been dealing with until now, we might say that the 'social' is a fluid that becomes visible when associations are happening. Further, everything that modifies a state of affairs, everything that makes a difference, is an actor, including objects. Interestingly enough, power relations or conflicts – which form the basis of theatre and notably social theatre – are mostly explained through psychological means, interactions, relationships or 'motivations'. Seldom is sufficient attention being paid to the objects involved into power relations and dynamics. And yet, most of the time it is objects that account for asymmetries and the exercise of power within associations we perceive as 'social', for example material resources of all types.

With these elements in mind, I would like to proceed to connecting what I have exposed until now with the practice of (social) theatre.

Section 2

Very often I hear social theatre practitioners regret not having been trained in some sort of psychological or counselling domain, and very often I have the feeling that they do not trust the power of their art when dealing with populations that are not in the process of becoming professional actors. It seems as if these social theatre practitioners think that their focus of attention should be psychological rather than artistic.

Right at the beginning of this section, I would like to formulate the hypothesis that when theatre is blurred with psychology or counselling it loses its artistic potential and its transformational power for groups and individuals. In the following, I attempt to offer the arguments that have led me to this conclusion.

Tasks before relationships

One important advantage I see in adopting the view of the 'social' exposed above is that it allows the researcher and the practitioner to concentrate on the subject matter without getting lost in relational group dynamics. Spolin invites the theatre practitioner to concentrate on the subject matter and the tasks ensuing rather than on the dynamics of the relationships between the players. She maintains that defining concrete tasks to be solved by the players within the play will direct their attention to the play and away from personal relationships, hence promoting concentration on the play and also allowing for the personal relationships to be transformed and forged through the play (Spolin 1993, pp. 35ff.).

The view above contradicts group dynamic principles as they have influenced our thinking since the 1960s. In therapy, social work, counselling, education and so forth, relationships are given primordial importance. It is believed that as soon as relationships are analysed verbally and tensions have been cleared, the group will proceed to solve the given tasks without problems. What we very often observe, though, is that more often than not groups get addicted to relationship discussions, spending lots of time on those and avoiding confronting the tasks to be tackled. Furthermore supervisors or facilitators find themselves with the dilemma of 'creating a good group atmosphere' and are tempted to lose distance and objectivity.

Concentrating on a task to be solved defines a point of concentration and creates a very different dynamic and 'social' context than if the players direct their attention primarily to relationships. Relationships emerge then and evolve, connected with the subject matter in question and the task to be solved. So, it is through concentrating on the task that the space is created within which the 'social' can be assembled.

As a sociologist, and with his view of the 'social' as I have exposed it above, Latour presents us with a new paradigm in thinking about 'social' and social relationships, a paradigm that allows us to keep away from psychology that is based on interpretations, as well as to understand and trust the power of a performance-oriented approach to 'social' matters.

Do it and show me!

What is 'doing' and what is it that needs to be done? Feelings, motivations and the like are fairly abstract notions that cannot easily be translated into actions. The challenge here is not only for the actors but also for the

director. As soon as the director – in our sense the social theatre practitioner – begins to interpret the feelings and motivations of the human
actors he or she gets onto slippery ground. She risks missing the various
factors – for example other, also non-human, actors and actants that might
be involved, act as mediators and will be deployed in the assembling of the
scene. More risky, yet, might be the fact that the director will not have
enough concrete elements to translate into showable and visible actions that
would make up a piece of theatre. And finally, he or she will find it difficult
to direct the players and the play for lack of concrete points of reference
that can be translated into actions.

The more concrete the actions and the better they can be expressed
through the body – I elaborate on this in Section 3 – the bigger the chance
that the players know what is to be done and can show the action on stage
and to the public, thereby allowing the 'social' space to emerge in its
full power, with all its connections, contradictions, interactions and
relationships.

The concentration on doing and showing allows the researcher and the
theatre practitioner to be freed from too many worries connected with
psychological interpretations and explanations. Instead, they can direct
their attention to finding and understanding the range and roles of mediators – human and non-human actors, actants and figurations – involved in
the play, affecting the actions of other actors and contributing to the
creation of the 'social' space assembled and presented.

The power of distance

By defining actors as we did above, namely as everything that makes a
difference to the subject matter, be it a person, a thing or an actant, we
depersonalize the action and make it objective, still preserving its fluidity.
This means that the many elements – human and non-human – allowing
the action to happen are being deployed, hence freeing the individual actor
or actress to play his or her role fully within the action that is happening
through the various configurations. Not only can inhibitions that might be
happening as a result of the players' own biography or their considerations
of other players be set aside, but the group's and the individual actor's
growth can be promoted since new associations can happen within the play
and within the new 'social' context that emerges through the play.

Players are often surprised by the power of the expressive capacity of
their body or the strength of their voices once they forget about who they
think they are and what they think they are able to do, once they concentrate on the action in the play. As I have mentioned above, the effects
experienced through the actions taken in the 'social' reality emerging in the
moment of the play last beyond that moment. In Section 3 I discuss in more
detail the lasting transformative effects of involving the body in theatre
practices for the individual actors.

The power of the moment

Thinking of the 'social' as a fluid, as a momentaneously happening association of things that influence the state of affairs is, of course, the basis for improvisation. Instead of concentrating on depicting given situations, it acknowledges the fluidity of associations and 'social' moments. It is through improvisation that mediators can develop their full potential and move the action forward. It is through a free and unencumbered reaction to the offers of other actors that actors can contribute to the dynamic making and showing of the 'social'. Even, or particularly so, when this means being a loser in the play. Giving in to the partner's wishes in the play is precisely what allows the 'social' to emerge out of the moment and enables the individuals involved to transform (Johnstone 2000, p. 90).

In the next section I would like to have a closer look at what happens on the level of the individual players while they are active with (social) theatre, and while they use their bodies in actions. Here, I offer some connections between acting, namely translating images into actions through the body (I owe this view of acting to Richard Nieoczym) and the growth and transformation of the individual player.

Section 3

We often think and read that social theatre promotes individual growth, yet we don't have a concrete idea of how this happens. Taking a look at recent neurobiological research should help us understand what happens during performative activities. What is particularly interesting in these findings is how images enter our mind through the sensory experiences of the body and how, on the other hand, the body perceives the world and reacts to it according to what has been mapped in the brain's regions through the body's experiences. Now let's see how images and feelings can be transformed through the body's activities in theatre work.

Usually, theatre work begins with a body warm up, and role taking also happens through the body. Theatre games are expected to help the actor overcome the division between body and mind (Barker 1989, pp. 29ff.), and hence ideally arrive at a point where the actor goes with the flow and responds on the spot to the exigencies of the moment in the play. Sue Jennings (1998, p. 121f.) proposes a three-phase model to describe the processes that take place in dramatic activities. According to this model, embodiment is the very first step through which every dramatic activity should be grounded, in order to allow – in a second phase called projection – the images to emerge that feed the roles embodied in the third phase. Also other theatre theoreticians and practitioners of the twentieth century put great emphasis on the actor's body and the connections between images emerging in the actor's mind and their bodily expressions (Grotowski 1999; Stanislavski 1989, pp. 36ff.). Now, if the actor's mind is – as Stanislavski has put it – her emotion memory (Stanislavski 1990, pp. 163ff.), the library that will feed her character, and if, as many (social) theatre practitioners know and postulate, role play enables her to enlarge her role repertoire in theatre as in life, how does this happen?

In his explorations of Spinoza's claim 'that body and mind are parallel attributes of the same substance' (Damasio 2003, p. 133), Damasio, a modern neurobiologist, examines these attributes under the microscope of biology in order to see how this single substance works and how the body and mind aspects are generated within it. His findings show a very interesting relationship between body states and feelings. According to his hypothesis 'a feeling is the perception of a certain state of the body along with the perception of a certain mode of thinking and of thoughts with certain themes' (ibid., p. 86). In other words, according to neurobiological hypotheses, and as Damasio states:

> the emergence of mental images from neural patterns is not a fully understood process . . . but we know enough to hypothesize that the process is supported by identifiable substrates – in the case of feelings, several maps of body state in varied brain regions – and subsequently involves complex interactions among (brain) regions.
>
> (Damasio 2003, p. 88)

'A feeling in essence is an idea – an idea of the body and, even more particularly, an idea of a certain aspect of the body' (ibid., p. 88). In the case of feelings, several maps of body state perceptions are mapped in the brain and 'the sensory regions designed to receive signals from the body' (ibid., p. 87). Hence, as Damasio concludes, the objects and events at the origin of feelings are inside the body and not outside of it. What is more important, yet, for our present exploration is that feelings are interactive perceptions. The brain can respond to an external object, as feelings unfold, because the object of the origin of the feelings is inside the body. The brain can act directly on the object it is perceiving, and it can do so by modifying the state of the object. This means that the object at the origin of the feeling on the one hand, and the brain map of that object on the other, can influence each other in a sort of reverberative process (ibid., p. 92). In other words:

> feelings are not a passive perception or a flash in time . . . there is a dynamic engagement of the body, almost certainly in repeated fashion, and a subsequent dynamic variation of the perception. We perceive a series of transitions. We sense an interplay, a give and take.
>
> (ibid., p. 92)

Let's apply these findings to our explorations so far. During play, theatre games and the embodiment of roles the emotional memory – the library that feeds the actor's role taking – might lead her actions and expressions in a particular direction. Suppose the director remains focused on tasks connected with the play and the role rather than worrying about psychological states and feelings. She will help the actor concentrate just on body expressions connected with the role(s). Instead of looking for the feelings and having them expressed through the body, we go the other way around: we bring the body into the position required by the play and the role and the feelings will follow. As Yoshi Oida and Lorna Marshall put it, 'working physically enables the performer to gain a deeper understanding of fundamental processes: through the body to learn something beyond the body' (Oida and Marshall 1997, p. 29). This helps the actor bypass existing brain body maps related to certain feelings and create new influences on the existing body maps, thus transforming them as well as the original feelings. This is why it is so important to keep focused on the tasks rather than on the psychological states of the players. And this is why players are so often surprised about their capacity for alternative actions, expressions and feelings during the play when this happens.

Last but not least, it is important to trust the learning and transformative power of the group of actors/players. As further recent neurobiological research has shown, humans are gifted with mirror neurons that enable them to learn by imitation (Bauer 2005). Thanks to the mirror neurons, humans repeat and imitate a great many body states, expressions and actions of others unconsciously. This is maybe what accounts in part for the sharing of the energy in the play. Thus, simple partner games and mirroring exercises can help change the mood of the players. The 'social' that emerges within a theatre activity can be manifold and offer many opportunities for learning and transformation.

Conclusion

Latour's performative approach to the 'social' in the frame of actor network theory seems particularly fruitful for the discussion on social theatre. It allows us to integrate constructivist/narrative approaches with realistic ones, postulating on the one hand that 'social' reality does exist and is not just constructed or narrated but happens, indeed, in the course of associations, and on the other hand acknowledging that this reality is momentaneously associated, fluid, a movement in need of continuation that changes and is constantly renegotiated through the actions that constitute it. Actions – doing – are what make up theatre and what make up the 'social'. And actions, actions that change the world, as Berchtolt Brecht would put it, are the stuff out of which social theatre is made. Actions as they happen through theatre practices emerge out of, and at the same time remodel, the brain mappings of the players, thus giving rise to innovative actions and transformations as well as newly assembled 'social' contexts.

As a closing word: I usually prefer the term 'applied theatre' to 'social theatre' because it seems to me that it keeps the emphasis on the power of the art rather than blurring it with social, sociological, psychological and similar components. But, after all, what's in a name? What matters is for us to be clear about what we are doing. What we are doing is using the transformative potential of the art in the most consequent way possible. As performative definitions of the 'social' are spreading, theatre seems to be going back to its original function of encompassing all domains of human life.

References

Barker, Clive (1989) *Theatre Games. A New Approach to Drama Training*, London: Methuen Drama.

Bauer, Joachim (2005) *Warum ich fühle, was du fühlst. Intuitive Kommunikation und das Geheimnis der Spiegelneurone* [*Why Do I Feel What You Feel. Intuitive Communication and the Secret of Mirror Neurons*], Hamburg: Hoffmann & Campe.

Brook, Peter (1987) *The Shifting Point. Forty Years of Theatrical Exploration 1946–1987*, London: Methuen Drama.

Damasio, Antonio (2003) *Looking for Spinoza. Joy, Sorrow, and the Feeling Brain*, Orlando, FL: Harcourt.

Grotowski, Jerzy (1999) *Für ein armes Theater* [*Towards a Poor Theatre*], Berlin: Alexander Verlag.

Jennings, Sue (1998) *Introduction to Dramatherapy*, London: Jessica Kingsley Publishers.

Johnstone, Keith (2000) *Theaterspiele, Spontaineität, Improvisation und die Kunst des Geschichtenerzählens*, 3rd ed., Berlin: Alexander Verlag.

Latour, Bruno (2005) *Reassembling the Social. An Introduction to Actor Network Theory*, Oxford: Oxford University Press.

Oida, Joshi and Marshall, Lorna (1997) *The Invisible Actor*, London: Methuen.

Spolin, Viola (1993) *Improvisationstechniken für Pädagogik, Therapie und Theaater* [*Improvisation for the Theatre*], 4th ed., Paderborn: Junfermann Verlag.

Stanislavski, Constantin (1989) *Building a Character*, London: Methuen Drama.

Stanislavski, Constantin (1990) *An Actor Prepares*, London: Methuen Drama.

2 Dramatherapy and social theatre

A question of boundaries

Anna Seymour

Introduction

Life is a state of continual flux, where change is at the core of everything. How do we think about, accommodate, absorb, adjust to, embrace, promote or resist change?

These are the profound and yet commonplace questions that those of us who take on the task of using, and creating drama professionally with other people, have to ask. There is a responsibility to account for both the definition and the process of practice, and inevitably these are subject to the thinking of our times.

In the UK, since the 1960s and the explosion of theatre that proceeded to break aesthetic boundaries and theatrical conventionality, it has been accepted among practitioners that theatre can be 'put to use' in many different ways. Very good. Theatre is no longer the preserve of the privileged and can give voice to discontent, take on new subject matters, be produced in all manner of settings, be made to do work other than entertain. Of course this is true if we think of formal theatre structures, buildings and patronage. However it also true that communities and individuals have *always* found ways of 'theatricalising' life experiences, to celebrate, mourn or mark life events, to work things out or simply to pass the time.

As dramatherapy scholars have argued (Andersen-Warren and Grainger 2000; Jennings 1992; Jones 2007; Pitruzzella 2004), drama is a fundamental part of being a human being.

Sue Jennings (1992) conceptualised the paradigm embodiment–projection–role (EPR) as the three stages of dramatic development that are essential for maturation and the growth of imagination. This framework parallels various models in developmental psychology, but it also characterises the essentially *dramatic nature* of human development, not by analogy but by clearly stating that drama is central to our being.

I use this paradigm as a vantage point to examine some of the creative tensions that are healthily embraced by dramatherapists, and from there look at what is peculiar to dramatherapy – what makes it different from applied or social theatre?

Social theatre and 'applied' theatre practices

These areas of practice are contested even in their naming. In James
Thompson's 2003 book *Applied Theatre, Bewilderment and Beyond*, there is
an extended discussion of the terms of 'applied theatre'. He makes no
mention of social theatre. Yet in 2004 in a special edition of *The Drama
Review* (Thompson and Schechner 2004), these practices have been shifted
under the heading of 'social theatre'. There is an acknowledgement at the
beginning of Thompson and Schechner's essay 'Why "Social Theatre"?'
(2004, p. 11) of the problematic of using the term:

> It is a familiar term in Italian ('*teatro sociale*') for a practice that in
> different Anglophone contexts has a diverse and bewildering nomen-
> clature: applied theatre (UK and Australia) community-based theatre
> (USA), theatre for development (certain Asian and African countries),
> or popular theatre (Canada).

For their purposes it appears that all of these 'practices' can be subsumed
under the banner of 'a practice' called social theatre, or rather the term is
being deployed performatively, 'as likely to *bring about* as it is to *describe*'
(ibid., p. 11). A broad differentiation is made between the 'aesthetic theatre'
and a theatre applied and performed in diverse locations and whose aim is
to 'interrogate' the status quo, which is social theatre. From then on
applied theatre becomes social theatre and presumably scoops up other
descriptions of community theatre and so on. For the purpose of economy
in this chapter therefore, I will do the same, using 'social theatre' as the
portmanteau term to cover this broad range of theatre. At the same time I
acknowledge a discomfort with this, being aware of the proud history of
community theatre, theatre in education and the like. Each is linked by
parallel histories but each has its own distinctive story.

Social theatre is accommodating in that it can adapt to the needs of
communities, commissioning bodies, funding organisations and govern-
mental directives. Its practitioners draw on local cultural practices, theoretical concerns that inform the particular context, and bodies of knowledge
outside the realm of theatrical practice such as understanding the education
and criminal justice systems and the history of war zones. At the same time
Schechner and Thompson emphasise the need to question this capacity for
accommodation and state that 'Restricting Social Theatre to definitions
determined by public policy discourses marginalizes the practice' (ibid., p.
13). Of course this opens up one of many contradictions around the sites of
this work 'being on the margins', and often the desire of practitioners to
associate themselves with practices that are inherently politically oppositional or artistically radical and at the same time maintain their own status
in relation to and even within public institutions. In other words, there is a
desire often to be both 'on the edge' and 'in the mainstream'. Of course this

luxury is more a mark of the privilege of the practitioner than the domain of the participants.

The struggle to define and redefine practice is the preoccupation of the academy. This is the job of academics, to think about things and reinterpret them according to the shifting circumstances of the time. The important thing here is to consider what are the implications of such shifts for practice.

In the 1960s and 1970s, the era that gave rise to social theatre, theatrical activity outside the mainstream was driven largely by a political agenda. Now the motivations and interests of practitioners cannot always be so clearly stated.

Practitioners have to ask, what do you think you are doing? In whose interests are you acting? And keep on asking these questions. In the UK as funding for arts projects disappeared in the 1980s, more focus was placed on particular contexts where there was funding and work with a specific goal was identified. From radical interventions, theatre in these settings took on more of a service orientation and the role of practitioners changed. In schools, prisons and health settings the beneficial aspects of working with drama were recognised. 'Purchasers' noticed such things as changed behaviours and so commissioned further input.[1] These developments had clear implications for the kind of work being done and raise questions about the boundaries and limitations of practice. Inevitably it seems the work strayed into areas more commonly associated with therapeutic practice. Yet with looser boundaries and the encouragement of interdisciplinarity against the background of postmodernist theories of fragmentation, it was entirely possible to pick and mix ideas, to play around with conventionality and generate new ideas about practice.

Earlier forms of practice with diverse communities were usually predicated on political commitment, on the tidal surge of optimism that it was possible to change the world. Suddenly there was no political compass. The harsh years of the 1980s gave way to the 'third way', a middle ground of consensus politics where old categories would be collapsed, old identities relinquished in a more 'even handed' society.

This less volatile climate in the UK nurtured the market economy and promoted its values universally. Cultural output was packaged, delivered and audited much as any other commodity. Some practitioners adopted the language, delivering training or treatment 'packages'.

In the theatre these shifts were reflected in a major swing away from linguistic text towards other kinds of 'texts' and ultimately a critique of the very nature of theatre itself with the collapsing of metaphor and the emergence of the new category 'performance'. The boundaries between theatre and everyday life are blurred by the notion of performance and this is significant in the discussion of social theatre:

> Prisons, refugee camps, hospitals etc are not empty of theatre nor do they only experience the theatrical when a Social Theatre project is

staged. These locations are arenas rich in performance moments – sometimes small and subtle and at other times huge and obvious. These places and the regimes of knowledge and practice that operate within them are performed. The dress demeanour and responses of people are performed – even more so in institutional and highly controlled situations such as prisons, hospitals, schools and refugee camps. Social Theatre uses one set of performance processes to make new sets at sites already full of performances.

(Thompson and Schechner 2004, p. 13)

Here, Goffman's (1990) analogy between theatre and everyday life becomes elided through the idea of performance so that life and art all become types of performance.

This presents an interesting challenge to dramatherapy: does universalising the idea of performance contradict or parallel dramatherapy's understanding of the drama of everyday life? The fact remains however that life is life and performance is performance. Just as what soldiers and politicians refer to as the 'theatre of war' is not theatre. It may *seem like* theatre or indeed be theatricalised with pomp, ceremony and rhetoric but it *is* war.

The analogy of life with theatre can be straightforwardly stated. We wear clothes that are like costumes to play out the many different roles of our lives. As we enact our parts we are witnessed by different audiences, who respond and modify our performances. We are given some scripts of parts to play and others we create. We may feel that our roles are too small or too big, too insignificant or too overwhelming. We may feel that we are not even allowed to step onto the stage sometimes but are left waiting in the wings longing to participate. And so the analogy can go on. This understanding provides a metaphorical distancing to enable the exploration of roles.

Identifying 'the performative' in everyday life similarly provides a useful analogy, suggesting the capacity for distancing, creating the space where insight and awareness can lead to change, whereas when life and performance are elided such distancing is not clear.

There is a difference between reading experience as 'performative' or through theatrical analogy, as opposed to actual engagement in theatrical process. This activity is boundaried by the performance space, a place that is set apart literally and metaphorically, using at the outset a different, self-consciously selected set of aesthetic practices implying choices and control. These choices, which are available within the theatre because of its constructed nature, are not so readily available or so readily changed in real life. The tendency to collapse the theatrical metaphor calls into question the whole process of dramatic distancing – which is central to the discipline of dramatherapy.

Dramatherapy insists on the maintenance of boundaries at a conscious level so that client material can emerge through metaphor in a non-interpretive way. This is because dramatherapy is a clinical practice.

Dramatherapy

Dramatherapy is a paradoxical practice that embraces the unknown as a potential[2] dramatic space. Just as some social theatre practitioners use the notion of the performative as a pervasive idea to inform their practice, so the dramatherapist may conceive of the relationship with their client(s) through theatrical metaphor. The everyday dramatic vocabulary of the client meets the theatrical and imaginative vocabulary of the dramatherapist.

The psychiatrist Murray Cox (in Jennings 1992, p. 28) talks about his own creative vocabulary, of 'being beset by literary metaphors that would not leave him alone'. He treats them as guides, but warns of the 'necessity to distinguish between concrete and metaphorical referents'.

It is the boundary between what Boal calls 'the fictional reality and the reality of the fiction' or between theatre and the 'drama of everyday life' that demarks the therapeutic space. We conceive of this both as a literal space for enactment and as a metaphorical space of relational exploration.

The place where the therapy is to take place is 'set aside' and the dramatherapist does all within their power to make sure that work cannot be overheard or seen from outside. This boundary then is 'protected'. In a similar way when an enactment space is defined, its boundaries are also protected. In each case there is a necessity to set a boundary from which to conceptualise – where is the 'edge' that marks the threshold?

Dramatherapy uses drama at the service of the client rather than expecting the client to serve the needs of the drama, though paradoxically it is through attention to the creation of the drama that the client becomes engaged in their own therapeutic process. An intimate space is created. This intimacy can be accounted for in the way a process of attachment and separation takes place between therapist and client that mirrors the processes of early child development. These may be accessed as a vocabulary of experience, as a set of skills or even places of absence, where the therapist may encounter the client(s) incapacity to 'act'.

It is worth now returning to Sue Jenning's EPR model as a core paradigm that suggests why the intensity of the dramatic experience can be so powerful, because it is what makes up one's selfhood. Of course, bearing in mind the *permanent* caveat that neglect, damage, trauma and circumstance can interrupt or utterly distort this process

Embodiment, projection, role

In the first year, the infant experiences life through physicalisation, everything is experienced through *its own* body. Infants learn through the quality of holding given, physical attachment and bodily sensation.

In the *projection* phase, the child has become aware of the parameters of its own body – this is me, this is not me – and is aware of a world outside of itself, where toys, objects and substances such as clay are organised and fashioned. Play becomes dramatic as the child allows these external objects to speak for it. Stories begin to be told and toys take on characters and enact drama, issues of morality and reasoning are worked through as the play becomes more complex. By the age of four the child itself is adopting *roles* having 'rehearsed' through the projection phase. The child dresses up, tries on shoes that are too big, and creates a sense of self and otherness through exploring the boundaries between pretend and reality.

It is through dramatic development that a sense of self and the other, of morality and conscience is established. It is how I can learn to feel for myself and imagine how the other feels. It is how senses of identification and empathy are acquired. The child can learn about the paradoxical nature of life – that it is possible to feel afraid and be a hero, that the strong can cry and beauty and pleasure can be found where we least expect it.

In action, this is Stanislavski's concept of 'as if', the suspension of disbelief as identification and separation from the other 'character' is achieved. This allows role flexibility, the freedom to move between senses of self, to experience comfort and to take risks through moving from everyday reality into believable fictional reality.

The possibility of working with the concrete expressive nature of theatre enables the projection of feeling onto objects, texts, spaces and characters. In relation to these aspects that can be considered as 'not me' but in reality become a projected part of me, decisions can be taken, witnessed, guided and supported. Suddenly the individual is not alone but held by the context of the theatrical frame.

The desire for 'holding' is embedded at a deep emotional level from the early years of life, and it seems to me that it is this process that theatre offers in a myriad of ways. We can also apply the theatrical conception to the whole nature of the encounter between practitioner and client. In the theatre, internal/external tensions between 'text', site, subject matter, personnel and historical context create a complex interaction. The theatre takes dramatic process and makes it into a formal constitution.

Generic forms apply specific aesthetic principles and set the boundaries for the construction of the drama and the broader context of engagement with it. This is both a self-conscious process and simultaneously one that can allow for the unexpected to take place.

However, in the dramatherapy process there is often a shifting point where our belief in the drama is tested. The client expresses doubt, feels afraid, in effect enacts the distresses that have brought them to therapy, but within the context of the metaphor. It is at this point, sometimes only through the belief of the practitioner in the 'reality of the fiction' that the client is able to do the work they need to do. Once the client has committed themselves to the theatrical framework and the metaphorical content, the task is to help them maintain these boundaries. The dramatherapist needs to defend the shape and boundary of the work because in this they are defending the *client themselves*, because this is the client's creation, the projection of themselves. This is in effect how the dramatherapist *holds* the client.

The dramatherapist needs the sensitivity to be able to be both firm and flexible in their approach to judge when is the time to move and when to 'stay put'. These are both artistic and clinical decisions.

Dramatherapy and social theatre

There are marked differences between dramatherapy and social theatre. Schininà suggests them in this way:

> The main difference between Social Theatre and the majority of theatrical-therapeutic techniques is that Social Theatre does not seek *catharsis* but *metaxis* (pluralisation). Its ultimate goal is to empower differences and create solidarity, not to purify and to 'normalize' them. In Social Theatre, the objective is to question society, with the living presence of its differences, rather than to be purified and be brought back to a 'normal' value system or social code.
>
> (Schininà 2004, p. 24)

I have tremendous sympathy with his implied political project but I want to take issue with him on three counts (aware that he does not specifically name dramatherapy). First, dramatherapy does not 'seek catharsis'. This may be the outcome of some dramatherapy sessions but it is not the ultimate goal of the therapy. The process is oblique and subtle, different theatrical approaches may be being used. Working with Stanislavskian identification with character may produce different effects from an approach that works 'from the outside', such as Meyerhold's constructivist theatre, or an approach that is not interested in the 'inner life' of the performer at all, such as the Commedia. Equally the dramatherapist may be working with myth, story or ritual.

Second, the term 'pluralisation' is confusing when set against catharsis. It seems to me that the aim of dramatherapy is to achieve both some sense of resolution[3] within the individual and at the same time the capacity to be 'outside of oneself', to experience the self in relation to others without losing a sense of the self. Personal boundaries in the literal sense of behaviour, sense of space and control are also mirrored within the individuals' imaginative conception of themselves.

Finally, the term 'normalisation' – it would be entirely unethical if the dramatherapist saw this as their task. Whose 'normality' would be evoked? But I must not be ingenuous here because what is implied is that therapy can be used as a form of social control. Of course working with vulnerable people and gaining their trust carries with it the responsibility to be clear about what the work is about. The therapist contracts with the client and makes sure that both understand the agreements they have come to. This contract is constantly under review because circumstances change. Always there should be clarity on the part of the therapist around any intervention they make. What are its purposes, what are its intentions? Having said that, often some sense of 'normality' is exactly what the client most craves – to 'be like other people' in order to have choices about how to be 'different'.

In the UK, dramatherapists are both held to account and protected in a number of ways. The profession has a code of ethics that governs practice and issues of consent. All dramatherapists must be in regular clinical supervision. The profession is regulated by the Health Professions Council. These controls exist to protect clients but ultimately any practice is only as good as its practitioners.

A key element in the training of dramatherapists is that they have to undergo their own personal therapy and be willing to return to therapy at any time after qualifying if the need arises. This means that the drama-therapist is not asking anyone to travel a road that they have not been prepared to travel themselves. The dramatherapist has had to face their own demons, their pitiful weakness and desire for love and recognition. The necessity for the dramatherapist to 'meet themselves' in an honest personal encounter is a continuing challenge to their practice and this scrutiny remains constant.

Conclusions

Arts practitioners make brief interventions into people's lives. Even if the client is engaged in long-term therapy over several years, nonetheless the actual time spent with the therapist is small. The work goes on outside the therapeutic space because this is where it 'really matters' in lived reality.

The confidence to propose such interventions must carry with it clarity of *purpose*. I believe that the practitioner, whether in social theatre or drama-therapy, must be honest about self-doubt but not make a virtue of it. The ability to bend and accommodate, to regard all situations as contingent, can mask the underlying reality that patterns of behaviour are repeated, not randomly but for *reasons* good or ill. Similarly, artistic and therapeutic practices owe their existence to *reasons*, traditions born of material circumstances.

If you are doing forum theatre, don't take it off the shelf like a piece of technical equipment. Consider that it is a theatrical form that may use different genres – it is not merely a dramatic device. Remember next time you hear someone say 'let's forum it' that the form is part of the 'Arsenal of the Theatre of the Oppressed', which has a deeply developed radical history. Why use blunted tools when you might use finely tuned instruments honed through experience? And if you do forum theatre, respect its shape, its discipline, its form. Let it do its work by keeping faith with its boundaries – if you suddenly decide to switch to another form, or 'bend the rules', how will you ever know what you have worked with?

Artistic practice celebrates imagination and the freedom to break boundaries. At the same time it needs to create boundaries in order to break others – this is the implicit tension of both the creative process of social theatre and dramatherapy, to investigate the expressive form that can articulate what needs to be done to make the theatre of use to people. My belief is that dramatherapy is an art form and struggles with this tension as endemic to its practice.

Marina Jenkyns (1996) states that it is the drama that holds the therapy: 'It is that moment of perfect tension between two realities in a moment of absolute sincerity and absorption.'

This chapter is dedicated to my friend and colleague Reverend Dr Roger Grainger whose work gives me joy and inspiration.

Notes

1 See for example Thompson's (2003) discussion of the use of cognitive behavioural techniques in the work of the TIPP Centre at the University of Manchester.
2 See Winnicott's (1971) discussion of potential space.
3 We do not aim to 'cure'. Sometimes the best a therapist can achieve is to help the client find life more bearable.

References

Andersen-Warren, Madeline and Grainger, Roger (2000) *Practical Approaches to Dramatherapy*, London: Jessica Kingsley Publishers.

Brecht, Bertolt (1960) *Brecht on Theatre* (ed. John Willett), New York: Hill & Wang.

Chesner, Anna (1995) *Dramatherapy for People with Learning Disabilities, A World of Difference*, London: Jessica Kingsley Publishers.

Cox, Murray (1992) 'The Place of Metaphor in Psychotherapy Supervision. Creative Tensions between Forensic Psychotherapy and Dramatherapy', in Sue Jennings (ed.), *Dramatherapy Theory and Practice 2*, London: Tavistock/Routledge.

Goffman, Erving (1990) *The Presentation of Self in Everyday Life*, London: Penguin Books.

Grainger, Roger (1990) *Drama and Healing, the Roots of Dramatherapy*, London: Jessica Kingsley Publishers.

Jenkyns, Marina (1996) *The Play's the Thing. Exploring Text in Drama and Therapy*, London: Routledge.

Jennings, Sue (1992) *Dramatherapy with Families, Groups and Individuals*, London: Jessica Kingsley Publishers.

Jones, Phil (2007) *Drama as Therapy, Theatre as Living*, 2nd ed., London: Routledge.

Nicholson, Helen (2005) *Applied Drama: The Gift of Theatre*, Basingstoke: Palgrave Macmillan.

Pitruzzella, Salvo (2004) *Introduction to Dramatherapy, Person and Threshold*, London: Brunner Routledge.

Schininà, Guglielmo (2004) 'Here We Are: Social Theatre and Some Open Questions about Its Developments', *The Drama Review*, *48*, 3: 18–33.

Seymour, Anna (2006) *The Contest of Identity and Form*, unpublished conference paper delivered at the 2006 annual conference of the British Association of Dramatherapists, University of Nottingham, UK.

Thompson, James (2003) *Applied Theatre, Bewilderment and Beyond*, Bern: Peter Lang.

Thompson, James and Schechner, Richard (2004) 'Why "Social Theatre"?', *The Drama Review*, *48*, 3: 11–16.

Winnicott, D.W. (1971) *Playing and Reality*, London: Routledge.

3 Like ham in a temperance hotel

Healing, participation and education in social theatre

Guglielmo Schininà

Introduction

Social theatre is a theatre for change. It is a theatre that facilitates individuals, groups and communities in finding their own ways to meet their own needs, improve their social functioning, and eventually overcome unhappy situations.

Social theatre is therefore a variety or an 'arsenal', to use Boal's definition (Boal 1990), of creative tools, communication techniques, and artistic ethics, derived from performance studies and the history of theatre (Bernardi 2004; Schininà 2004a). These used in combination can bring people to express themselves freely, communicate better than before, redefine safely their own roles, discuss peacefully possible changes, and enact socially these personal and collective changes.

Over the last few years, however, social theatre has been mainly identified with theatre for healing and cure and prevention, rather than with theatre for participation. For the most part, social theatre has become an important – and sometimes indispensable – component of what is known as psychosocial intervention, and has therefore been affected by the same set of contradictions and limitations pertaining to this particular activity.

Throughout this chapter I argue that healing, participation and education cannot be understood as separate concerns in social theatre interventions. When they are, the risk of partiality, elitism, lack of ethics, exploitation of the beneficiary, subservience to dominant political discourses becomes extremely high. I substantiate my argument by discussing a number of observations, mostly drawn from my experience as a psychosocial manager and trainer in war-torn situations, in particular during the Kosovo, Iraqi and Lebanon crises.

Social theatre, psychosocial interventions, and war

Theatre in general, and social theatre in particular, is about working on limits and borders. Any theatre activity results from an urgency of some kind. For the human species, war probably represents the uppermost confrontation with its individual and collective limits, and the ultimate emergency. In tackling the issue of social theatre and healing, I have therefore decided to refer mainly to the use of theatre for psychosocial interventions in war-torn situations. The ethical, social, political implications become indeed more obvious in these contexts. However, the insights developed here could apply, to a varying extent, to any social theatre project in the mental health and psychosocial fields anywhere.[1]

The psychosocial theory, and theatre in psychosocial interventions: Participation and healing

A basic definition of 'psychosocial' can be found in the *Oxford English dictionary* (OED 1997), where it reads as 'pertaining to the influence of social factors on an individual's mind and behaviour, and to the inter-relation of behavioural and social factors; also and more widely pertaining to the interrelation between mind and society' (OED 1997).

The psychosocial perspective highlights the interrelation between psychological and social factors. It cannot be limited to either a psychological understanding of social factors, or a social understanding of psychiatric and psychological needs and healing, as is still common among mental health professionals worldwide. In my view, the scope of psychosocial work is much wider and much less fragmented, and its ultimate meaning lies precisely in the fundamental interconnectedness of the individual and the collective dimensions. Psychosocial programmes should aim at readjusting the role of individuals, groups and communities inside a given society.

The key word in psychosocial theory is 'role', a notion that situates itself at the intersection between individual construction and collective perception, psychological beliefs and social norms and habits. For this reason, the psychosocial approach proves especially useful in situations where individual, group and community roles are questioned, annihilated, in need of reconstruction and/or readjustment, as is the case with social settings affected by war, disasters, displacement or social disruptions. In all these contexts the four domains (individual–collective–social–psychological) cannot be compartmentalized, nor can one be given prominence over the others.

The readjustment and rehearsal of personal and collective roles, relationship and communication, limits, creative responses to unexpected situations, the self/context relation, and the process of ritualization are central topics in psychosocial work, especially when operating in war-affected situations. It would therefore seem all too natural that there should be a role for theatre, and especially for social theatre, in psychosocial interventions, given that drama addresses exactly the same issues and can boast a time-honoured record of responses across a wide range of cultures and circumstances. And yet, during my practice in psychosocial and social theatre in war-torn situations, I have been confronted with a number of problems and contradictions.

The psychosocial practice, and theatre in psychosocial interventions: Healing versus participation

The dominant psychosocial discourse in war-torn situations has been medical, pathological, individualistic and based on pre-packaged research and response frameworks that are not necessarily tailored to local realities, cultures and understandings. Psychosocial work often becomes a thera-peutic branch of humanitarian interventions that, from Kosovo onwards, have been a key component of international military interventions that were labelled 'humanitarian' (Kosovo) and 'preventive' (Iraq). A sort of transi-tive relation has been established between humanitarian war and humani-tarian intervention, which however raises a number of ethical dilemmas.

Is it appropriate for the international forces to bring war to a country or region, and simultaneously the therapeutic tools to investigate and eventually cure its effects? Is it ethical? And what can be the role of social theatre within this context? Can social theatre afford to be critical of the dominant political paradigm, or would it just be used to maintain the *status quo*, entertaining, distracting, appeasing, and relieving the suffering of the people? Should not social theatre instead foster the participation of beneficiary communi-ties in the humanitarian project, and thereby empower them to react?

I do not have definitive answers to these questions, but I can try to pinpoint what I feel to be the most urgent issues according to my experience in the field and to the international literature on the subject.

Mass trauma in conflict: The Kosovo case

In many recent international psychosocial programmes, mass trauma in conflict was taken for granted. During the Kosovo crisis, it was at a certain stage assumed that 75 per cent of the population had been severely trau-matized by the war – a notion that several closer assessments later failed to support. As Vanessa Pupavac highlights, 'the appearance of clinical con-ditions in war remains particular, not universal', and 'appearance of clinical trauma rendering people unable to function is relatively rare' (Pupavac 2004: 7). These early estimates, however, had the effect of bringing psycho-social response and mental health issues to centre stage. 'Trauma' readily became a 'buzzword' among fund raisers within many organizations. And, sadly, a lot of theatre projects were graced with the additional label of 'Trauma Response projects'.

PTSD and other western models: Kosovo and others

Most interventions were based on the notion of Post-Traumatic Stress Disorder (PTSD) syndrome. This was certainly the case in Kosovo, Sri Lanka and Iraq, where the unchallenged western presumption that there is a universal response to highly stressful events, and that this response can be categorized as a diagnosable form of mental disorder, resulted in cultural insensitivity. PTSD was conceptualized while dealing with Vietnam war veterans; it therefore refers to a very specific geographical, cultural, historical and social environment (Summerfield 2001) and cannot be applied per se to all war-related distress. While it is true that the PTSD approach was often criticized by many scholars and practitioners in the field, this was usually done in order to promote the use of alternative models – conversational versus medical-biological, psychotherapeutic versus cognitive-behavioural, and others (Losi 2002) – and not to endorse the empowerment of the beneficiaries and their active participation in identifying, prioritizing, and devising a response to their psychosocial (and not merely psychological) needs.

And what was the role of social theatre within these projects? On the whole, it provided entertainment, an alternative therapeutic tool, and the opportunity to involve people in high visibility events. Very often, social theatre was employed to get people to relate their life stories through autobiography, storytelling, metaphors, according to the western practice of counselling or talk therapy, rather than inviting them to create new stories or a new history. This was just another case of unquestioned reliance on foreign explanatory models that failed to acknowledge cultural specificity. In some societies, for instance, silence and avoidance are preferable to remembrance. In the case of Kosovo, this particular use of social theatre resulted in the validation of collective political narratives of suffering and war, which tended to disregard individual specificity and promote violent discourse. Was it indeed feasible to work on people's roles in the context of a military and humanitarian intervention that took for granted their role as victims or perpetrators and inevitably cast foreign experts as their saviours? Should not these fixed roles have been targeted and readjusted by theatre interventions in the first place?

Normal reactions to abnormal situations: Iraq

By disregarding individual and collective coping and resilience mechanisms, many international programmes risked 'pathologizing' entire communities. As Derek Summerfield puts it, 'features of post traumatic stress disorder are often epiphenomenal and not what survivors are attending to or consider important: Most of them remain active and effective in the face of continuing hardship and threat' (Summerfield 2001: 123). Moreover, certain psychological reactions are just normal reactions to abnormal situations, and as such they should not be cast as mental pathologies. Quite to the contrary, they are a healthy sign of people's capacity to assess their situation. People living in Iraq today and suffering from fears, anger, and nightmares are simply showing an awareness of their predicament. Considering them ill would be unethical and would only corroborate the mistakes of the international intervention.

What is the current use of social theatre in Iraq? It serves to divert people, especially children. It creates safe spaces. That is all that can be allowed in the present security circumstances. But is it ethical to create fictional safe spaces in what has become one of the unsafest places on earth? Is this not liable to harm, rather than help, the populations involved? And does it not amount to a paradox, considering that it comes along with and from the very same cultures that occasioned those security circumstances?

Training as propagation of ideas: Anywhere

Education and training have played a rather prominent role in most psychosocial programmes in emergency and war-affected contexts, mainly because of the need to ensure the sustainability of the programmes themselves. Training local people means, first, the possibility of relying on local staff who would be fully knowledgeable of the project during its implementation; second, having someone to hand over the project to when budgets become too low to fund an international presence; and third, the chance for organizations and aid workers to leave a lasting mark of their presence in the field, thereby laying the foundations for long-term professional international networks. Training, however, is grounded in foreign models and expertise, while the relevance of local experience, training and knowledge is usually downplayed. It is also generally based on priorities identified by agencies that are often more concerned with the implementation of their projects than with the local population's actual needs.

One could argue that training programmes are often successful, attract large numbers of participants, and are evaluated positively by those who attend. It should be kept in mind, however, that international interventions create a labour market with which the local one cannot compete in terms of opportunities and salaries. Job offers and training tend to come from the same sources. In this sense, it results obviously that education comes across as a field where the boundary between capacity building and cultural colonialism tends to become blurred. And what is the role of theatre in these circumstances? It is used instrumentally, as an effective method to transmit and validate through experience new concepts and tools over a short period of time. It is more and more common to see social theatre become a subject matter to be learned. But social theatre is an experience more than a technique, and aims at participation. How can it fit in ready-made training modules that aim at remodelling local expertise to suit pre-planned projects, rather than facilitating the creation of new scenarios?

The internationalization of ethics: Iraq

In 2005 I conducted on behalf of the International Organization for Migration (IOM) an assessment of the psychosocial situation of displaced communities in Iraq (Schininà 2005). I was particularly worried and impressed by some coincidental results. First, it emerged clearly that the Iraqis were reporting their psychological (or better, spiritual) concerns to traditional – mostly spiritual – healers and not to local professionals. Second, all the people interviewed were noticing an unexpected deterioration (orchestrated from above, according to them) of the relations between different religious groups: Sunni, Sh'ia, Catholics, and so on. Third, societies were being religionized, because religious leaders had also suddenly turned into political authority figures. Moreover, assuming religion-based values and habits offered people an effective way of becoming accepted into a wider community. Finally, many people felt that they were in need of spiritual help, such as the one provided by psychosocial counselling, especially to cope with the consequences of the Operation 'Iraqi Freedom'. And yet what can one do in a situation where people have pressing psychosocial needs, but the only response they are prepared to accept is a religious one, in a context where the therapeutic, social, religious and political responses alike are all concentrated in the same hands?

In a broader perspective, I started to wonder whether my concerns did not smack of arrogance, and whether the same crooked logic was not at work behind all international interventions. Any international psychosocial intervention attached to humanitarian relief operations risks turning into the therapeutic side of a single political, cultural, and sometimes ideological and military discourse. The 'Iraqi Freedom' intervention was justified and informed by a distorted or even perverted concept of democracy, on which the ethics and practice of the military, political, informational intervention were based. My assessment, too, was grounded in a democratic understanding of psychosocial needs, and its validity was therefore undermined by the same paradoxes and contradictions.

The risk management approach

Finally, psychosocial programmes can be seen as an internationalization of the risk management approach, defined by Pupavac (2004) as the nonparticipative preventive actions that inform the social policies and activities of many western governments. Over the past few decades, the risk management approach has progressively reduced the value of politics and participation, promoting instead the therapeutic governance of societies. People have been turned from political subjects into the recipients of administrative actions, and as a result they have increasingly renounced active participation by delegating decision-making to politicians.

The most glaring example of this process and of its consequences was seen in the USA in the (mis)management of the armed intervention in Iraq and in the failure of the preventive and rescue operations during the Katrina flood. In both cases, risks were not properly assessed, priorities were arguably determined, and the responses claimed more human lives than all the terrorist attacks ever suffered by the USA. In both cases, the US government manifestly failed to deal responsibly with national and international crises, and this caused the current administration's popularity to drop dramatically. What seems to have proved particularly bewildering for Americans was their leaders' incapability to perform a correct risk analysis, as a result of sheer incompetence or of the misleading influence of ideological beliefs and vested interests. And yet, the risk management approach to politics, according to which societies hand over to a ruling elite the task of setting security priorities and social agendas, still goes unquestioned.

So far, the theatre has been unable to change the general perception on these issues.

A step forward? The Lebanon crisis

The Lebanon crisis of 2006 produced a drastic and positive change in the psychosocial approach to conflict and war. While the war was still being fought, an Inter-Agency Technical Committee on Mental Health and Psychosocial, comprising 12 of the more active international agencies in the respective fields (among them, WHO, UNICEF, the IOM and many others), issued technical advice for the emergency (2006).

The document stated that while wars produce a number of distressing factors, only in a small percentage of the population is the distress so severe that it limits the basic functioning of individuals. The committee therefore discouraged the medicalization of communities and advocated the promotion of a safe and supportive environment, through the access to basic rights such as health and education, water and sanitation, shelter and livelihood, and the preservation of family unity to avoid displacement. It was also emphasized that the key programming principles should focus on human rights, participation, resiliency, normalization of daily life, a community-based approach, capacity building and integrated multidisciplinary support. Interventions should comply with the rule of 'DO NOT HARM' – that is, avoid culturally inappropriate tools, or inappropriate explorations of distressing events – and perform two necessary and concomitant actions:

1   They should provide social and protective activities for the entire population, including: access to services and to psychosocially aware humanitarian assistance; help to communities in re-establishing their normal activities and rituals, including grieving rituals; psychosocial training for community members; information; promotion of recreational, sporting, artistic and cultural activities, group discussions and support groups; reduction of children's exposure to the representation of violence; life skills and vocational training; psychosocial care for humanitarian workers and avoidance of widespread and short-term trauma counselling.

2   Psychological treatment for people in acute distress and people with pre-existing mental disorders, including: psychological first aid;

psychotropic help in exceptional cases only and always in combination with non-medical forms of support; avoidance of programming focusing on a single diagnosis (e.g. PTSD), and support for programming considering the wider range of urgent neuropsychiatric needs.

Finally, the document recommended avoiding the terms 'trauma' and 'therapy', which were deemed inappropriate in the Middle Eastern context, and using instead 'distress', 'stress', and 'structured activities'. Drama was mentioned as a necessary psychosocial tool.

The Inter-Agency Technical Advice is undoubtedly a step forward from the theoretical point of view.

In practice, though, it has to be noted that the document was written by international organizations and only endorsed by local authorities. The issue of participation was at last addressed in theory, but the process was initially non-participatory. Ironically, the Lebanon crisis found the local professionals and political movements highly prepared. While hostilities were still ongoing, the Khyam Rehabilitation Centre for Victims of Torture had already issued its Ten Commandments for Mental Health, instructing people to respond to the crisis by resorting to notions of heroism, God and martyrdom.

Education and healing

So far I have investigated the dangers involved in a therapeutic use of social theatre that disregards the importance of participation, or in contexts that hinder participation. By contrast, when it comes to social theatre and education the healing value that training experiences have or might have on the participants can hardly be overestimated. To illustrate my argument, I turn to an episode that occurred during a training programme in social theatre that was held in south-eastern Sicily in 2005.

The programme consisted of six modules of 20 hours each. The group of participants included 27 theatre practitioners, social workers, activists, psychologists, teachers and educators, as well as actors aged between 19 and 64. The modules covered the full range of social theatre practices, following a progression from individual empowerment and expression in the group (dramatherapy), to group building (social theatre, complex circle), to self-identification of problems and resources in the group (complex circle) or identification by the group of problems and resources within society (theatre of the oppressed; TdO), to direct social action, including dramaturgical actions (TdO, dramaturgy of the group). The training emphasized the value of participation (Nemoprofeta 2006).

Given the professionally oriented curriculum, and the background and expertise of most participants, I had expected the technical component to come to prominence. This was not the case. For instance: at the end of the 'theatre of the oppressed' module, participants were asked to divide into subgroups, identify an oppressing situation, and present it in a forum theatre. The topic had to be chosen according to specific guidelines designed to ensure that the dramatized story would focus on social rather than personal issues.

One group presented the episode of a car crash: a man driving his car, another man crossing the road on a bicycle; the rider gets run over by the car and dies, the driver bursts into frantic crying; a policeman intervenes, and two symbolic figures, one representing guilt, the other a positive attitude, comment on the scene and interact with the driver. In selecting this particular story, the group had ignored all the instructions they had received. The performance counted more as the first scene of a psychodrama session, the one where the problematic scene is presented, than as anything resembling a theatre forum. Needless to say, it dramatized an event that had actually occurred to one of the participants a few weeks earlier. It was obvious to all that the participant's need to share this story and his feelings about it in order to obtain help from the group was extremely pressing, and prevailed over any technical consideration or direction. The other group members, perceiving his urgency to emotionally ventilate the experience, initially chose not to interfere. After a while, however, I asked the group to modify the scene so that the forum could eventually take place. The setting then changed to the oppressive situation brought into being by the accident within the driver's family.

This episode left me deeply perplexed and raised the following dilemmas: (1) Is it possible to actually train people in social theatre, given that the experience of social theatre involves first and foremost working on the self? (2) Can a training programme in social theatre concentrate on participation only, ignoring the psychological needs of the participants? (3) If the answer is no, then is there any difference between a group in training and an informal group? Is there any difference between a trainer and a facilitator? (4) Is it possible, within a social theatre learning context, to use pre-packaged training material, or can this material only come from the specific experience of each group? Was it appropriate in this particular case to ask the group to change the story to make it fit in with the technical description of the module (theatre forum)? Or would it rather have been more effective, in educational terms, to keep the scene as it was and work on it using a psychodrama approach, thereby meeting the obvious need of the group member from which it had originated? After all, the aim of social theatre is allegedly that of serving real, self-identified needs, not abstract techniques. I still have not found a definitive answer to these questions.

Conclusion

This chapter offers doubts rather than certainties, dilemmas rather than conclusions, but it does take a clear-cut stance on the importance of understanding the interconnectedness of the therapeutic, participatory and educational facets of social theatre. Even in extreme situations, as in war-torn societies, social theatre should aim at social empowerment and participation; otherwise there is a real danger of corroborating questionable therapeutic and political approaches, and of becoming instrumental to the internationalization of the therapeutic governance of societies. Conversely, even in a protected educational environment, any social theatre experience inevitably comes to include personal involvement and the venting of intimate feelings and stories. Here, concentrating on participation while downplaying the therapeutic dimension of social theatre could amount to placing technique and ideology above the needs of the individual. Healing, participation and education should be one single, indivisible realm of action within social theatre practices.

Note

1 Projects using a different approach have existed even if unaccounted for in this chapter. Limiting our observations to the emergencies discussed here, we should refer, at least, to the International Consortium of Solidarity (ICS) psychosocial projects in the Balkans area (see Schininà 2004b; Rubbioli 2006), to the IOM project 'Psychosocial and Trauma Response in Kosovo' (see Losi 2002), and to IOM's and some UNICEF funded programmes during the last Lebanese crisis.

Bibliography

Bernardi, C. (2004) *Il Teatro Sociale. L'arte tra disagio e cura*, Rome: Carocci.
Boal, A. (1990) *L'Arc en Ciel du Désir*, Paris: Ramsay.
Inter-Agency Technical Group (2006) *Mental Health and Psychosocial Protection and Support for Adults and Children Affected by the Middle Eastern Crisis: Inter Agency Technical Advice for the Current Crisis*, unpublished document.
Khyam Rehabilitation Center for Victims of Torture (2006) *Ten Commandments for Mental Health*, Tyr.
Losi, N. (2002) 'Psychosocial and Trauma Response in Kosovo', in R. Papadopoulos (ed.), *No Place Like Home*, London: Karnac, Tavistock.
Nemoprofeta (2006) *Report of the Training Path: Più teatro per Tutti*, available at: www.nemoprofeta.org/teatrosociale/piùteatropertutti/report/download, accessed 15 January 2006.
Oxford English Dictionary (1997) Oxford: Oxford University Press.
Pupavac, V. (2004) *Therapeutic Governance: The Politics of Psychosocial Intervention and Trauma Risk Management*, available at: www.odi.org.uk/hpg/confpapers/pupavac.doc, accessed 21 July 2006.
Rubbioli, C. (2006) *Teatro e Guerra, L'intervento di Guglielmo Schininà nei centri collettivi in Serbia*, University thesis, Educational Sciences Faculty, University of Torino.
Schininà, G. (2002) 'Cursed Communities, Rituals of Separation and Communication as Vengeance. A Redefinition of Artistic Intervention in War and War-torn Situations. The Kosovo Case', in C. Bernardi, M. Dragone and G. Schininà (eds), *War Theatres and Actions for Peace: Community-Based Dramaturgy and the Conflict Scene*, Milan: Euresis.

Schininà, G. (2004a) 'Here We Are. A Background on Social Theatre and Some Open Questions about its Developments', *The Drama Review, 48*, 3: 18–33.

Schininà, G. (2004b) 'Far Away, So Close. Psychosocial and Theatre Activities with Serbian Refugees', *The Drama Review, 48*, 3: 34–50.

Schininà, G. (2005) *Psychosocial Needs of ID Populations in Iraq. An Assessment*, Amman: IOM.

Summerfield, D. (2001) 'The Invention of Post Traumatic Stress Disorder and the Social Usefulness of a Psychiatry Category', *British Medical Journal, 322*, 13: 121–6.

4 *Ah pava! Nathiye*

Respecting silence and the performances of not-telling

James Thompson

'Trauma relief' is a dominant mode of practice and discourse (a 'master term'[1]) that has become an explanatory tool for many artistic programmes with individuals and communities in crisis. With its connections to the field of Holocaust Studies and origins in body of knowledge emerging from the First World War through to the post-Vietnam research on post-traumatic stress disorder (Argenti-Pillen, 2003, p. 7; Caruth, 1995, pp. 3–11), it has become an important paradigm from which a range of micro-practices, including much applied and social theatre, find their theoretical rationale. This chapter argues that these culturally particular theories and practices, emerging from a certain historical moment, have led to treatment demands that have at times been uncritically adopted by social theatre practitioners. The assumptions emanating from the 'trauma diagnosis' have led to many demands for people 'to express themselves' with the prescription of 'telling one's story' often viewed as a key method and necessary precondition for 'relief', 'liberation' or 'healing'. The argument presented here is that the prescription has then transformed itself into a proscription as the binary opposite of silence or 'not-telling' is somehow denigrated as a dangerous retreat, a failure, or the site of continued harm. Theatre makers have recognised an apparent congruence between their storytelling forms and the telling urged in projects with trauma survivors and have subsequently sought to make a rapid alliance between the two fields of practice.

This chapter seeks to question that alliance. It suggests that the insistence that survivors 'tell their stories' is a culturally particular approach that can become problematic if applied universally. I believe that *tell your story* can become an imperative rather than a self-directed action. This results in a set of practices and assumptions that inculcate themselves into relief operations in many locations, ignoring and potentially interrupting culturally particular modes of mourning, coping or crisis management. And in being a popular framework for social theatre, simplistic demands for storytelling can be in danger of having a similarly problematic impact on this range of local practices.

This chapter proposes a flexible ethos that respects culturally particular processes. An ethos that, for example, validates silence as a possible form of resistance, that accepts numerous artistic forms as appropriate responses to horror and that respects multiple context specific modes of dealing and living with the appalling. This might, of course, include storytelling but the argument here is that this should not be the default position for social theatre makers.

Example 1

After the Asian tsunami in December 2004, a huge relief effort channelled resources into the disaster-affected countries. As the second worst-hit country,[2] Sri Lanka received financial aid but also a plethora of specialist teams dealing with all aspects of disaster relief. Prevalent in these groups were a large number proposing a bewildering range of therapeutic or psychosocial interventions. Some of these were invited, but the majority simply arrived with their elaborate plans for offering relief to the 'tsunami-traumatised population'.[3] My example here originates in the sense of disbelief expressed by Sri Lankan colleagues who were working in development and psychological services prior to the tsunami.[4] Conversations with these individuals, who rapidly became gatekeepers to the newcomers, indicated that:

- Many of new teams considered all Sri Lankans to be in need of psychosocial support or trauma relief by the very fact that they were living in areas touched by the tsunami.
- The *telling of stories* was a dominant approach and used indiscriminately in chaotic settings.
- Communities were frequently asked to *tell their stories* with next to no follow up or clarity as to what was to be done with the stories told.

Example 2

While the first example is general, the second refers to a specific moment from a theatre-based intervention. In February 2005, a British arts organisation was running a series of projects in a tsunami displaced-people's camp in the south of Sri Lanka. While they ran sessions involving a range of art forms, they also brought two registered dramatherapists to conduct theatre workshops with children. The dramatherapists worked in the camp for several weeks with a somewhat transient group of school age children. Early in the project one of the practitioners, having played some theatre games, asked the children to tell their stories of the day that the tsunami hit. One child started to cry and left the group and later the dramatherapist complained, somewhat at a loss, that they were 'not prepared tell their stories' and 'all they want to do is play'.[5]

A woman from the camp came to the drama group asking for money to help rebuild her house. She was informed by the dramatherapist that they had no money to give and that they were only there to do drama. She responded in Sinhala, '*Ah pava! Nathiye*' – loosely translated as a sarcastic, 'Oh great [literally *sin*]! Theatre.'[6]

Trauma – 'a cut into the soul'[7]

A *trauma* was originally a medical term for a wound in the flesh that during the course of twentieth century was adopted by psychiatric and mental health professions as a psychological injury. Although a definition of trauma as a 'cut into the soul' indicates a somewhat dubious religious framework, it is the relation between specific psychological definitions and subsequent treatment procedures that are important here. Cathy Caruth defines it as:

> [a response] sometimes delayed, to an overwhelming event or events, which takes the form of repeated, intrusive hallucinations, dreams, thoughts or behaviours stemming from the event, along with numbing that may have begun during or after the experience, and possibly also increased arousal to (and avoidance of) stimuli recalling the event.
>
> (Caruth, 1995, p. 4)

Traumatic incidents thus overwhelm the memory-making facilities of the person to create a numbness close to the event and then an uncontrolled revisiting at periods sometimes long after. Traumatic events are thus the most extreme moments of horror, loss or violence that disturb usual patterns of memory to create affective memory traces that may appear unpredictably in the future. The Caruth definition above is commonly linked to diagnoses of PTSD where past incidents continue to disturb an individual in the present. This chapter does not claim that PTSD symptoms are not real for those that suffer them but makes three related observations. First, that the meanings attached to these symptoms are vastly different across cultures, and dreams or hallucinations for example cannot be detached from cultural systems of interpretation. Second, that because the meanings are so different, the treatments must engage with those differences and not ignore, minimise or deny them. Finally, PTSD is a particular diagnosis that cannot be mapped onto all individuals who experience uncomfortable or terrible events. For many, as is fully acknowledged in the literature, involvement in an appalling incident does not lead to any PTSD symptoms.

The tendency of the definition of trauma to confuse what it claims to be universal psychological traits with the culturally particular can be seen starkly in the following quotation from Schauer *et al.* For these writers, the 'core' of psychological trauma is:

the alienation from life of a wounded soul. In the moment in which pain and harm is purposefully inflicted by one human being onto another, breach of humanity has occurred. Trauma destroys the human kernel that resides in moments or acts that occur within a social context: communication, speech, autobiographical remembrance, dignity, peace, and freedom.

(Schauer *et al.*, 2005, p. 1)

I in no way want to minimise the 'pain and harm' caused by many appalling events, but concepts such as 'soul', 'humanity' and 'human kernel' coupled with 'dignity, peace and freedom' seem to mix the quasi-religious with a human rights discourse, all under the umbrella of a medical diagnosis. Although this throws doubts onto the 'universal' claims of PTSD, the same book assertively claims that 'there is no evidence for the hypothesis that the prevalence and validity of PTSD depends on cultural factors' (Ibid., p. 12). If the very definition used for trauma already relies on concepts that are self-evidently not automatically translatable to different cultural communities (ask a Sri Lankan Buddhist about human kernels for example), I would argue that the universal claims are suspect.

This link is far from obvious, but the consequence can be that treatment specificities from PTSD slip easily into protocols for all who experience events that are labelled traumatic. In both examples, there is an assumption that all people living in tsunami-affected areas of Sri Lanka, or war regions more generally, are affected by trauma and will therefore need a treatment approach that emerged from the specific problems with memory noticed in people who suffer from PTSD. Although 'trauma professionals' may deny this slippage is made, in the often chaotic, difficult to manage and highly complex moments of crisis with huge numbers of disrupted people, I would argue it happens frequently. The result is that a minority response to awful and terrible incidents, based on particular, culturally located moments, is transformed into a near universal set of theories and practices.

The imperative to tell

One of the many symptoms of PTSD is that individuals will struggle to explain or describe a past incident in detail. The awfulness of the experience is somehow beyond sense and therefore beyond the bounds of recalling in any easily structured way. Much of the treatment for PTSD seeks to overcome these difficulties so that a troubling, easily triggered, reliving can become shaped into less injurious forms of memory (ideally one that permits the events to be contained within a narrative form that the person is more able to control). Moving too rapidly from a respect for the difficulty to an emphasis on a solution once again jumps dangerously from the case-specific analysis to an over-simple universalised response. This can be seen in the trauma literature where the accounts of the strength of those people who are able to speak of their histories is transformed into an imperative that the telling must be undertaken. For example psychiatrist Dori Laub creates a proscription in the following:

> [T]he survivors did not only need to survive so that they could tell their stories: they also needed to tell their stories in order to survive. There is [. . .] an imperative need to *tell* and thus to come to *know* one's story, unimpeded by the ghosts from the past against which one has to protect oneself. One has to know one's buried truth in order to be able to live one's life.
>
> (Laub, 1995, p. 63; emphasis in original)

Although the imperative here seems to start as a desire among the survivors of past horrors, it is possible to see how the desires of some become projected as the needs of all. The 'imperative to tell' becomes validated so strongly in the literature that it is easy to see how this shift from the *imperative within* the survivor to an *imperative without* – from the therapist to the client – emerges. An example of this can be seen in another quotation from Laub:

> This imperative to tell and to be heard can become itself an all-consuming life task. Yet no amount of telling seems ever to do justice to this inner compulsion [. . .] The pressure thus continues unremittingly, and if words are not trustworthy or adequate, the life that is chosen can become the vehicle by which the struggle to tell continues.
>
> (Laub, 1995, p. 63)

By way of example from a theatre practitioner, Jane Moss explains the link between PTSD and storytelling in the following way:

> [T]he symptoms of post-traumatic stress disorder – recurring dreams and hallucinations – are involuntary returns to the horrific events in which the person experiences the anxiety not present before and confronts the enigma of survival . . . To work through the trauma, the person must speak of it, bearing endless testimony to the impossibility of survival.
>
> (Moss, 2001, p. 174)

They do not struggle to speak or maybe only have a desire to speak – now *they must* speak. So while telling is clearly represented as difficult, it is also proposed as necessary. Laub writes that 'one *has* to know one's buried truth' (my emphasis) suggesting this requirement. Although telling for some people can be an 'all-consuming life task', what is important to acknowledge is that an internal condition problematically becomes an external compulsion. What is a specific response is in danger of turning into a Golden Rule – an imperative. Not that you do tell but that you *must*.

Trauma, the 'importance of storytelling' and the connections to theatre

In a discussion about the importance of the Fortunoff Video Archive of Holocaust survivor testimony, Dori Laub makes the following comment:

> Yet it is essential for this narrative that *could not be articulated* to be *told*, to be *transmitted*, to be *heard* [. . .] Such endeavours make up for the survivors' need for witnesses, as well as for the historical lack of witnessing, by setting the stage for a reliving, a reoccurrence of the event, in the presence of a witness.
>
> (Laub, 1995, p. 69)

While I do not seek to deny the relevance of this archive as a remarkable and vital collection, this quotation once again seems to place the need to tell one's story as essential: as ahistorical and not something constructed by the world we live in today. The relevance of these comments for the argument here however, is the connection they make to the practice of theatre. In announcing that the archive is 'setting the stage for a reliving, a reoccurrence of the event, in the presence of a witness' he establishes a set of terms that can easily – and problematically – link this process to the construction of a performance. This dynamically illustrates why the practice of creating theatre with certain groups of people can very easily find an explanatory framework within the discourse of trauma and specifically research on testimony. Theatre makers have borrowed from these disciplines to justify and explain their theatre practice because they already use quasi-theatrical terminology that emphasises the repeat and the staging of that repeat: because they emphasise the importance of telling a story in front of witnesses (whether that be the therapist, archivist or audience). The danger of this interdisciplinary borrowing is that 'making theatre' as a response to traumatic experiences uses a theory that is, as has been argued above, particular to a specific form of traumatic stress experienced in a minority of people and in a particular historical and cultural moment. If theatre borrows from this discourse and seeks to transfer its logic to other cultural and geographical settings, it too is in danger of universalising and prescribing how people should respond to appalling incidents.

This borrowing can be seen in an account of Kurdish and South African performance by Kimberly Segall. It is worth quoting her at length to see the move from particular account to general framework of analysis in action.

> In another scene, a young boy in the video described the way everyone in his village was brought to a large bulldozed pit and shot [. . .] These stories, related through oral and media forms, also circulated in songs, were reworked with ancient legends, emerged in poetic laments at funerals, and were redesigned as songs of Kurdish courage to be played

during festive dances. Similarly, in South Africa, stories of the apart-
heid police raiding and burning homes [. . .] emerged in performances
and songs [. . .] instances in both groups where performances move
individuals from debilitating isolation (personal trauma) to com-
munally embraced mourning.

(Segall, 2005, p. 138)

The parenthesis in the final sentence is vital. A complex account is reduced to
a particular mode of understanding and, although there is no way of
knowing whether in these highly diverse communities there were examples of
the symptoms of traumatic stress, their experiences become labelled as such.
She relies on the trope of 'stories' because this is a familiar way of understanding fluid and multiple cultural performances and she seems to shoehorn
radically different practices into that over-convenient category. Stories
'circulate' as songs and are 'redesigned' as songs or as dances without it
being clear how exactly they *remain* as stories. Because trauma studies, and
the sub-set of theatre practice that borrows from it, requires storytelling as
its treatment and dominant practice-based strategy, cultural acts of a
community in crisis are interpreted as various forms of storytelling rather
than the multiple acts of cultural expression that they in fact appear to be:

[T]he cultural practices of rituals, songs, public storytelling, and funeral
laments that perform the past in a new context emphasize the distinction between the traumatic past and the present moment. The embodied
memory of well-known verses shifts out of the cognitive mode – since
cognition is often disrupted by PTSD – to a physical, rhythmic release
of tension, and the improvisation and spontaneity accompanying
storytelling and singing – in juxtaposition to the helpless state of torture
and terror – offers a measure of artistic choice and control.

(Ibid., p. 139)

People are all given the diagnosis of PTSD when it is acknowledged that a
minority of people in crisis situations suffer from the associated symptoms
(Schauer *et al.*, 2005, p. 12) and the performances are still understood as
either variants of or 'accompaniments' to the dominant mode, which is
storytelling. What is in fact most remarkable about the practices outlined in
the Segall article is that there are multiple art forms mentioned and many of
them might have no formal 'telling' or narrative structure (songs, laments,
rituals and dances) that would be the usual 'requirement' or 'imperative' in
trauma relief work. The apparently universal need to tell is met here with a
whole range of arts practices, many of which it could be argued are as much
about forgetting as about remembrance. They are perhaps not contained
within either a 'telling' or a 'not-telling' framework, and instead exist as
multiple means of actively displaying, ignoring, remembering or forgetting
experience.

In their work on forms of remembrance Simon *et al.* discuss what they call the strategy of the *difficult return*, where projects of remembrance do not seek to heal the 'cuts to the soul' with over-neat forms of resolution. Instead:

> remembrance as a difficult return then becomes a series of propositions of how to live with what cannot be redeemed, what must remain a psychic and social wound that bleeds.
>
> (Simon *et al.*, 2000, p. 5)

Although the imagery here is quite brutal, the suggestion is that the past can find a place to live problematically in the present rather than be cured: that the struggle of that past's difficultness can be validated rather than always becoming a problem to be overcome. Recognising that struggle, and seeking to work with it in culturally meaningful ways, seeks to break the link that welds the 'people are traumatised' cause to the 'they must tell their story' solution. In the account from Segall, what is described is a community using multiple artistic methods that have complex relations to the problems of the past. This I would argue is perhaps an artistic version of that *difficult return* and could just as easily not be connected to discourses of PTSD. What the writer does is try to create a neat categorisation that in fact fails to contain this plethora of practices. In practice, people have multiple reactions to terror that cannot be reduced to a radically passive 'helpless state' or a 'debilitating isolation'. My suggestion here is that perhaps arts programmes need to step out of the umbrella of trauma studies in order for their varying effects to be realised. The more fluid concept of the *difficult return* might be a place from which to start these analyses.

The 'failure of silence'

The word *proscription* has been used here in the critique of trauma studies' reliance on a formula that people *must* find ways of having their stories told. The suggestion that in certain circumstances people do want to tell their stories, or that by telling they receive some relief from the debilitating memories of the past, becomes, through iteration, a rule. By creating a rule, a certain sense of righteousness and disdain for those who disobey becomes evident. This disdain was seen in the teams of 'trauma specialists' who descended on Sri Lanka and criticised the resistance to their work as evidence that people did not know what was best for them, and in the shock of the dramatherapist who did not know what to do with her rule-breaking charges. The operation of the 'rule' is also dynamically shown in the way that the binary opposite of *tell your story*, not-telling or 'silence', is discussed. It is important to examine this briefly because by recognising the strength of the disregard for not-telling, the potentially authoritarian nature of the trauma industry can be demonstrated. I would argue that it is from this dismissal of an ill-defined *silence* that the refusal to acknowledge the possible alternatives embedded in local practices stems.

To illustrate the argument a series of quotations from psychiatrist Dori Laub will be used.

> That the speakers about trauma on some level prefer silence so as to protect themselves from the fear of being listened to – and of listening to themselves. That while silence is defeat, it serves them both as sanctuary and as a place of bondage.
>
> (Felman and Laub, 1992, p. 58)

> None find peace in silence, even when it is their choice to remain silent.
>
> (Ibid., p. 64)

> Survivors who do not tell their story become victims of a distorted memory [. . .] The 'not telling' of the story serves as a perpetuation of its tyranny.
>
> (Ibid., p. 64)

> The events become more and more distorted in their silent retention and pervasively invade and contaminate the survivor's daily life. The longer the story remains untold, the more distorted it becomes in the survivor's conception of it, so much so that the survivor doubts the reality of the actual events.
>
> (Ibid., p. 64)

In these quotations we discover that 'silence' is a place in which 'none find peace'; it is a 'defeat' and a 'place of bondage'. Although Laub does permit silence to be a 'sanctuary', the overall emphasis here is easily read as punitive. Silence is not healthy, not a place that those that have suffered should remain. It is ultimately damaging, a contamination and a perpetuation of tyranny. And by extension those that either support not-telling, or communities that seem not to realise its importance, are by implication guilty of committing these acts of tyranny. Again, to emphasise, the argument here is not a dismissal of the importance of telling stories per se. Rather, it is a reaction to how this discipline has embedded within it a set of assumptions that when put into operation can lead to a denial and at worse a disregard for alternative and possibly multiple responses to crises. When telling becomes essentialised as an act against the tyrannical in a discipline that has a problematic global reach, how can a specific community that has variant local methods of survival and resistance, develop explanatory regimes that can compete?

There are two points against this marginalisation of silence that are made here before the fuller defence in the next section. First, there is a tendency to create a binary between speaking and silence that forgets that both are part of processes that many engage with at different times in their histories. By positioning silence against speaking, it reduces it to a passive failure rather than giving it any possibility for agency. Silence in fact could be an *active* means of coping at certain points in the history of a person's relation to an appalling experience. It is not only the dwelling place of the feeble and deluded but also potentially the tactic of the strong.

Second, it is important to emphasise that Laub here is discussing Holocaust survivors and it is difficult to tell whether the account is peculiar to certain individuals or an accurate description of them all. While the particular is to be respected deeply, it does appear that from the experience of some a generalisation is made. The argument of this chapter is that it is problematic to make a case that these experiences are translatable to all survivors of horror, at all points in history and across all cultures. Laub is not necessarily doing this, but one of the dangers of the dominance of western visions of survival and healing is that the specificity of one set of survival processes becomes the recipe for others.

Respecting the paradox

Writing on psychodrama with trauma survivors, psychodramatist Peter Kellerman notes the following:

> Frequently, there is a contradictory (and largely paradoxical) effort to both remember and to forget, both to approach and to avoid the traumatic event in a compulsive, repeated fashion.
>
> (Kellerman and Hudgins, 2000, p. 24)

This chapter has argued for a respect for this paradox and an acceptance of the past's place in the present as a complex and not easily solvable *difficult return*. Kellerman however cannot resist a desire to resolve this paradox when he elaborates later:

> Getting the traumatic experiences out into the open is in itself a liberation from the earlier tendency to repress the emotional impact of the event.
>
> (Ibid., p. 28)

Similarly, in Schauer *et al.* the paradox is recognised but then overcome with a compulsion:

> From an outsider's perspective, it might seem that 'Narration' and 'Trauma' are radically opposed, and mutually exclusive, as people suffering these crimes are in too much pain [. . .] to share their stories. However, these two concepts are intimately connected. The atrocities cannot remain buried forever and eventually the victim will be

compelled to speak. It is this dichotomy that creates the foothold for this approach.

(Schauer et al., 2005, p. 2)

It is not clear whether they are compelled to speak by their own motivation, but in placing this statement in a manual proposing 'exposure' to narrative, I would contend the compulsion has external drivers. Similarly Kellerman's liberation might work for some, but in insisting on it, writing it and creating professions from this basis, the complex reality of different communities' suffering becomes overridden with a dictat.

This is not to argue that silence is better than speaking or that theatre practitioners should only be interested in the performance of non-stories rather than stories, but that all cultural activities are potentially appropriate responses, if they are understood from within the contexts in which they emerge.

A Sri Lankan response?

I now propose to turn briefly to one such context by returning to the examples from the beginning. In order to respect the specificities of a particular setting, a detailed understanding of how talking, storytelling and grief are exhibited and given meaning within that society is vital before decisions are made as to the different communities' needs. For Sri Lanka we need to ask what storytelling means to Sinhala young people. We need to know how bad events are remembered or forgotten within their community. What processes already exist to deal with, live through or manage crises? And in terms of the arts, what forms of cultural expression are already in place?

While there are numerous anthropological studies of Sri Lanka that are relevant to this argument (Brow, 1996; Kapferer, 1988, 1991; Daniel, 1996; and Obeyesekere, 1990), the work of Alex Argenti-Pillen is perhaps the most revealing as a starting point to answer some of these questions. She offers both a critique of trauma studies and 'a detailed critique of the ways in which the notion "war trauma" has been exported to non-Western societies through the implementation of humanitarian counselling services in war torn societies worldwide' (Argenti-Pillen, 2003, p. xii). Her analysis gives both a methodological response to the problems raised by the examples here and also an insight into how the specificities of Sri Lanka might challenge the assumptions they contain. Her overall study seeks to explore how 'the trauma paradigm has reached rural communities in southern Sri Lanka' and by doing so she aims to reveal 'the effect of trauma counselling programs' on these areas (Ibid., p. 8). The suggestion here is that practices based on the trauma model are not benign in their interaction with these communities but in fact have an adverse effect. The resistance met by the dramatherapist is not therefore merely an issue of intercultural translation but a fundamental clash of what storytelling may mean in this community. Argenti-Pillen demonstrates how speaking straightforwardly of troubling events for many Sinhalese is understood to cause harm to the speaker. Her detailed analysis of discursive practices within a village affected by the conflict in the late 1980s indicated a delicate interrelation of violence 'containment' processes around speaking that would be disturbed by any uniform demand for people to 'tell their story'. The thrust of her argument is that 'the discourse on trauma poses a threat to the culture-specific strategies of containment of violence' (p. xii). 'Speaking' therefore is not a panacea but a peculiar demand that in this case interrupts strategies where 'not talking' about disappearances allowed violence to be held back. The practitioner in the opening vignette asked people to tell their story of a crisis in a place where explicit telling of that story was understood to do you harm.

Methodologically Argenti-Pillen offers an ethnographic approach that should perhaps be shared by social theatre practitioners. Rather than adopting the trauma paradigm as the explanatory framework and then constructing projects from within its logic of practice, we should start from the systems of knowledge already in place. Argenti-Pillen explains:

> The narratives of the women from Udahenagama [. . .] engage us to think about how survivors of wartime atrocities reconstruct their communicative worlds and interrupt the cycle of violence in ways that may be difficult for Euro-American professionals to imagine [. . .] I base my critical analysis on the extensive presentation of empirical material I gathered in southern Sri Lanka, and I show how the discourse on trauma poses a threat to the culture-specific strategies of containment of violence that Udahenagama women use on a daily basis.
>
> (2003, p. xii)

As mentioned above, social theatre practitioners perhaps need to withdraw from forms of practice determined by 'Euro-American' trauma studies and discover how 'survivors of wartime atrocities reconstruct their communicative world and interrupt the cycle of violence'. From this culturally specific location we then might build performance and artistic approaches with artists from the communities that extend, develop and maximise the potential for violence to be interrupted and for worlds to be reconstructed. And the art forms that are most appropriate will emerge in this negotiation. They may be silent dance, expressive song, wild lament, craft-making and of course they may be storytelling.

Conclusion

This chapter has sought to emphasise that the paradoxical relationship between telling and not-telling is manifested in culturally specific ways, and the place of artists in situations of crisis depends on the narrative, healing and performative cultures in which those crises happen. This is recognised after the tsunami in Sri Lanka when activists and local mental health workers tried to protect their communities from external therapists who descended and urged people to talk about their experience, with little acknowledgement of what speaking of the past and the dead might mean in these communities. It was not recognised by the British practitioner whose belief in the 'importance of the story' took no account for how storytelling was understood or might already be practised.

Perhaps the *difficult return* is a search for a relation with the memory of crisis that does not insist that telling a story will mean that pain will be healed and the problems put to rest. Social theatre should be searching for examples of practice that are alternatives to the rhetoric of the trauma relief programmes – programmes that forget that telling is not always the best solution to people's suffering. Social theatre's repertoire should include projects that respect silence and speaking out as different actions made necessary by different circumstances. This is a mission that, returning to the opening examples, rejects the arrogance of the therapists who assume they have the best approach to 'helping people' or the social theatre practitioner who cannot cope with the fact that the children will not speak about their tsunami experiences.

The final quotation comes from a student paper on the Holocaust where the writer seems to hold onto the idea that there is a paradox in people's response to crisis, and the word 'literature' here could be replaced by theatre or performance by social theatre practitioners:

> Literature has become for me the site of my own stammering. Literature, as that which can sensitively bear witness to the Holocaust, gives me a voice, a right, and a necessity to survive. Yet, I cannot discount the literature which in the dark awakens the screams, which opens the wounds, and which makes me want to fall silent. Caught by two contradictory wishes at once, to speak or not to speak, I can only stammer.
>
> (Quoted in Felman and Laub, 1992, p. 56)

So the contradictory wish – to speak and not to speak – led this person to stammer. Perhaps these stammering responses are the complex reactions to crises that social theatre practitioners should engage with as we search for ways for theatre and performance to contribute to the plethora of ways to meet, contain, resist, reveal, avoid, relieve and hide from suffering in its varies guises. An engagement that hopefully ensures that the disdain of *Ah pava! Nathiye* never again challenges the arrogance of those that thought theatre might be useful in these settings in the first place.

Notes

1 From Appadurai (2003, p. 8).
2 The north-western Indonesian province of Aceh was the worst hit.
3 These comments are based on interviews/discussions with people working directly within psychological and mental health services in the country.
4 Sri Lanka had over 20 years of civil conflict prior to the tsunami and there were therefore many local agencies working with war-affected communities.
5 Conversation with the author. While they were dramatherapists, this critique could be made of many social theatre practitioners. Clearly there are many forms of dramatherapy that are not based on storytelling.
6 The final part of this story comes from a translator and theatre practitioner who worked with the dramatherapist – Premalatha Sam Pradeepan. I would like to thank her for the inspiration for writing this chapter.
7 Schauer *et al.* (2005, p. 5).

References

Appadurai, Arjun (2003) in Alex Argenti-Pillen, *Masking Terror: How Women Contain Violence in Southern Sri Lanka*, p. 8, Philadelphia: University of Pennsylvania Press.

Argenti-Pillen, Alex (2003) *Masking Terror: How Women Contain Violence in Southern Sri Lanka*, Philadelphia: University of Pennsylvania Press.

Brow, James (1996) *Demons and Development: The Struggle for Community in a Sri Lankan Village*, Tucson: The University of Arizona Press.

Caruth, Cathy (ed.) (1995) *Trauma: Explorations in Memory*, Baltimore, MD: Johns Hopkins University Press.

Daniel, Valentine E. (1996) *Charred Lullabies: Chapters in an Anthropology of Violence*, Princeton, NJ: Princeton University Press.

Felman, Shoshana and Laub, Dori (1992) *Testimony: Crises of Witnessing in Literature, Psychoanalysis, and History*, London: Routledge.

Kapferer, Bruce (1988) *Legends of People, Myths of State: Violence, Intolerance, and Political Culture in Sri Lanka and Australia*, London: Smithsonian Institution Press.

Kapferer, Bruce (1991) *A Celebration of Demons: Exorcism and the Aesthetics of Healing in Sri Lanka*, Oxford: Berg Smithsonian Institution Press.

Kellerman, Peter Felix and Hudgins, M.K. (eds) (2000) *Psychodrama with Trauma Survivors: Acting Out Your Pain*, London: Jessica Kingsley Publishers.

Laub, Dori (1995) 'Truth and Testimony: The Process and the Struggle', in Cathy Caruth (ed.), *Trauma: Explorations in Memory*, Baltimore, MD: Johns Hopkins University Press.

Moss, Jane (2001) 'The Drama of Survival: Staging Post-traumatic Memory in Plays by Lebanese-Québécois Dramatists, *Theatre Research In Canada*, 22, 2: 173–89.

Obeyesekere, Gananath (1990) *The Work of Culture: Symbolic Transformation in Psychoanalysis and Anthropology*, Chicago: University of Chicago Press.

Schauer, Maggie, Neuner, Frank and Elbert, Thomas (2005) *Narrative Exposure Therapy: A Short-term Intervention for Traumatic Stress Disorders after War, Terror, or Torture*, Toronto: Hogrefe.

Segall, Kimberly Wedeven (2005) 'Stories and Song in Iraq and South Africa: From

Individual Trauma to Collective Mourning Performances', *Comparative Studies of South Asia, Africa and the Middle East*, 25, 1: 138–51.

Simon, Roger I., Rosenberg, Sharon and Eppert, Claudia (eds) (2000) *Between Hope and Despair: Pedagogy and the Remembrance of Historical Trauma*, Oxford: Rowman & Littlefield Publishers.

5   On the dramaturgy of communities

Claudio Bernardi

What community?

Social cooperation is fundamental to our lives. It has played historically, and still plays today, a key role in the effort by human beings to protect, feed, and look after themselves, and therefore in the survival of the species. Relationships provide meaning, support and opportunities. Deficient or defective social interactions are a major source of physical and mental disorders and of daily stress. Good relationships, on the contrary, are crucial to people's well-being. Positive feedback from others and interpersonal attachments strengthen one's capabilities, autonomy and self-esteem. The environment where we form our earliest connections is the family. Social bonds begin in the family and are the basic building blocks of the larger process of socialization. Friendships and school then extend the child's social world. Social interactions and attachments to other people develop the adult's aptitude for relationship and community.

A community is usually defined as an association of people sharing common values, goals, lifestyles, with some degree of constancy in membership as well as attendance. A more comprehensive definition would involve a group of individuals who have learned to communicate among themselves, to create positive feelings, whose relationships go deeper than their masks, who have grown intimate enough to take pleasure in each other's company, who experience strong solidarity, a minimum level of suffering, and a high sense of purpose. These communities, be they religious or ethnic, are very close-knit, actively enforce their boundaries, and exclude outsiders. Violation of norms by community members brings about exemplary punishment.

From the nineteenth century onwards, two competing notions of community have begun to clash. The traditional one refers to a social unit the size of a village (smaller than a town or a nation) where face-to-face relationships are possible and a sense of immediacy and locality is still in place. In the global era, instead, the term community has been employed to indicate adherence to a common or hegemonic set of values within society at large; group living based on alternative lifestyles; or even just people who share a purpose of some sort (religious, political, etc.).

The early notion of community has not wholly disappeared: it has been transformed. Communities no longer define themselves according to the place where people live, but rather according to what they do for each other. Women and men form social connections of their own choosing, and build up relational networks with people like themselves. These are self-oriented and privatized ties. Personal communities, ranging from virtual networks to real-life interactions, promote the interests of individuals and groups, but not the common good.

A virtual community is a community that we take with us wherever we go. Technology enables us to connect with people or groups all over the world, often to the detriment of traditional communities that rely on face-to-face interaction (Bruhn 2005: 233). Enlarged opportunities to connect with other people, however, do not necessarily entail enlarged opportunities to engage in common projects, to take part in political, cultural or social schemes of action. In other words, the West is nowadays full of solitary or individualistic communities with only limited interest in becoming involved in other people's communities as well as in any kind of public concern, except for purposes of expediency (ibid.). The common good, instead, depends on civic commitment and public participation. Pollution control, international security, peace and the like remain impossible missions, unless self-interest societies and closed communities give way to open, connected communities committed to the common good or to *res publica* at a local, national and international level.

McLuhan has described our world as a global village, but one would be tempted to say that it is rather becoming a global corporation (Bull 2005: 17). Attempts by nation states, deriving their sovereignty from a territorial basis, to counter globalization and neo-imperialism have proved ludicrously ineffectual. Global economy is not counterbalanced by a global or universal policy. A way of overcoming the impotence of single countries would be the establishment of an international community – that most fragile and unstable entity. Inside nations, citizens voice their protest and defend what they perceive to be their rights through, on the one hand, the interventionism of the no-global movement pleading for a just, caring world, and on the other, the extreme self-assertion of national, religious, ethnic, social and local identities and communities. The crisis of the modern state, based on the fundamental trinomy of (democratic) sovereignty, territory, and citizenship, points to a failed reconciliation, in recent western history, between *pactum unionis* and *pactum subiectionis*. The handing over of the citizens' individual power to the state in order to guarantee their security and welfare (*pactum subiectionis*) has overshadowed, incorporated, or even shattered the notion of *pactum unionis*; that is, the founding of personal and social life, as well as of national and global economies and policies, on principles of amicability, relationship, association, dialogue, social creativity, all that is defined by Putnam (2000) as social capital.

In conclusion, we are in dire need of local communities, of virtual communities produced by our own interactions (Bruhn 2005: 233), and of a 'community of communities' that will promote individual, local, as well as common good.

Community theatre models

The concern over lack of community in modern society is over one century old. While several scholars have put forward multiple reasons behind this phenomenon – the rise of individualism, bureaucracy, consumerism, competitiveness, institutional and economic changes, television, time pressure, mobility, the breakdown of families and family traditions, and so on – only a few have attempted to point out the means to create, rebuild or strengthen the community and its fuel; that is, social capital. Among the ways available today for the invention, empowerment or restoration of community, '*community theatre*' has gained remarkable credit. John Bull has proposed a tentative list of nine community theatre models (Bull 2005: 9–11).

- The motivation of amateur *Community Theatre* groups is to participate in dramatic and social production. Popular plays (comedies, thrillers, musicals, etc.) are performed in the groups' own theatres, in hired premises or in local professional theatres before an audience consisting of the participants' families, friends and supporters.
- *Youth Theatre* groups have as their primary aim the development of theatre skills as well as the exploration of themes that are particularly important to local youth and communities.
- *Community-based Theatre* within professional theatre encourages local participation in productions tackling specific socio-cultural issues or targeting specific community sections.
- *Theatre in Education* brings companies into schools. The productions often raise particular issues (bullying, racial equality, etc.); they require strong participation on the part of the audience, create a sense of community, provide motivations and suggest strategies to cope with life's demands.
- Reaching targeted community audiences outside institutions is the goal of *Educational Community Groups*, whose activity also comprises courses in 'community-based theatre' practice.
- *Special Interest Theatre Companies* include specific theatre for people with disabilities (theatre for the blind, the deaf, etc.). Most often the targeted persons themselves are involved in the production.
- *Theatre in the Workplace* is made by people within a given profession who produce work (frequently interactive) on specific issues and themes relating to the activities of the organizations or institutions.

- One-off *community celebrations, festivals, pageants*, and so on are forms of local participation in national or local events. Back in time, it was here that 'community theatre' found its highest and most genuine expression – see, for example, the York Corpus Christi Cycle (Beckwith 2001). John Bull and many other scholars or practitioners who ignore the historical reasons behind the decline of ritual and feast in modern Europe seem to underestimate their power and the importance of reviving and strengthening these traditions.
- *Theatre from Within and Theatre for the Community* are, respectively, theatres created by and for a specific community, or productions mounted by resident or touring companies in and with a designated community. In the latter case, the aim is usually to link up specific local issues with wider political problems, in particular lately capitalism and globalization.

Many other types of theatre and performance deal with work for, with and from within communities (Van Erven 2005; Boon and Plastow 2005), such as for instance Augusto Boal's Theatre of the Oppressed, dramatherapy, or community dance. In many cases, however, a narrow or limited understanding of community, deriving from ideological, cultural, historical or professional biases, may undermine 'community-based' drama's stated purpose of promoting relationships, creativity, socio-cultural change, and the common good, or at least weaken its potential impact. The greatest difficulty, particularly within 'old' Europe, is a consequence of the failure to identify a social and public domain beyond that of the state or market (in France, for example, 'community' is still a taboo word). As a result, the community becomes the means, or indeed the Trojan horse, to achieve other goals, to implement the performing art in question and not so much the community. In Britain, for instance, the community dance movement has become an influential and flourishing area within the dance profession (Thomson 2005: 116). Among recent developments within community dance is the promotion of social inclusion. Initially, the main aim of community dance was to free art from the shackles of institutional venues and professional entertainment and to open it up to groups of ordinary people. It soon met with great success among people with disabilities, inmates in prisons and hospitals, the very old, and many other marginal groups. But here the positive effects of dancing pertain to individual socialization: the development of self-confidence and self-esteem, body awareness, mental health, well-being, the improvement of communication and social skills, the gradual release from social isolation, and so on (Thomson 2005: 126). That is all very well, but what about the community?

In more conservative 'community theatre' practice, the celebration of one's particular values and history shuts the door on other communities, people and groups, and makes it very difficult to develop dialogue, carry out common projects, or pursue the common good. Often, the ritual celebration of the group's identity entails hostility towards, and an incitement to violence against, other groups, peoples and cultures (Schininà 2002: 101–16). In a democratic context, this is not completely unlike what happens in interventionist 'community-based theatre'. Here the community is engaged in a political action, such as opposing and fighting the empire of western capitalism, and radical theatre becomes a weapon of political struggle, a means of raising awareness and mobilizing people. Generally speaking, however, 'community theatre' simply offers to those involved an opportunity to take action and to experience comradeship, care, support and refuge (Bull 2005: 15). Politics, business, art are necessary and very important elements in the community's life, but they are not everything.

The dramaturgy of communities

Two interesting symptoms of the growing importance of the community can be detected in the recent changes within the business world and in the movement of American communities. As Edmund M. Burke explains, in the business world the business of business is no longer just business, but rather corporate citizenship. Today, the belief is widespread that corporations have the obligation or even the right to become involved in the community. In public relations as well as in corporate planning and strategy, the role of the community manager is becoming more and more prominent (Burke 2005).

From the 1980s onwards, several cities and communities have become involved in the Healthy Communities movement, which promotes partnerships at local, regional and state levels in order to improve environmental quality, social equity, economic welfare, social cohesion, trust, and in the attempt to foster a deeper sense of community.[1] The features of a healthy community bear a striking resemblance to the principles and the dynamics of social theatre. The building of relationships among residents or community members is only possible if there is a shared vision of what a community is, what it should be and how to get there. The means usually employed are dialogue and face-to-face interaction, in order to produce a shift from outcome-oriented communication, based on the rule of 'what's in it for me?', or on the Latin motto *mors tua vita mea* (in modern terms: 'I win, you lose'), to process-oriented communication, where sociability and affability are considered essential. Process-oriented communication and community building benefit from face-to-face interactions and non-verbal communication (Bruhn 2005: 235). For these and other reasons, the best and most effective instrument of community building turns out to be the theatre. Outcome-oriented communities are solitary or self-interest communities. Process-oriented communities are healthy and open communities concerned with the common good.

While the traditional community is actively exclusionist, too attached to social values and hence indifferent to individual needs and rights, the virtual community is intrinsically exclusive, too self-interested and hence adverse to social values and lasting ties. Traditional and virtual communities have a very poor record of connection and exchange between them, and have developed a culture of fear that increases social distance and encourages distrust in institutions. The first common good to be aimed at, therefore, is a community of communities at the local, regional, national and international level. The envisaged community, epitomized by the slogan 'better together', should retain all the positive elements of traditional and modern communities, and discard all the negative ones. How can this be achieved?

The dramaturgy of communities is a complex model of social theatre devised and tested by Guglielmo Schininà (2004a; see also Bernardi 2004). His methodological approach is based on the ritual model of the complex circle:

> The basic principle here is to perceive theatre as a system of communication, which, whatever the activity carried out, establishes a circle of barters and encounters and is also able to show these barters and encounters to the world outside the circle. This, in its turn, promotes a change in the perception of certain problems and favours the inclusion of multiple voices and narratives in collective communication.
>
> (Schininà 2004b: 54–5)

Everything starts with a number of individuals, who are members of different groups or communities. Each individual has his or her own characteristics, that reflect the cultural and social influence of his/her community. 'The individual always remains him/herself and free, and his/her individual action interacts with the actions of others' in a free relationship. When the interactions come to include the entire group, 'a ritual circle is created, in which each person develops individual relationships, expressing feelings and ideas that the entire group is made aware of. The group thus becomes a site where each and every kind of diversity and each and every personal or collective relationship is known by everyone and therefore is pluralized and shared'. The group then develops as such through the pluralization of the problems, possibilities and resources of each individual and of his/her community, 'as well as through their solidarity and consideration towards problems and resources that cannot be pluralized'. The same circular approach also has to be established between groups, communities, and institutions (Schininà 2004b: 55).

The most important difference between social theatre and 'community-based theatre' or dance is that the first is a 'psychosocial-educational model based on creative arts and focusing on the different rituals and specific cultural features' of each community involved. 'At the basis of this model stands the concept of the limit as a creative passageway between cultures' and communities (Schininà 2004b: 54). Art is the vehicle: a means, not an end in itself. The real creativity is social creativity, the establishment of new and satisfactory connections, interactions, ties, friendships, relationships, agreements. Social theatre includes the two different perspectives suggested by the etymology of 'theatre' and 'drama'. The first is vision, the second action, and both are necessary in the dramaturgy of communities; just like 'I' thinking or individualism is necessary in traditional communities, and 'we' thinking or sociality is necessary in solitary communities. The village (local, virtual, global) is a complex social texture and we are its weavers – or its dramatists.

Note

1 See www.healthycommunities.org

References

Beckwith, S. (2001) *Signifying God. Social Relation and Symbolic Act in the York Corpus Christi Plays*, Chicago and London: The University of Chicago Press.

Bernardi, C. (2004) *Il teatro sociale. L'arte tra disagio e cura*, Rome: Carocci.

Boon, R. and Plastow, J. (eds) (2005) *Theatre and Empowerment: Community Drama on the World Stage*, Cambridge: Cambridge University Press.

Bruhn, J.G. (2005) *The Sociology of Community Connections*, New York-Boston-Dortrecht-London-Moscow: Kluwer Academic-Plenum Publishers.

Bull, J. (2005) 'Introduction: On Interventionist and Community Theatre', in P. Billingham (ed.), *Radical Initiatives in Interventionist and Community Drama*, Bristol: Intellect Books.

Burke, E.M. (2005) *Managing a Company in an Activist World. The Leadership Challenge of Corporate Citizenship*, Westport, CT-London: Praeger.

Putnam, R.D. (2000) *Bowling Alone. The Collapse and Revival of American Community*, New York: Simon & Schuster.

Schininà, G. (2002) 'Cursed Communities, Rituals of Separation and Communication as Vengeance. A Redefinition of Artistic Intervention in War and War-torn Situations. The Kosovo Case', in C. Bernardi, M. Dragone and G. Schininà (eds), *War Theatres and Actions for Peace: Community-Based Dramaturgy and the Conflict Scene*, Milan: Euresis.

Schininà, G. (2004a) 'Here We Are. A Background on Social Theatre and Some Open Questions about its Developments', *The Drama Review*, 48, 3: 18–33.

Schininà, G. (2004b) 'Social Theatre and Artistic Interventions in War-torn Societies', in C. Dente and S. Soncini (eds), *Conflict Zones: Actions, Languages, Mediations*, Pisa: ETS.

Thomson, C. (2005) 'From Idealism to Acceptance: the Development of Community Dance in the UK 1976–2004', in L. Delfini (ed.), *Beyond the School . . . Community Dance*, Granarolo dell'Emilia: Mousikè.

Van Erven, E. (2005) *Community Theatre. Global perspectives*, London: Routledge.

Part II

Theatre, social theatre and change

An exploration of texts and contexts

Introduction

It is an interesting shift of experience for the reader moving from Part I to Part II. Here there is an immediate dynamic that takes us into several performance spaces; all very different but all with their own particular charge.

Mady Schutzman's chapter (Chapter 6) chronicles the development and production of *UPSET*, a play mainly about Rodney King and the 1992 riots in Los Angeles. It is written by Schutzman and makes use of the Joker System of August Boal. It argues for young people's ability to tackle complex and controversial issues and language, (see also Hickson's Chapter 11 in Part III). Schutzman maintains that the process must promote respect, debate, empathy, multiple interpretations and 'endless curiosity'.

By complete contrast, John Casson (Chapter 7) looks at seventeenth-century theatre therapy in six Jacobean plays written between 1613 and 1625, which deliberately use drama and theatre for therapeutic purposes. He places the therapeutic methods within a context of ideas about mental health at the time, with reference to *The Anatomy of Melancholy* (Burton 2001). He points out that theatre could be therapy three hundred years before the emergence of dramatherapy and psychodrama, and two hundred years before the development of psychiatry!

Salvo Pitruzzella (Chapter 8) creates what he terms 'a necessary dialogue' between theatre and therapy through the device of two characters standing under a pergola: one represents theatre and the other one therapy. This dialogue mirrors Pitruzzella's own process where he recently changed his own view of theatre and therapy after involvement with a group of people with learning difficulties in a theatre company. His chapter is a testimony to this change and illustrates a confrontation between theatre and therapy that finally shows that theatre and therapy influence each other at a profound level of 'unawareness'.

Tom Magill and Jennifer Marquis-Muradaz (Chapter 9) describe the filming of a modern version of *Macbeth* in a maximum security prison in Northern Ireland. This chapter proposes that active engaged participation in creative drama affords prisoners a unique opportunity to confront and transcend their own violent pasts through the safety and distance of fiction (of related interest, see Jennings in *Shakespeare Comes to Broadmoor* 1992). Furthermore the authors believe that Shakespeare and film in combination provide both academically and socially acceptable ways for prisoners to examine the causes and effects of their behaviour.

> Somewhere we have fallen short of the demands of experimental theatre. And although it is going to be uncomfortable we have to ask ourselves the question: how truly experimental are we? We have done something new, refreshingly novel – but have we been guilty of confusing novelty with experimentation? Have we failed to realize that real experimentation goes much deeper and much beyond than merely a new form/or novel content. It is a light that illuminates one's work from within. And this light in the spirit of quest – not only aesthetic quest – it is an amalgam of so many quests – intellectual, aesthetic, but most of all, spiritual quest.
>
> (Elkunchwar 1995: 29–30)

Aanand Chabukswar (Chapter 10) quotes the above to pinpoint his own journey through programmes and projects, traditional theatre and educational initiatives to discover 'theatre in search of healing'. He feels that training needs to allow the individual to live life 'as a practice of self-evolution'. We need to have the ability to lead as well as to follow, to enable others to build a relationship with the arts, to draw out norms. He talks about nudging and supporting insights, and the important role of the witness. Chabukswar works as a dramatherapist as well as performer, and his writing is also echoed in some of Schininà's writings about the healing role of theatre in psychosocial intervention.

In Part II several common experiences are echoed, either in the healing context where there is the possibility of emotional repair, or in the social context where participants have the opportunity to confront themselves as well as society. Indeed theatre and therapy seem to be coming much closer together in this section.

References

Burton, R. (2001) *The Anatomy of Melancholy*, New York: Review Books Classics.
Elkunchwar, M. (1995) 'Experimentation in Marathi Theatre', in *Marathi Theatre*, New Delhi: Maharashtra Information Centre.
Jennings, S. (1992) in M. Cox (ed.), *Shakespeare Comes to Broadmoor*, London: Jessica Kingsley Publishers.

6   What a riot!

Mady Schutzman

Chorus: To what is denied and must come forward
To who is erased and must be seen
We dedicate this show to Rosa Parks

There comes a time when there's some force or some power
The spirit of history that tracks you down
And selects you to be that person, to be that vessel,
To be the one to get in the way

Sometimes you gotta sit down to stand up
You gotta sit tight where it says WHITE
You gotta break the law that breaks your back

'Cause when you're on the street, it's your street
When you're in the school, it's your school
When you're in the family, it's your family
When you're in the church, it's your church
When you're on the bus, it's your bus

To someone who got in the way
Montgomery, Alabama, December 1, 1955
To Rosa Parks.
Claudette: And Claudette Colvin.
Chorus: Claudette who?[1]

In September 2005, I was invited by the Community Arts Partnership (CAP) at the California Institute of the Arts (CalArts) to write the annual play for the Plaza de la Raza Youth Theatre Program. Plaza is a multi-disciplinary arts center located in East Los Angeles and as a CAP 'partner' is a site for workshops for teens in art, theatre, dance, music, writing, and film taught by CalArts' students and faculty. The theatre program at Plaza was entering its sixteenth season when I was asked to participate; *UPSET!* was written in conjunction with the Latino youth (ages 13–17) who enrolled in the Plaza program and met three times a week (even more as we neared show time) for 22 weeks before performing at Plaza and a downtown

Los Angeles theatre, REDCAT. This chapter chronicles the making of *UPSET!* toward contributing to the critical discourse on community-based theatre.

The theme of *UPSET!* was decided in large part by the youth themselves. I asked them to come up with a list of historical characters they would like to know more about or celebrate. Their original list had as many as 40 figures as diverse as Che Guevara and Paris Hilton. After several pedagogical sessions (to educate the youth about the nominees they didn't know), the students voted on Rodney King and Claudette Colvin. Most everyone remembers Rodney King as the unfortunate African-American man brutally beaten by four white LAPD officers in 1991. Their acquittal, a year later, instigated widespread rioting in Los Angeles. Perhaps less known is Claudette Colvin, a 15 year-old African-American girl who in Montgomery, Alabama, 1955, refused to give up her seat to a white passenger nine months before Rosa Parks did the same. Claudette Colvin – who has never received acknowledgement for her act of resistance – comes to hijack the show from Rodney King, someone who is getting a lot of attention for having done, in Claudette's opinion, nothing very remarkable for the civil rights movement. As each of their stories unfold, we learn about the historical complexities of racism and resistance in US history and meet a slew of characters including Rosa Parks, Emmett Till, Fannie Lou Hamer, Malcolm X, and Donald Rumsfeld, to name just a few. By the end of the play, Claudette receives her due with a full-cast 1950s rock-gospel number honoring her courage in 1955, after which she and Rodney, united as odd-couple in their status as anti-heroes, give the audience a lesson in civil disobedience. Well, Claudette does, and Rodney, giving activism a try for Claudette's sake, follows her lead.

Joker: Ladies and gentlemen, boys and girls of all ages, we are here today to tell you a story. It is a story of what has happened and what will happen again. It is a story full of truth telling and lying as well, and we won't be telling you which is which. That's for you to decide . . . And who am I you might wonder, wearing this funny hat and carrying a big stick? I am the Joker. Like in a deck of cards, I belong to no particular suit, I'm on no one's side – though I have my opinions! I interrupt, upset, question, undo and remake, all for the common good. No one escapes my interrogations or my lectures, not all of which are very smart, but I try!

Chorus: Close your eyes! Hold on tight! 'Cause the Quality of your Life is about to take a remarkable turn, hovering on the edge of reason, dissolving at the tips of your fingers, pooping from the rears of your rabid dogs!! Are you on the bus or off the bus?

Joker: Friends and neighbors, today we tell a story for you to enjoy. A story of civil rights, a story of scoundrels and do-gooders, and it's quite easy to mix them up. A story of Los Angeles and many other cities as well. If you like it, give us a big hand! If you don't, keep your opinions to yourself!

UPSET! is modeled, stylistically, after the Joker System of Brazilian theatre director, Augusto Boal. A Joker System play is meant to be a spectacular discussion, or even a trial, where different ideas and feelings about a historical character or event can be presented and debated. The ultimate goal is to raise questions, offer multiple points of view, and encourage dialogue. The techniques of the Joker System, and of the entire Boal oeuvre, come from circus and carnival, agit-prop, Brecht, Freirean pedagogy, newspaper theatre, and journalistic investigating. There's always a Joker, or an MC, and a big Chorus (sometimes two) that sings, dances, complains, rallies, and talks directly to the audience.

One of my primary interests – before and during my residency at Plaza – was to write an original Joker System play, something that to my knowledge has not been done since Boal and his colleague Gianfrancesco Guarnieri did so over 40 years ago. As a practitioner and scholar of Boal's Theatre of the Oppressed (TO) for nearly 20 years, I have been intrigued by the dramaturgical methodology of the Joker System that preceded the interactive techniques of TO for which Boal is internationally known. In these early plays, the following is customary: the story is a composite of commentaries, lectures, exhortations, news clippings, and transcripts; the characters are interviewed mid-scene, sometimes mid-speech, by the Joker; the Chorus expresses its joy or discontent with how the story is unfolding and proposes alternatives; the Joker steps in and plays different characters as he or she pleases; actors themselves change characters; scenes are staged in very different styles from one another promoting aesthetic eclecticism; paradox and irony and humor are everywhere; everyone gets a chance to tell it as they see it. And yet the bad guys and good guys tend to remain easy to tell apart.[2]

Pooh: (*friend of Rodney King*) Everything changes after tonight. Even some good things happen. If good things happen from a really bad thing, is it still a mistake?

Rodney: (*to audience*) I just wanted to head downtown to pick up some girls. We were speeding a bit, yeah, but when I heard those sirens, man, all I could think was, I don't want to go back to jail. I was scared and I just thought if I could lose them, I thought the problem would just go away.

Freddie: (*friend of Rodney King*) How about we go to Hollywood and check out that new club. You drive Rodney, I'm trashed.

Pooh: You're drunk, Rodney, and you've got a wicked temper when you're drunk. Just sit down and stay down.

Rodney: But I am down, brother. I'm really down.

Joker: (*enters, holding mike to Pooh like a reporter*) You sound like a
            very reasonable young man, Pooh. Are you?
Pooh: No, not at all. But I thought for the show I'd try to be, you know,
            smarter, be the one to stand up and say, Hey, no drinkin' and
            drivin'! I mean Rodney here drives like a maniac even when he's
            sober. I thought maybe for the record I'd try to come out looking
            a little less stupid.
Joker: But in real life, you're pretty stupid?
Pooh: Yeah. But nothing like Rodney.

I was interested in writing a play that included the young people's experience learning about the characters they were to portray; their reactions and
questions to the often brutal and terrifying events in the characters' lives
were as compelling to me as the events themselves. How were these young
people processing the murders of so many black people whose acts of
resistance constituted the civil rights movement? What connections were
they making between these seemingly remote historical characters of the
past and their current lives as Latinos in Los Angeles, particularly at a time
when an immigration movement was fermenting and the South Central
Farm[3] was being threatened (and eventually razed) by real estate developers? Donald Amerson, production manager of *UPSET!* said, 'The story
of the farmers was so powerful because it was a link. What did Claudette
say? "This rage is not a one-day thing?" Well, this rage is not a one-color
thing either.'[4] The Joker System provided a perfect aesthetic vehicle to tell
not only the story of Rodney King and the ensuing uprising, but a larger,
ever-changing and yet ever-the-same, story of violence, racism, and resistance in the US. Creating *UPSET!* in the mode of the Joker System
provided a means to incorporate the teens' curiosity, dismay, outrage,
confusion, fear, and inspiration in relation to the subject matter of the play
within the play. Speculation, even fiction, collective brainstorming, writing,
dreaming, and image-making joined the facts to became critical characters
in our representation of the 'truth.'
    In the scene transcribed above in which Rodney and his friends are
drinking just before heading downtown on that fateful night of 3 March
1991, it was *my* choice to rewrite Pooh as a more sympathetic character
and to have the Joker interrupt the scene for a character interview.
However, several other such interventions in the play were scripted
entirely by the Plaza students. For instance, as I relayed the story of
Claudette Colvin's act of resistance in Alabama in 1955, I invited them to
ask questions of any and all of the historical players at each step in the
story's unfolding. I provided them with critical historical information that
informed the scene, such as the prevailing law at the time that designated
seats on public buses for black passengers at the back and for whites at
the front; black people were allowed to occupy the indistinct middle
section only if white people did not use them. It was the students'

questions that fueled the spirit of my writing of the scene as well as providing all the actual questions of the Chorus members within the final script. In the following excerpt from that climactic scene, the Joker starts off referring to the preceding scene of the play in which four white supremacists[5] mock Rodney's infamous line ('I felt like a crushed can') and rant proudly about crushing cans – 'Afro-*cans*, Jamai-*cans*, Domini-*cans*' – as a Ku Klux Klan (KKK) member dressed in full KKK regalia performs a wild stomping dance, literally crushing aluminum cans scattered across the stage.

Joker:	Our show and our bus have made a very serious turn. Spinning around and turning us this way and that. We hardly know where we're headed! That last scene, for instance. That was terrifying! But do we have anything to really worry about? It's just the theatre, after all. It was very dangerous, indeed, but then, POOF! the danger is all gone! (*to the Chorus*) Is it here? Or is it gone? That's for you to decide.
Chorus:	(*debating with each other*) It's still here, I think. (*others*) No, I think it's gone.
Joker:	So shall we all get on the bus?
Chorus:	(*all, scared*) NO!!
Joker:	How tragic! The bus of the past, the bus of the future, the bus we have been waiting for, is an empty bus, stuck between then and now, between as-always and what-if, a real Could-Have-Been-A-Great Bus but instead just sitting here with nowhere to go and no one to get it there. (*everyone looks at each other, no one moves*)
Claudette:	I'll get on the bus!
Chorus:	YEAH!!
Claudette:	My name is Claudette Colvin, and I'm 15 years old.
	[CLAUDETTE gets on bus and sits in the middle section. BUS DRIVER gets on bus. As BUS RIDERS get on bus they receive either a WHITE MASK or a BLACK MASK.]
Bus driver:	(*to CLAUDETTE and BLACK MASK sitting beside her*) Move to the back of the bus.
	[The BLACK MASK moves quickly to back. CLAUDETTE remains.]
Chorus:	Claudette, are you blind? Claudette, why don't you listen? Claudette, are you going to let them walk all over you?
White mask:	You got to get up.
Black mask:	She ain't got to do nothing but stay black and die.
Chorus:	Claudette, are you being an uppity black girl? Claudette, are you brave enough to do the right thing?

[BUS DRIVER moves and stands beside CLAUDETTE. In slow motion, we see CLAUDETTE buckle up, holding her stomach. BUS DRIVER returns to his seat.]

Chorus: Why doesn't anyone help her?
Is it still worth it, Claudette?
Bus Driver, aren't you afraid that the black people will come to your house and murder you?

[BUS DRIVER laughs.]

Chorus: White Mask, what makes you better than her?
White Mask, do you deserve that seat?
Claudette, do you deserve that seat?
Bus driver, can't you give her a break and just let her sit down?

White mask: If she gets away with this, they will take over.

[POLICEMAN enters bus.]

Policeman: Don't you think you ought to get up?
Claudette: No, sir.

[CLAUDETTE buckles over again as if hit in the stomach.]

Black mask: Oh God.

[POLICEMAN takes CLAUDETTE off bus. Exit.]

Chorus: If I were on that bus, where would I have to sit?

The strategic inclusion of these questions posed by the youth in the rehearsal process into the play itself was a gift proffered by the Joker System. But the actual acuity of the questions can be credited only to the youth themselves. It was José Velasquez who, during our writing/rehearsal session about that fateful day in 1955, asked the profound question, 'If I were on that bus, where would I have to sit?' As he sat in Lincoln Heights, CA, in 2006, traversing time and history, making sense of his identity as a young Latino *vis-à-vis* the life of a young black girl born over 50 years before him in a place he has never been to, José was exposing the very fragile understanding that fear, like rage, is not a one-day or a one-color thing. What would I do in her circumstances, which are not, perhaps, so different than what I might face tomorrow?[6]

Why did the youth select Rodney King? Most of them were born in Los Angeles the year in which Rodney King was in the news, when the amateur videotape of the beating played over and over on national TV, or a year later when the policemen charged with excessive force were found not guilty and the city went up in flames. They listened carefully as the adults in the room told stories of where they were when the riots broke out. They went home and asked their parents. And these teenagers began to envision themselves as newborns or toddlers whisked out of smoke-filled rooms, enveloped by fearful cries, thrown into car seats by desperate parents to pick up siblings unable to get home from school or music lessons. It's not talked about much in Los Angeles but the legacy of the uprising of 1992 pervades contemporary Angelinos, no matter what age. It was clear that these retellings captured the imagination of the youth, as did the mere spectacle of violence and fire that ravaged the city for most of six days.

Why Claudette Colvin? Her appeal was, in part, her age; she did a very brave thing when she was only 15 years old, the age of many of the performers. Her courage became a standard, and a high one indeed, against which to measure their own commitment and audacity regarding any number of challenges. Claudette's apparent bitterness as a 66-year-old also may have been instructive, providing an image of dreams unrealized, efforts unrecognized, pride buried beneath frustration. The questions abounded regarding who she was, exactly what happened on that bus, why she was abandoned by the National Association for the Advancement of Colored People (NAACP) as well as the white community of Montgomery, what her relationship was to Rosa Parks, how she survived after moving to New York City as a single mother, and what she was doing now. It was as if they were comparing this woman to their own grandmothers and teachers, community leaders and politicians, trying to assess how this woman made sense in their day-to-day world and where her values and actions were or were not echoed.

Rodney: Someone meeting me for the first time would say I threw my life away, like I had a chance to do something important and let it go by. I dunno. I like watchin' TV with my buddies, I like girls, I like baseball a lot. I was an usher at Dodger Stadium once. Ozzie Smith, Wizard of Oz, he was good, played short-stop. I like Willie Green, too, but that's just because me and him have the same birthday. I'm Rodney King. I know I've done bad things. I drink too much. I'd like to turn my life around, I guess. Someone meeting me for the first time, they'd know I'm no Jesus Christ for Black people. But I'm still the King. . . .

Claudette: Someone meeting me for the first time would think I'm just a tired old lady, don't know about politics and the street life. But I've been doing the right thing for a long time now. Why's nobody watching me at all? How come all the good I do goes unnoticed? You think Jesse Jackson's is going to pray over my dead body in the Rotunda? Aretha Franklin going to sing for my soul? Not even Montgomery, Alabama is remembering me at all. I'm Claudette Colvin. And I'm going to find the spirit of my history. . . . Right here on this stage!

The production manager, Donald Amerson, mentioned to me one day that several of the students approached him and said that they 'didn't want to play poor Latinos anymore.' Interestingly, while a few previous Plaza shows focused on Latino history and struggles, rarely were the teens portraying 'poor Latinos.' All the same, the youth live their everyday lives in Los Angeles feeling so cast and their comment struck us as healthy (albeit nascent) political defiance and artistic curiosity; in the spirit of what the theatrical arts have to offer, they wanted 'a different part.' 'We want to be black people or rich people,' one of the teens had blurted out. While I'm not certain how well their escape fantasies were met (though, in fact, no one in *UPSET!* was cast as a 'poor Latino'), the students seemed to intuit that they might get a glimpse into the spirit of their own history by exploring that of others.

Making a play about Rodney King and Claudette Colvin inevitably required an investigation of how to stage violence – not just physical violence but the violence embedded in language, law, and the media that functions to deny people their constitutional rights on the streets every day. One way of handling the violent and racist nature of the material of the show, as already suggested, was through the Joker System, allowing students to literally step into the imagined bodies and voices not only of outraged and frustrated rioters but also of the racist police, commissioner, and KKK. 'They loved it . . . the permission to be as violent as they liked. But on the other side of that, they were speaking to racism *as racists*. They got it from the beginning, just reading the script they understood this sophisticated kind of critique' (Dodge). The Brechtian distance was an opportunity to critique the violence precisely as one embodied it.

Another approach we took in dealing with this delicate material was to borrow from popular theatre in the fashion of San Francisco Mime Troupe and Teatro Campesino. For performers and audiences alike, use of popular song, dance, and humor already marked as entertainment serve as a platform through which grim realities can be made consumable without necessarily anaesthetizing them. One recurring motif in *UPSET!* was a bastardized version of the popular TV show Wheel of Fortune in which we pit a radicalized Vanna (now feminist historian, Vanna White of Civil Rights) against an evil Spin Doctor (conservative media incarnate in a blinding gown made of glimmering CDs) who spins the Wheel and twists the obvious into the dubious and the dubious into a reality. The Spin Doctor would stand by the Wheel – a demographic map of race in Los Angeles – and make sure that bad luck would always fall on a black piece of the pie. In appropriating popular culture we could assume a common language associated with fun and entertainment within which to stage more probing questions of social politics. Is it really chance where the pointer lands? Who authors fun and entertainment? What is the game behind the game? Through the spin of TV's Wheel-of-Fortune we could speculate about other kinds of spins and other kinds of fortunes – such as, what kind of spin did the media put on the videotape of the King beating captured by George Holliday? Marvin Tunney, the production choreographer, reminds us that 'the [media] spin was in everyone's face. But when the Holliday tape was shown with the whole thing captured on video, the public still didn't see it.' The good or bad fortune of the Los Angeles Police Department (LAPD) officers on trial were, to an extent, in the hands of various spin masters who turned the Holliday tape into numbing 'wallpaper,' just as Claudette's fortune was measured by an NAACP seeking a viable national icon.[7]

Other times, when the storyline got particularly rough, the Joker and Chorus took comedic interludes (providing relief for themselves as well as the audience):

Joker:	Is it getting exciting yet?
Chorus:	Yes, it's getting exciting.
Joker:	Where are the people?
Chorus:	They are hypnotized in their houses.
Joker:	Is it time then to bring out Defense Secretary Donald Rumsfeld?
Chorus:	Donald Rumsfeld? What is he doing in our play?
Joker:	We don't want people to think that spin doctors only look like that (*points at SPIN DOCTOR*).
Chorus:	(*nodding with understanding*) OH!
Chorus member:	Donald Rumsfeld, come on out and tell us what you have to say!
	[Full-size cardboard figure in likeness of RUMSFELD enters and crosses stage.]
Rumsfeld:	(*audiotaped*) I believe what I said yesterday. I don't know what I said, but I know what I think, and, well, I assume it's what I said. Reports that say that something hasn't happened are always interesting to me, because as we know, there are known knowns; there are things we know we know. We also know there are known unknowns; that is to say we know there are some things we do not know. (*RUMSFELD exits.*)
Chorus:	Oh no.

In spite of the Joker System providing a platform to feature the voices of the youth, the production team of *UPSET!* was charged (by some parents, Plaza staff, and CalArts students working as teaching assistants) with proselytizing the youth, thrusting our biased values (primarily mine, as playwright) on young vulnerable minds. Of course we know that all playwrights put words in people's mouths. I raise this here, however, not to defend myself or to cast aspersions, but to underscore a problematic in community-based theatre work – that is, the relationship between author and community participants/performers. To whom and to what is the author beholden when writing a play for a specified population that has been invited to contribute to the playwriting process?

The Joker System plays written by Boal and Guarnieri, *Arena Conta Zumbi* and *Arena Conta Tiradentes*, exhibit clear boundaries between right and wrong in what Boal refers to as a Manichean format. Both, written in the mid-1960s, revisited turning points in Brazilian history in order to envision 'correct' contemporary behavior – that is, exemplary oppositional leftist politics in resistance to the military dictatorship in leadership at the time. Interestingly, the aesthetic choices of the Joker System complicate any easy dualism. In *Zumbi*, no actor played any one character for the length of the play; at various intervals the Joker would direct all actors to change roles. Though the approach is Brechtian (and thus roles are played with 'alienating' distance), and the audience is never asked to sympathize with a torturer or dictator, Boal's techniques, as we have seen, invited a degree of empathy; actors and audiences were asked to put themselves in the position of not only the protagonists but their antagonists as well. In *Zumbi*, the bad guy remains a bad guy and yet because all performers, at some point, play the bad guy, they are asked to locate the potential for 'badness' within themselves. The Joker System embraces the mutability of identity, reminds us that our identities, as well as others', are constructed and thus available for reconstruction. This philosophy is enacted in several ways beyond those I have already outlined: selected music of scenes contradicting the seeming pace or seriousness of the scene; reversals in chronology; staging effects of actions before the action itself; and the constant interruptions of the Joker not only to interview characters but to rally the audience toward one and then another side of the debate, give a lecture, criticize a performance, or redirect a scene. All of these techniques betray (to an extent) the very Manichean polarity to which the authors themselves were apparently devoted.[8] This became evident in *UPSET!* as well: 'Stacy Koon? [one of the LAPD officers who beat King]. I didn't think of him as a human being before this play started. Afterwards, he just became a flawed human being' (Amerson). Dodge put it like this: 'Nobody's a monster here. That's the thing that makes it tragic, that these characters are human beings.'

One of the most explicit and effective applications of this critical empathy occurred in the scene representing the beating of Rodney King. All cast members had an opportunity to become Officer Laurence Powell, the LAPD officer who delivered the most blows to Rodney King. While in his shoes, baton raised and ready to strike King, the youth expressed what they imagined Powell was feeling or thinking: (1) I am scared to death; (2) I'm not sure why I'm doing this but my buddies aren't stopping me so it must be okay; (3) I hate how black people want to move in and take our jobs and change the way we do things: (4) I don't get paid to lose street fights; (5) It's wrong but I don't know how to stop it; (6) I feel powerful; (7) I don't feel anything; (8) He looks like a criminal to me; (9) I feel like a criminal; (10) I hate my job.

In many youth-theatre productions employing a community-based theatre model, the priority is to stage the stories and experiences of the youth themselves, using their words almost exclusively. That is not the model that CAP and Plaza have used over the years. In other words, while incorporating the language and culture of the youth is always encouraged, and while being attentive to their abilities, concerns, limitations, and demographics is absolutely vital, Plaza regularly hires a professional playwright. Also, in selecting King and Colvin, the youth, knowing very little about either, rendered themselves students and respondents from the start. As dramaturge/playwright, I would not be weaving any first person accounts, unless the youth wrote of parallel experiences in their own lives (which some did and were included in the play).

With the onus this placed on me as playwright, one choice I made from the start was to not 'dumb-down,' neither in language nor structural complexity. Young people can handle difficult material and non-conventional staging. Did they have a dramaturgical understanding of the entire play? No. Did they fully comprehend how we were using the Joker System as a way to process the subject matter? (B.J. Dodge, in her unflagging bent for the comedic, put it this way: 'For these kids process is like – processed. Is that cheese?') Did they understand the Joker as a character? Very few. Were they at times confused and frustrated by how to work in an ensemble, playing one character for only five minutes before moving on to the next? Yes.[9] Did they feel safe enough to express their frustrations as they were asked to explore uncomfortable material in unfamiliar ways? Yes. 'The program pushes them up and holds them, allows them to be who they want to be, or naturally be the people they are becoming' (Risha Hill). Were they able to comprehend the innuendos and double entendres that pervaded the more stylistically sophisticated scenes? Some of them, some of the time. Did they fully appreciate the historical meaning of the LA riots on contemporary LA? I doubt it (though I hardly know any adult who does either). Did they understand all the words they spoke? Definitely not. We spent many hours explaining terms such as 'integration', 'melting pot,' 'chokehold,' 'NAACP,' 'KKK,' and so on. Were community and human relations prioritized over professional training? Yes.[10]

The Joker System is built to incorporate all varying points of view as they arise in the process of making the piece; questions, disagreements, even moral outrage, have a designated place (usually through the Chorus) within the structure. That said, how else might we alleviate concerns regarding proselytizing, particularly when dealing with charged political material? Every play is a world that actors, and then by proxy audiences, inhabit. Often, when the play is 'unmarked' – that is, when it reiterates convention and sanctioned social values – there is no challenge of the authors' intentions; *The Wizard of Oz* is not recognized as espousing or proselytizing ideological tenets of home and family. That is, *The Wizard of Oz* portrays a politic that by virtue of being engrained, mainstream, is deemed apolitical.

When the values of a play are visibly 'marked' – re: contrary to convention – their otherness is occasion to fault. Levi Brewster, CalArts alum and designer of *UPSET!*, put it succinctly (and more confidently than I could have when the production team got together to discuss the criticism) when he said:

> there are plenty of people out there who are pushing their agenda forward. I don't know why our agenda, whatever that is, shouldn't have it's time. . . . [The youth's] voices were there. Yes, our voices were there, too, and I don't think that's a problem. Yes, we brought our politics into the process . . . and they are important politics to put into circulation, right alongside all the others.

Dodge framed it pedagogically, emphasizing the pedagogical priorities of the Plaza process:

> We are indeed practicing propaganda if we don't inform her [the actor] what she is saying, who said it first, why she's saying it. But we do inform her. That kind of educational responsibility is indigenous to this program.

Finally, I wonder if, in spite of the methodological 'democracy' and seemingly deconstructive stance that the Joker System allows and advocates (by virtue of its fluid, self-critical, Brechtian nature), it is simply easier, perhaps safer, for audiences to recognize and then censure the progressive leaning of *UPSET!* than to embrace the ambiguity that such democratic dramaturgy inspires. Perhaps, not surprisingly, the penchant for black and white, if even hinted at as a viable paradigm of interpretation (and this we certainly did· hint at in keeping with Boal's Manichean leanings), will always triumph over shades of gray.

From the opening *Dedication* (to Rosa Parks) to the very final scene, *UPSET!* followed and fueled a bus motif. Borrowing from Tom Wolfe's famous line from *Electric Kool-Aid Acid Test* ('You're either on the bus or off the bus'), the motif suggested that there is no middle road, and that one must act without compromise in accord with the right set of principles or you are off the bus. In *UPSET!* we were lucky to have a real historical bus in the story to more literally drive home the principle. Cast and audience alike were being asked what they would do if they were in Claudette's shoes. In effect, they were asked to consider how and what their color means in their community, city, country. As the play progressed, there were all kinds of lessons cum puzzles to chew over: who do we trust in moments of crisis?; are we getting all the information we need from media, teachers, leaders in order to make the right decision?; how do I make choices amidst all the contrary information?; are the police there to protect me or to suspect me?; do I have the courage to make the right decision given the probable consequences?; what is the difference between agency and heroics, or, when is it foolish to perform acts of resistance and when is it courageous?

For nearly 90 minutes of show time, we waited for this real and symbolic bus to arrive, tried to solve the riddle of responsibility and ethics that it was posing, pondered our own spins of the Wheel of Fortune. By the time the bus appeared we were all aware of its import, and we were faced with a question that all the waiting did not really prepare us for: What role do we want to play at this moment? And on entering the bus, within whose theatrical shoes will we learn what we need to learn? Claudette's? The bus driver's? One of the White Mask's? The policeman's? We wait for the bus and when it finally comes, we do not get a free ride but a big predicament, not an easy choice but a tough test. A test not necessarily passed or failed but rehearsed over and over again.

	[CLAUDETTE stands beside RODNEY and takes his hand.]
Rodney:	(*sings*) I have tried in my way to be brave and important But I've learned I have nothing to offer If I could, I really would, I would stand up and deliver I don't know how to turn, to turn things over
Claudette:	(*sings*) I was once, someone strong, and I feel the longing in me To move on, to do good for another Don't give up, don't despair, we can take small steps here to there I'm sure, if you try, you'll recover
Rodney and Claudette:	Times are tough, change is slow, but there's still so many roads to go It can't just be the same, the same old story It's my life, not a play, got to work for justice everyday They're dreams, but we feel, to rehearse will make them real, We feel that we can make them real
	[RODNEY and CLAUDETTE walk towards each other.]
Chorus:	Oh no. Don't tell me this show is going to end as a love story?
Chorus:	(*debating with each other*) YEAH! (*others*) BOO!
Joker:	It's never a bad thing when a show becomes a love story!

> [RODNEY and CLAUDETTE give each other a hug. RODNEY acts interested in CLAUDETTE, leans forward for a kiss. CLAUDETTE gently pushes RODNEY away.]

Claudette: (*to audience*) Don't worry, he's not my type. (*to Rodney*) Come on, Rodney. Let's rock the bus!

Notes

1 All play excerpts in this essay are from *UPSET!*, written by Schutzman (2006) in conjunction with the youth of the Plaza de la Raza Youth Theatre Program, 2005–06 season.

2 The most well-known Joker System plays that Boal and Guarnieri co-authored were performed by Arena Theatre in Sao Paolo: *Arena Conta Zumbi* (*Arena Tells the Tale of Zumbi*) in 1965, and *Arena Conta Tiradentes* (*Arena Tells the Tale of Tiradentes*) in 1967. For descriptions of Boal's Joker System (its philosophies and techniques) and the above plays, see Boal (1979: 159–197).

3 The South Central Farm refers to 14 acres of vacant land in South Central LA offered by the City of Los Angeles to the people as a site for community healing after the riots. Over 14 years, the land was cultivated by community residents into what is presumed to be the largest urban farm in the nation.

4 All non-play citations in this chapter are from a roundtable discussion (Schutzman *et al.*, 2006) that I conducted with the production team of *UPSET!* three months after it closed. We discussed various subjects related to the production, the Joker System, the Plaza Youth Theatre Program's philosophies and practices, and our personal experiences. Those in attendance were B.J. Dodge (director), Donald Amerson (production manager), Marvin Tunney (choreographer), Levi Brewster (designer), and Risha Hill (assistant director). The second assistant director, Amber Skalski, was unable to attend.

5 The students performing this scene decided themselves who they wanted to portray as a white supremacist. They chose Hitler, a cowboy, a housewife (in a clambake apron), and a Viking.

6 It may be interesting for readers to know that José is the same actor who played the KKK member stomping cans in the white supremacy scene mentioned earlier.

7 Claudette Colvin was thought to be too poor, young, and dark-skinned for her arrest to serve as a test case to end segregation on public buses. When it was discovered that she was also pregnant (and unmarried), there was no chance the NAACP would use her as a spokesperson.

8 This seeming contradiction between Boal's spoken intent of the plays (as Manichean) and my understanding of the techniques (as producing far more fluid categories of identity) might be attributed, at least in part, to my inability to read the plays in their original Portuguese.

9 It became clear as the rehearsal process began that this was a huge challenge for the youth. They were not familiar with plays in which an actor did not play one character all the way through. In a way, playing all these different characters was something like playing no one at all. At first, many missed what they thought all theatre offered in playing a singular character with clear motivations, psychology, story line, realistic dialogues, costume; without the grounding in a steady identity, many had trouble engaging at all. Adding to this, most of the teens were in the Chorus and on stage for the entire length of the play with no

downtime backstage. This resulted in a kind of manic frenzy as if the lack of a consistent character translated – after a certain threshold of time – into bursts of collective and contagious attention deficit disorder! (It made for a very dynamic riot scene, the actors' sense of mayhem finally finding its calling!) These concerns notwithstanding, the youth learned *in their bodies* how to change channels without losing the subtleties of each character. 'One reason I like these techniques is because they ask you to develop a capability to be "neutral" so that you can move in all directions' (Brewster). To their credit the youth intuited early on that they were engaged in an experiment, one that offered them a different set of opportunities than they came in expecting: to convey a recurring and dynamic plot about power, to tell a story that contained within it many stories (including their stories, their questions), and to learn complexity, flexibility, and teamwork. As difficult as this ensemble mode was for them, for the most part they embraced these opportunities.

10 For a full account of the Plaza Youth Theatre Program, see Dodge (2008). B.J. Dodge has been the director of the Program since its inception in 1990.

References

Boal, A. (1979) *Theatre of the Oppressed* (trans. C.A. and M.-O.L. McBride), New York: Theatre Communications Group.

Dodge, B.J. (2009) *Plaza de la Raza*, Valencia, CA: Community Arts Partnership, CalArts.

Schutzman, M. (2006) *UPSET!*, produced at REDCAT, Los Angeles. Community Arts Partnership, CalArts.

Schutzman, M. *et al.* (2006) Unpublished roundtable interview, Los Angeles.

7 Seventeenth-century theatre therapy

Six Jacobean plays

John Casson

Introduction

Between 1613 and 1625 six plays containing scenes in which theatre is used therapeutically were staged. These plays are connected and are the first to demonstrate the therapeutic power of theatre.

Shakespeare and Fletcher: *The Two Noble Kinsmen* 1613

This play, based on Chaucer's *Knights Tale*, is the very last play we know Shakespeare wrote. However the scenes that concern us are not in Chaucer; they are created by Shakespeare and Fletcher.

Palamon and Arcite are the two noble kinsmen who are imprisoned. They declare their friendship and loyalty to each other but this is tested when they see Emily, with whom they both fall in love. Arcite is banished, leaving Palamon in prison. The Jailer's daughter falls in love with Palamon and helps him escape. She follows him and yet he does not return her love. She goes mad. While the main business of the play is the working through of Palamon and Arcite's struggle for Emily's hand, the scenes of the Jailer's daughter's love and madness are a significant subplot. The play's central themes are love/war, loyalty and compassion: the compassion we feel for her is a vital element that integrates the two plots.

The Jailer's daughter's decline into madness is progressively and carefully charted. In a scene believed to be by Shakespeare, a doctor assesses her madness but fears he cannot help. He diagnoses her as suffering from a profound melancholy. Learning that she has been distracted from her impending betrothal by seeing and falling in love with Palamon, the doctor then prescribes the following treatment:

> This you must do: confine her to a place where the light may rather seem to steal in than be permitted. Take upon you, young sir, her friend, the name of Palamon; say you come to eat with her, and to commune of love . . . Sing to her such green songs of love as she says Palamon hath sung in prison . . . Learn what maids have been her

companions and playferes, and let them repair to her with Palamon in their mouths, and appear with tokens, *as if* they suggested for him. It is a falsehood she is in, which is with falsehoods to be combatted.

(4.3.70–88)

He is in effect following on from the uncle's prescription that they play along with her metaphors and delusions. He is deliberately using the dramatic '*as if*'. The doctor then reveals that this is not an innovation but normal clinical practice:

> I have seen it approved, how many times I know not, but to make the number more, I have great hope in this.

(4.3.91)

The next time we see the doctor he asks: 'Has this advice I told you done good upon her?'

Wooer: Oh, very much. The maids that have kept her company have half persuaded her that I am Palamon. Within this half-hour she came smiling to me, and asked me what I would eat, and when I would kiss her. I told her presently, and kissed her twice.

(5.2.1–6)

The doctor encourages the continuation, indeed the intensification, of the role playing, encouraging the wooer to take her to bed, somewhat to the outrage of the father. When she appears she is still rambling, but playfully, and her father plays along with her. She talks with her Wooer about marriage but is still convinced her father is to be executed and that her Palamon does not care for her: there is still some way to go in the cure. Interestingly she puts the Doctor into the role of Arcite and he immediately responds, with appropriate spontaneity, as such (5.2.91). She asks him if Palamon (the Wooer) will have her and he confirms her hope. She then notices that the doctor is taller than Arcite: 'Lord, how you've grown!' (5.2.96) The doctor stays in role as Arcite, even suggesting he has to go off to the coming tournament. He is now confident that within three or four days she will recover. The scene ends in tender, playful intimacy between her and the Wooer. We don't see her again but hear that 'she's well restored and to be married shortly' (5.4.27).

These scenes are amongst the very last Shakespeare wrote in his career. Their message is of compassion, therapeutic optimism, playfulness, humour and hope.

Fletcher: *The Mad Lover* 1616

This comedy tells the story of Memnon, a war hero, who returns to the court of King Astorax of Paphos, after his triumph over the enemy,

Diocles. Despite his great skills and confidence in military matters Memnon is tongue-tied when meeting the King's proud and beautiful sister, Calis, with whom he falls instantly in love. Being a blunt soldier, lacking the social graces of courtly manners, he eventually blurts out that he loves her. She is startled and frightened by his abrupt manner. In a later meeting when she and her ladies are teasing him, he tells her that he has a loving heart. She asks for his heart. He takes her request literally and promises that she shall have it, delivered in a glass. He asks various military friends, starting with his old loyal soldier Chilax, and then a surgeon, to cut his heart out. Memnon believes he will thus find himself in Elizium, a land of everlasting love where Calis is bound to join him. His friends fear for his sanity and Polydore, his brother, devises a plan to help Memnon step back from this suicide. He begins with a funeral procession, pretending to present Memnon's heart to Calis, angrily confronting her with her cruelty in the hope of moving her to love Memnon. Polydore succeeds only in attracting her attention onto himself: she falls in love with him!

Meanwhile Memnon is in the care of Stremon, his favourite singer. Stremon notes that Memnon 'has divers times been calling upon Orpheus to appear and show the joys' (of Elizium). Stremon therefore creates a masque in which Orpheus appears, singing about the suffering of those who die in despair for unrequited love, and so pass not into Elizium but into Hell. He then introduces Charon, the boatman of the underworld, who refuses to take Memnon across the Styx into Elizium if he commits suicide. Orpheus shows him a series of ridiculous figures who have become trapped by love. These enactments buy time, holding Memnon back from desperate action and calming him. When Memnon meets the whore who has been disguised as Calis and guesses the trick because of her rank smell, he turns the tables on the actors and bursts into laughter. Later Chilax (who has disguised himself in a priestly robe in the temple of Venus for his own purposes) is mistaken by Memnon for the ghost of his old enemy Diocles. Spontaneously playing along with his delusion Chilax succeeds in buying more time, further postponing the suicidal heart operation.

There are other twists and turns of the plot until Polydore performs a last theatrical act: he pretends to die and when all are gathered round his bier, sits up and asks Calis to accept Memnon as her husband. She chooses Polydore instead but all ends happily.

In these therapeutic masques images and actions that the 'patient' suggests are dramatised: the heart in the glass, Orpheus, the land of Elizium, a death/funeral, the ghost of Diocles; and people play real and symbolic roles. Crude though it may seem (and this is a comedy!) it works and the suicidal man is brought back from the brink. The informal and spontaneous efforts of Polydore, Stremon and Chilax to use drama therapeutically in this play are followed in the next two plays by the deliberate and planned therapeutic theatre of two doctors: Dr Paulo and Dr Corax.

There are thematic connections between *The Two Noble Kinsmen* and *The Mad Lover*: both have a struggle between War and Love: in the first play this is symbolised by Mars and Venus and in the second Venus herself appears in a vision. The continuity between the plays is hardly surprising as Fletcher wrote parts of the first and all of the second within a period of three years (1613–16). After another three years, in 1619, Fletcher and Massinger were working on the next play to demonstrate the healing power of theatre: *A Very Woman*.

Fletcher and Massinger: *A Very Woman* 1619–22

A Very Woman is a story of youthful arrogance humbled and the recon-ciliation possible between people when such humility is accepted. Don John Antonio, Prince of Tarent, is a suitor to Almira but she arrogantly dismisses him as she is in love with Don Martino Cardenes. The latter contemptuously challenges Antonio who eventually is provoked into a fight, seriously wounding Martino. Antonio escapes but is captured by pirates and sold into slavery, eventually finding himself a servant in the court of Almira. She falls in love with this disguised stranger. Meanwhile Martino is seriously ill and ruminates on his fault in challenging Antonio. He is treated by a Doctor Paulo who uses a story and two dramas to help Martino, who resolves to make amends if he lives. Eventually Antonio's identity is revealed, Martino asks for forgiveness and gives up his interest in Almira, who marries Antonio. (There are other characters and story lines but this is the core of the plot.) The play is interesting, dramatic, funny and serious by turns and it is sad that it has not been performed since 1661. I will now concentrate on the scenes with the Doctor.

He first appears after Martino's wounding, summoned with two surgeons to administer to the patient. He tells his employers, Martino's father and the Viceroy, that they have just begun the healing journey and there are still dangers ahead:

> Though his hurts,
> I mean his outward ones, do promise fair,
> There is a deeper one, and in his minde,
> Must be with care provided for. Melancholy,
> And at the height too, near of kin to madness,
> Possesses him; his senses are distracted,
> Not one, but all; and if I can collect 'em
> With all the various ways, invention,
> Or industry ever practis'd, I shall write it
> My master-piece.
>
> (2.2.77)

This diagnosis, that Martino is now suffering at least as much from a psychological hurt as anything physical, is of the utmost interest:

melancholy we might translate as depression but Paulo suggests further that he is on the borderline of madness.

Martino, in a soliloquy, ruminates on his fault: berating himself he concludes he was taught by a woman to act as he did and so must abjure women and love. The Doctor tries gently to reason with him and concludes that his melancholy will lessen by degrees. Of his treatment the Doctor says:

> I do apply myself, checking the bad,
> And cherishing the good. For these I have
> Prepar'd my instruments, fitting his chamber
> With trap-doors, and descents; sometimes presenting
> Good spirits of the air, bad of the earth,
> To pull down, or advance his fair intentions.
> He's of a noble nature, yet sometimes
> Thinks that which by confederacy I do,
> Is by some skill in Magick.

> > (4.2.11)

Here the Doctor is explicitly telling us that he is using theatrical means, symbolising psychological polarities, dramatising inner conflicts. It is interesting also to note he does this deliberately, using theatrical illusions. He hides Martino's father and the Viceroy as a secret audience to the theatrical cure that follows. Martino appears in bed, musing on the nature of the soul, still blaming himself for his behaviour and condemning himself to an isolated existence, even to a living death in despair. The Doctor enters disguised as a Friar. He tells Martino he has been sent by the Doctor, saying, 'Thou art too cruel to thyself'. He then tells him a story about his own youthful errors and how he has repented and accepted forgiveness. He leaves Martino to further reflect on how he is persecuting himself. This use of story is repeated later in the play with similar results: Antonio (while still disguised) tells Almira a story to help her change her mind. Fletcher and Massinger understood the power of story to alter consciousness.

Martino continues his moral ruminations and considers suicide. In a scene believed to be by Massinger, the Doctor returns to his dramatic treatment, next appearing as a soldier with one of his slaves dressed as a courtier. Clearly these roles have been chosen to dramatise Martino's mental state:

> My thoughts are search'd and answer'd; for I did
> Desire a soldier and a courtier
> To yield me satisfaction in some doubts . . .

> > (4.2.121)

Martino questions the two figures, seeking guidance as to correct behaviour in Love and Honour. There are moral lessons here. The Doctor ends with:

Who fights
With passions, and orecomes 'em, is indu'd
With the best vertue, passive fortitude.

(4.2.153)

These scenes move Martino:

The discords of my soul
Are tun'd, and make a heavenly harmony:
What sweet peace I feel, now! I am ravish'd with it.

(4.2.158)

We hear music and the Doctor re-enters as a philosopher. There is a masque of good and evil spirits, singing and the doctor exits to return as himself. Martino greets him with:

Doctor, thou hast perfected a bodies cure
T'amaze the world; and almost cur'd a mind
Neer phrensie. With delight I now perceive
You for my recreation have invented
The several objects, which my melancholy
Sometimes did think you conjur'd, otherwhiles
Imagin'd 'em Chimeras . . . In your moral song
Of my good genius, and my bad, you have won me
A cheerful heart, and banished discontent.

(4.2.170)

Martino later meets Antonio. He is humble, wiser and achieves reconciliation. Dr Paulo is much admired for his skill. In telling this story I have reduced it: my aim here has been to convey the elements of the dramatic cure the Doctor achieves through theatrical means.

Fletcher and Middleton: *The Nice Valour* 1615–25

This comedy uses masques in an attempt to cure a 'Passionate Lord' who is mad for love, indeed erotomanic, and melancholic with mood swings and delusional jealousy. He is the brother of the Duke who describes him as in the following extract:

Duke: A man so lost
          In the wild ways of passion, that he's sensible
          Of naught but what torments him!
La Nove: True, my lord,
          He runs through all the passions of mankind,
          And shifts 'em strangely too: . . . in's melancholy again . . .

> . . . Then on a sudden he's so merry again, . . .
> And in the turning of a hand, so angry . . .

Duke: I pity him dearly,
> And let it be your charge, with his kind brother,
> To see his moods observ'd; let every passion
> Be fed ev'n to a surfeit, which in time
> May breed a loathing: let him have enough
> Of every object that his sense is rapt with.
> And being once glutted, then the taste of folly
> Will come into disrelish.

(1.1)

The Duke therefore is prescribing that the madman's fantasies be satisfied (a view that Burton was later to subscribe to as a treatment option, see below). To achieve this La Nove employs masquers and one woman plays the role of Cupid. Again the method is to dramatise and fulfil the psychotic fantasies, just as Moreno was to do in psychodrama from the 1930s onwards (Casson, 2004, p. 72). The first time we see the 'Passionate Lord' he ridiculously mistakes La Nove for a woman and the latter plays along with this misapprehension to comic effect: he even pretends to be pregnant! Cupid also plays along with the mad fantasies: at his erotomanic behest shooting amorous arrows at women who he imagines love him. Fulfilling his fantasies gives Cupid some power over the madman so that he is pacified and follows her. Unfortunately for the woman playing Cupid, she believes the Passionate Lord's promise of marriage so she loses her virginity: she has obviously allowed herself to go too deeply into her role! The project to heal the Passionate Lord continues despite this but he becomes violent, beating up a clown called Galoshio, who provides a comic catalogue of his injuries. Eventually, as the Duke predicted, the Passionate Lord has had enough of erotic pleasures and banishes Cupid to sink into melancholy with a song:

> Hence, all you vain delights, . . .
> There's naught in this life sweet,
> If men were wise to see't,
> But only melancholy,
> Oh, sweetest melancholy! . . .

(3.3)

His brothers however expect further trouble, namely that anger will emerge from depression:

> . . . the tail of his melancholy
> Is always the head of his anger, and follows as close
> As the report *[bang]* follows the *[gun]* powder.

(3.4)

This explosive military metaphor indeed is proved accurate as the Passionate Lord enters with a truncheon and beats a man (Lapet) who has previously suffered throughout the play as other people's scapegoat. We next see the Passionate Lord with Base, his jester, laughing uproariously about these beatings. Together they sing and laugh. They are joined by the masquers in hilarious comedy and dance. Sadly this happy occasion in interrupted by a soldier bent on revenge who stabs the Passionate Lord. This shock, which at first seems fatal, restores him to sanity and he marries the now pregnant Cupid.

Thus the playwrights show that whatever the best efforts of the masquers to achieve a healing drama, yet life may find unusual ways of bring people to their senses!

This is perhaps the least satisfactory text in this series. I have much reduced the plot to highlight the therapeutic masques. As a comedy it is hardly a serious manifesto for therapeutic theatre: nevertheless the masquing does contain the Passionate Lord's manic fantasies and allow him a creative space where he can sing and play despite his madness. We must remember that laughter is also healing and comedy has a place in healing theatre.

Ford: *The Lover's Melancholy* 1621–5

This play recapitulates themes, explicitly, through textual echoes, reaching back to Shakespeare's *King Lear* and *Tempest*. Ford has clearly studied Burton's *The Anatomy of Melancholy* (1621). Some scholars have suggested that Dr Corax in the play is a portrait of Burton. Before the play starts the previous king, Agenor of Cyprus, had attempted the rape of a woman, Eroclea, betrothed to his son, Palador. Her father Meleander rescued her but he was accused of treason and imprisoned in his own castle. Eroclea escaped with Menaphon to Greece and survived by being disguised as a young man, taking the name Parthenophill. Agenor dies and Palador takes the throne but is melancholic and unable to rule effectively. The play begins with Menaphon and Eroclea, still disguised as Parthenophill, returning to Cyprus. Meleander is still lost in grief: indeed he is considered mad. Dr Corax cures both Meleander and Palador of their melancholy using dramatic interventions. The other aspects of the plot are less relevant but are about the psychological education and trials of lovers before they can be united: the play has a moral theme concerning the proper management of strong feelings, including lust, so that these result in harmony rather than conflict. Music and musical metaphors play a significant role in this exposition.

When we first meet Dr Corax he exchanges banter with courtiers. These joking exchanges refer to the current practice of medicine (with a quotation from Burton's *Anatomy of Melancholy*). The doctor recruits the courtiers for his planned therapeutic drama. He says: 'I'll shape ye all for a device before the prince; we'll try how that can move him' (1.2.155). This statement shows his intention is that the drama be cathartic. We next meet Dr Corax when he confronts Prince Palador for not following his prescription of healthy exercise. He asks to return to his university; for if the prince will not follow his prescriptions he cannot help and indeed he is himself caught up in the Prince's 'wilful dullness' and 'almost mad' himself (2.1.61, 66). This might be understood as an example of countertransference, though Corax is perhaps being sarcastic. Later in the play, when working with the mad Meleander, Corax says:

> There is so much sense in this wild distraction
> That I am almost out of my wits too,
> To see and hear him; some few hours more
> Spent here would turn me apish, if not frantic.
> (4.2.130)

Corax allows himself to enter into the madness of his patients, finding meaning and empathy for them.

Senior courtiers confront the Prince with his responsibilities and Corax fearlessly challenges him. Aretus guesses that there is a hidden element in the Prince's melancholy (2.1.26). When alone with the prince, Rhetias discovers this is his pining for his lost love, Eroclea. We next see Dr Corax when he stages his first therapeutic drama: *The Masque of Melancholy*. This is a series of figures who symbolise different types of melancholy beginning with the wild wolf man of Lycanthropy, followed by a paranoid figure of Hydrophobia, a poor philosopher representing Delirium, a mad woman as Phrenitis (mania) and a madman as Hypochondria. After nonsensical dialogues they dance together with a sea nymph and exit. Prince Palador has grudgingly enjoyed this show but is in for a shock. He asks Corax what is the meaning of the empty space at the end of the masque and the doctor replies,

> One kind of melancholy
> Is only left untouched; 'twas not in art
> To personate the shadow of that fancy.
> 'Tis named Love Melancholy. As, for instance,
> Admit this stranger here – young man, stand forth.
> (3.3.94)

Corax invites Parthenophill, the disguised Eroclea, onto the stage. She/he is embarrassed, Thamasta is outraged, and Palador rushes out. Despite the upset, Corax knows he has succeeded in his plan to move the prince. The mystery of the cause of his melancholy has been revealed.

The next time we see the Doctor he is congratulated on his diagnostic skills by Rhetias, who tells him that Meleander is in a frenzy. Corax replies:

. . . 'tis not a madness, but his sorrow's
Close-griping grief and anguish of soul
That torture him; he carries hell on earth
Within his bosom. 'Twas a prince's tyranny
Caused his distraction, and a prince's sweetness
Must qualify that tempest of his mind.

(4.2.11)

Thus he diagnoses that the root of Meleander's mental ill health is in the previous king's injustices and that the cure must come from Palador correcting these. Meleander enters in a rage with a poleaxe. Corax is ready for him, wearing a Gorgon mask. In effect he shouts, 'Freeze!' using the Gorgon's mythic power to petrify, and so halts Meleander in his homicidal tracks. Meleander accepts the dramatic metaphor and gives up his weapon.

In their subsequent conversation Meleander discloses his suicidal thoughts. Corax joins him in his thoughts, seeming to accompany him in his plan to hang himself, then asks him to wait, as he wants to say farewell to a lost daughter before they hang themselves. Meleander immediately recollects his own lost daughter and complains to Corax that while mad he did not feel the grief of her loss. His speeches have a Lear-like pathos. He brings in his other daughter Cleophila, who begs him not to let 'passion overrule you' (4.2.162). Corax has arranged for a sleeping potion to be prepared and Meleander drinks it. While asleep they cut his long, unkempt hair and beard and change his clothes. Corax wakes him with music and in a dramatic masque presents a series of figures who gradually restore to Meleander what he has lost: the honours of courtly and government roles of the Marshalship of Cyprus and the Grand Commander of the Ports, then a miniature painting of Eroclea, his lost daughter, before she herself appears. His intention is to gradually reintroduce him to health through this ritual. At first Meleander cannot believe these promises but gradually he is restored and the play ends in three joyous marriages as long-divided lovers are reunited.

Reflections on the therapeutic processes in **The Lover's Melancholy**

Ford based much of his treatment of melancholy on Burton's encyclopaedic study. Burton lists the following therapeutic measures that Ford uses in the play:

1 not to leave the patient alone (friends working together can help);
2 exercise;
3 occupation;
4 distraction;
5 change of life, giving security and satisfaction;
6 quietness and gentleness, proceeding little by little;

7   relieve disgrace and loss;
8   helpful letters;
9   hope and counsel;
10 confession of secret concerns to a friend.

Burton however does not mention theatre as a method of treatment. He has sections on music and dance, and suggests 'mirth' will be useful, even 'witty devices' and does mention examples of dramatising the delusions of the mad. Ford deliberately shows the value of diagnosis; the meaning of seemingly irrational behaviour; the metaphors people use in their distress; the value of a gradual process of restoration; the therapeutic use of dramatic distance; the deliberate use of mask, costume, roles and music. Ford shows that transgenerational injustices, loss and grief and the inability to speak of these are what have made Palador and Meleander ill. 'What makes the patient ill is silence' (Forrester, 1980, p. 31). This accords with our understandings as demonstrated by Schutzenberger (1998) and my own research (Casson, 2004).

Ford and Dekker: *The Sun's Darling* 1624–5

The protagonist of this masque is Raybright, who is the child and 'darling' of Phoebus, the Sun. To treat his melancholy, he is given a year to experience the earthly pleasures of the four seasons. The priest of the Sun diagnoses his condition:

> Tis melancholy, and too fond indulgence
> To your own dull'd affections . . .
> Your fantasie
> Misleads your judgment vainly . . .
> These are but flashes of a brain disordered.
> Contain your float of spleen in seemly bounds,
> Your eyes shall be your witness.

Raybright falls under the deceptive influences of Folly and Humor (the latter is to be taken in the medieval sense of the four humours: phelgmatic, choleric, melancholic and sanguine: perhaps these might be considered now as moods, temperments or complexes) and his search for satisfaction is unfulfilled. In the end the Sun warns Raybright that he must resist Folly and Humor to attain harmony.

The masque is not a play with human characters but a series of scenes in which symbolic figures represent the seasons and aspects of the world and human experience. Raybright is himself not so much an individual human as a representative figure: the bright soul of humanity that is dulled by depression and unsatisfied even when desires are fulfilled. The title page of the 1656 edition describes the work as a 'moral masque' – an accurate description, in that the drama combines the characteristics of the traditional morality play with those of the seventeenth-century masque. Indeed it is more a moral exposition than a demonstration of the therapy of an individual through drama. In *The Sun's Darling* we see the use of story, myth, metaphor and symbol; the satisfaction of fantasies and wishes through dramatisation; the differentiation and representation of roles, presenting different aspects of the psyche.

Theatre therapy in a connected sequence of six plays

There are clearly links between all these plays: Fletcher was part author of four of them. The recurrence of melancholy, madness, lovers and masques connects their plots and characters thematically and technically. For example there are links between Fletcher and Massinger's *A Very Woman* and Ford's *The Lover's Melancholy*: the pride of Almira is echoed by the haughty Thamasta. In the later play Rhetias tells Palador a story just as Doctor Paulo uses a story to help Martino, and Antonio tells Almira a story in similar circumstances. In both plays doctors design and direct the therapeutic dramas with auxiliaries playing roles.

Theatre confronts audiences with psychological truths through showing and telling stories. It can be healing and enable people in denial to gradually emerge into acceptance. These plays show the importance of accurate diagnosis, the development of mental illness from significant life events, disappointments, loss, grief and injustices, and the benefits of witnessing theatre.

We can see the following therapeutic processes deliberately used in the plays:

1 The use of dramatic distancing;
2 The use of story, myth, metaphor and symbol;
3 Concretising and externalising inner psychological experiences in symbolic enactments;
4 Satisfying psychotic fantasy through dramatising delusions;
5 Promoting catharsis through dramatic action;
6 The differentiation and representation of roles, presenting different aspects of the psyche;
7 The potential value of spontaneous enactments, including the spontaneity of ordinary, untrained auxiliaries;
8 Prompting reflection in the patient through stimulating their observer ego (or audience ego) by showing them scenes that explore their world and the consequences of their actions;
9 The value of these therapeutic dramas not only for the identified patient but also for the other actors and the audience;
10 Music and songs are also important in all these plays and have healing power.

Conclusion

These six playwrights, with their vast collective experience, showed that theatre could be therapy. While it might be argued that they were using a comic, dramatic device to entertain, they were also presenting a serious hypothesis: namely that people with a range of psychological disorders, from psychosis to neurosis, could be helped by being presented with theatrical metaphors, enactments of their condition, guidance from real and symbolic roles. They demonstrated the success of the method. These six plays demonstrated that theatre could be therapy three hundred years before the emergence of dramatherapy and psychodrama and two hundred years before the development of psychiatry.

Bibliography

The text of *The Nice Valour* is available at: www.tech.org/~cleary/nice.html
Further information on the play is available at: http://en.wikipedia.org/wiki/The_Nice_Valour
Some material is drawn from: http://en.wikipedia.org/wiki/The_Sun's_Darling

Bowes, F. (ed.) (1982) 'The Mad Lover', in *The Dramatic Works in the Beaumont and Fletcher Canon*, Vol. V, Cambridge: Cambridge University Press.
Burton, R. (2001) *The Anatomy of Melancholy*, New York: New York Review Books Classics (original work published 1621).
Casson, J. (2004) *Drama, Psychotherapy and Psychosis: Dramatherapy and Psychodrama with People Who Hear Voices*, Hove, East Sussex: Brunner-Routledge.
Casson, J. (2006) 'Shakespeare and the Healing Drama', *Journal of the British Association of Dramatherapists*, 28, 1, Spring.
Edwards, P. and Gibson, C. (eds) (1976) 'A Very Woman', in *The Plays and Poems of Philip Massinger*, Vol. IV, Oxford: Clarendon Press.
Forrester, J. (1980) *Language and the Origins of Psychoanalysis*, London: Macmillan.
Hill, R.F. (ed.) (1985) 'The Lover's Melancholy' by John Ford, Manchester: Manchester University Press.
Pearson, J. (1873) *The Dramatic Works of Thomas Dekker*, Vol. Four, *The Sun's Darling*, London, Brawn.
Schutzenberger, A. (1998) *The Ancestor Syndrome*, London: Routledge.

8 Theatre and therapy

A necessary dialogue

Salvo Pitruzzella

Introduction

As a dramatherapist working mainly in the mental health field, I am not usually concerned with performance. During the last three years, however, I have been involved in an experimental theatre project with a semi-professional company, composed of a group of young adults with learning disabilities and a group of volunteers (mostly psychology and education students). This experience has set in motion a profound change in my own view of both theatre and therapy, a change which is still in progress. The present article is a testimony of such a change.

A perplexed conversation

(A town near the Mediterranean Sea; a warm summer night. Standing under a pergola of jasmine are two persons, engrossed in a lively conversation. One is a dramatherapist, the other a theatre director. They are friends, and they have just started working together in a theatre project involving people with learning disabilities. They talk about a play they had been watching an hour ago, whose protagonist is a well-known actor with learning disability. Every now and then, the smell of the jasmine flowers seeps into the clouds of cigarette smoke, conjuring up visions of Arabian flavour.)

A: I think he is the greatest actor I ever saw. I had a gut feeling about him before knowing it with my heart and mind. He expresses the pain of being alive that he bears within himself in such a piercing way, yet he is so light.

B: Is he aware of all this? Is he an actor or only a pitiable person, just doing what he's been told? Aren't they using him as a puppet, to create an effect?

A: Nevertheless, his being a puppet tells us of our human condition, of our 'puppetness'.

B: But what about the man behind the performance? If people are unaware of what they express, they become like fools in the eyes of others, objects of scorn, and their humanity is diminished.

A: Actors have always made a sacrifice of themselves. And how can you know how he feels? He might be happier than you and me, for reasons we could not even imagine. If you think you know what is good for him better than he himself does, as he can't understand what people says, and he can't even speak, you claim to be more than him.

B: This is exactly what his director does. He uses him, and he justifies himself by saying he knows that he likes to be an actor, because he knows him in a way other people cannot understand. It could even be a sort of or moral subjugation.

A: And this is exactly what therapists do.

B: Therapists have an ethical code.

A: Who made that code? Clients? The deaf and dumb?

B: We try to be scientific.

A: Science! *There are more things in heaven and earth. . .*
(Pause)

B: Anyway, I must admit that sometimes there is some pressure toward 'normalization', which is in contrast even with what the therapist thinks and feels. But there is always a choice. . .

A: Is giving up a choice?

B: I didn't mean that. The choice is between pushing people to behave as they are expected to, and helping them find their own way of being. It is a question of freedom.

A: Theatre is free. . .

B: I don't think so. Theatre must conform to countless rules: current aesthetics, critics' judgement, the urge to satisfy the audience, money, censorship and so on. Creative freedom of the artist is nothing but a myth.

A: So, we are both caught in a trap, aren't we?

B: This is not the crux of the matter. We are all tangled up in a web of necessities, which influence our being in the world. Neither theatre nor therapy exists in a void. But what I want is to get near to people, feel them and get in touch with their true needs. I want to help them to discover those needs. I try to let them find their own ways to manage them.

A: But you make diagnoses, don't you? You put a label on them, storing them in a pigeonhole.

B: You must have some hypothesis to start with.

A: A diagnosis is not a hypothesis; it is a judgement.

B: Kant would argue that it is more an analytic judgement a posteriori than a synthetic judgement a priori. But that is not the point. I don't mind labels. I try to meet people openly, and to know them close up. When you select an actor for the stage, you make a *sterner* judgement. Sterner and more whimsical.

A: That is my job.

(Pause. A big yellow moon is peeping over the horizon.)

B: Therapy is not devising a remedy for an illness. Therapy is service.

A: Theatre too is service. We serve art.

B: There is no art without people. People are art. Unless you are a Gordon Craig-like director, wishing for a Super-Marionette.

A: Which is not far from Nietzsche's Super-Man.

B: Don't try to baffle me. You know well that you can't just tell the actors 'do this and that'. You must help them to look inside themselves; to do this, you must establish an authentic relationship with them.

A: Like Socrates with his disciples. . .

B: Right.

A: Socrates went on trial for undue influence. And he drank hemlock.

B: So, we reached a dead end.

A: Or a vicious circle.

B: The more you caress a circle, the more it becomes vicious. . .

(Pause)

A: We need a new start.

B: Let's talk about purposes. I told you what I expect from my work: I cannot be certain all the time, but I am used to being sensitive to some cues that tell me that something is growing. I constantly question myself if I am right or wrong, but I can't help thinking that I must try.

A: What kind of cues are you talking about? Are they visible?

B: Yet they express what is invisible.

A: Just like theatre: the truth is not only in what is told or shown, but in the gap between what can be seen and what is unspeakable and unfathomable.

B: It might be an abyss.

A: The audience can fill it.

B: Yes, but the audience cannot return it to the actors, except in the form of applauses and cheers. That is the actor's pay: an ephemeral glory, a moment of excitement that is soon over.

A: I don't care about glory. But let's go back to purposes. Mine is . . . I don't know. It's something coming from inside. I want to create a thing living by itself. Jean-Louis Barrault has said that theatre is first of all an art that moves.

B: And drags actors along with it. Where to?

A: Heaven or hell, of course. Where else?

B: Or both. . .

(Pause)

A: Who are the actors?

B: Who are they?

A: Me and you, aren't we the actors of this staged conversation? Is not that old man passing by over there an actor in this play?

B: You mean *All the world's a stage* and all. . .?

A: No, not really. I was saying. . .

(Pause. Perfectly round, the full moon hangs in the middle of the sky.)

B: Something about truth. . .

A: Yes. An actor tells the truth. Peter Brook said that it's just because theatre is an illusion, it shows us what lies behind the dangerous illusions we are attached to.

B: That's interesting: you mean that the real catharsis is not a relief from bad feelings, but the breaking of illusions, don't you? It sounds a bit therapeutic.

A: In a certain sense. . .

B: Yes, but – again – what about actors? Are they just a cog in the illusion machine?

A: They are more than that. They are both the officers and the gate-keepers of this ritual where illusions are destroyed. They deserve great respect. They deserve awe.

B: Should directors have this respect and awe towards the actors?

A: Yes, they should. A director is not a tyrant, he is a pedagogue.

B: Perhaps he must learn to be one.

A: Yes, he must learn from the actors.

B: Just as the therapist learns from his clients. I ask people: teach me how I may help you.

A: Well, at last there is something we both agree upon.

B: But you also teach form, don't you?

A: I help people to understand that a shape is necessary.

B: A shape for experience.

A: What is formless can be dreadful.

B: And forms can be shared. If there is no form, no communication is possible.

(Pause)

B: That is another delicate argument. Finding shapes needs time. And the theatre business is penny-pinching about time. The risk is that you impose your own forms, instead of waiting for them to experiment until they find their own forms, the forms they really need.

A: You can't keep hanging around with experiments forever; you need to reach a point. If a more demanding effort is needed, well, it is just what happens in life.

B: Trying to be as careful and gentle as you can. . .

A: Of course.

B: It can be hard when you are under stress yourself.

A: If we face it together, it may become a strong experience of sharing. It can empower people, helping them to find an inner strength so that they may go on coping with life's challenges.

B: Now, you're talking just like a therapist. . .

A: So it's your turn to speak as a comedian.

B: 'I will see you tomorrow at the rehearsal. Please, be on time'.
(The two men laugh. They embrace and part. The moon is hiding behind the jasmine pergola.)
(The curtain falls)

Ten propositions for an encounter

1   Although they might conceive it in different theoretical ways, the practices of theatre and dramatherapy share the use of drama as a vehicle to reach further objectives. According to the dramatherapy model, drama is both a frame of experience and a constituent feature of the person. For theatre, drama is both the groundwork on which a work of art can be constructed, and the form of the work of art itself.

2   In the last five decades, some theatre started leaving its ivory tower of bourgeois entertainment and looking at society not only as a potential reserve of audience, but as a living body to relate with. In recent years, many directors have trained laypeople, including social outcasts and minorities, to put themselves on stage, drawing artistic material from people's own life experiences and their actual expressive talents, although the ways to reach this aim are of all sorts, and are sometimes hazy or contradictory. For these actors, drama has become mainly a place where their condition can be expressed and declared, but can also be shared with the audience, tending towards an overcoming of the marginalization and a more rooted presence in society.

Dramatherapy, for its part, has been aware from the beginning that the wellbeing of individuals, as well as their chances to defeat the hindrances that keep them from their self-realization, are strictly tied in with their being part of families, groups, communities. So, we share the idea that therapy must be put into context, although sometimes the effective consequences of this idea are not entirely clear. Yet drama is considered a place for the transformation not only of the internal balance of individuals, but also of their relationship with society.

3   In spite of this potential confluence, a profound gap between drama-therapy and theatre (even in its declination as 'Social Theatre') remains, emphasized by a concrete element: the use or not of the public per-formance as a ritualized ending of a journey. This has led to the consideration of drama as process-oriented and of theatre as product-oriented. This can be true as far as theory is concerned, yet there are many overlaps on a more practical level. Two examples follow. First, theatre has lately incorporated within itself the idea that dramatic work is an open-ended research, and this manifests itself in a new awareness of the process. As professor Dalla Palma has written:

> in the intimacy and intensity of the life of the *ensemble*, the group, through its members, sets up not only form arrangements, acts charged with a precise artistic intentionality, (. . .) but also acts that are extremely pregnant from the point of view of deep meanings'
> (Dalla Palma, 2001: 143)

Second, the process of dramatherapy is always punctuated with performance events, and, what is more, every so often groups have opened their performances to the presence of some kind of audience. As Renée Emunah recounts: 'I felt that these dramas *had to be seen on the outside*, as a healing force for the larger community'. And she reminds us also that 'the therapeutic impact of performance is different from, and often greater than, process-oriented drama therapy' (Emunah, 1994: 251–3).

4   Therefore, it seems that the main difference is not to be found in the processes, which present many similarities, but rather in the conscious purposes lying at the core of the two forms. For theatre, the main purpose is art; for dramatherapy, it is healing.

5   Gregory Bateson has clearly demonstrated how conscious purpose is both bliss and a curse. It helps us to pursue stubbornly a fixed objec-tive, channelling our energies towards an outcome, but at the same time it makes us blind to any side effects and to possible imbalances in the systems in which we operate: the destruction of the environment is a case in point. Conscious purpose needs a corrective. Art can be healing, and healing can be art.

6   For theatre, a positive effect of conscious purpose is a concentration of people's energies, in order to make a leap together; a negative one is subjugating people to the iron rules of the artistic project. For

dramatherapy, a positive effect of conscious purpose is focusing on people's needs; a negative one is gauging them for their illness rather than for their resources as persons.

7 A theatrical approach may influence dramatherapy; a dramatherapeutic approach may influence theatre. Such a mutual influence, when managed creatively and with a sense of responsibility, may serve both fields, converting the negative effects of conscious purpose into positive ones, recovering some vital guiding principles that might have been lost in a mindless routine.

8 For theatre, a dramatherapeutic influence may help directors to increase their sensitivity to the psychic state of the individuals and groups, and to develop an empathic attitude towards them. This may extend the aesthetic boundaries of the work and produce different kinds of performance. But above all it may allow directors to reach further insights about their own feelings, thus developing a renewed awareness in their relationship with the actors, so that they may avoid compelling them to conform uncritically to a prearranged project, preventing the risk of hindering people's liberty.

9 For dramatherapy, a theatrical influence may help therapists to restore their ability to address people's creativity rather than taking into account mainly their distress or their pathological sides. This may allow therapists to get in touch with their own inner sources of creativity, using this influence as a means to learning more about themselves and their clients, allowing themselves to be open to unforeseen developments of their progress, and preventing the risk of hindering people's liberty.

10 Letting theatre and therapy influence each other may present an amount of risk; nevertheless it is indispensable for the refreshment of both the fields, and in the assistance of people in search of new answers to old questions: what is Healing? And what is Art?

Like an epilogue

She moves
Like she never moved before.
She smiles
Like she never smiled before.
She covers her face and talks from the depth
Saying the unspeakable; not saying anything
Anything at all, at all.
She cries
Like she did before.
She aches
Like she did so many times before.

Where are we? What kind of world do we tread on?
Is it a world where pain is non existent?
My pain is a sting, your pain is a wound.
We bleed together and we are so far apart.
Give me a space, oh, give me a little space
Where our pains can be seen
And roll over the mountains, and plunge into the sea
And laugh a big laughter as only pain can do
wrenching leaves from the branch, wrenching branches from the tree
leaving flowers floating and floating
over the world astounded
wide asunder from pain to pain.
Will they bear fruit? Will they wither to become clay?
Will anybody be a witness, will anybody tell
About the injuries and the scars and what cannot be healed?

She says I want.
She sits and she's silent.
She is.

What is healing? What is art?
        (Poem written by A or by B, I can't remember exactly)

Bibliography

Barrault, J.L. (1954) *Riflessioni sul teatro*, Firenze: Sansoni.

Bateson, G. (1972) *Verso un'ecologia della mente*, Milano: Adelphi, 1976.

Brook, P. (1987) *Il punto in movimento*, Milano: Ubulibri, 1988.

Dalla Palma, S. (2001) *La scena dei mutamenti*, Milano: Vita e Pensiero.

Emunah, R. (1994) *Acting for Real*, New York: Brunner/Mazel.

Fiaschini, F. (2000) 'Bobò e la cognizione del dolore', in G. Badolato, G. Innocenti Malini, F. Fiaschini and R. Villa, *La scena rubata*, Milano: Euresis.

Jennings, S. (1998) *Introduction to Dramatherapy*, London: Jessica Kingsley Publishers.

Pitruzzella, S. (2004) *Introduction to Dramatherapy. Person and Threshold*, Hove & New York: Brunner/Routledge.

Pozzi, E. and Minoia, V. (eds) (1999) *Di alcuni teatri della diversità*, Cartoceto: ANC.

9   The making of *Mickey B*, a modern adaptation of *Macbeth* filmed in a maximum security prison in Northern Ireland[1]

Tom Magill and Jennifer Marquis-Muradaz

It is important that education, rather than trying to deny risk, encourages men and women to take it.

(Freire, 2004: 5)

Making a film adaptation of *Macbeth*, with the 'godfathers' of Maghaberry Prison was a risky idea, and anyone who has ever attempted anything risky inside a prison soon learns all about prison staff resistance. Maximum-security prisons are risk averse. Fear and distrust are the dominant motivations that underlie almost every decision. Daily airtight procedures produce a monotony that numbs the senses in the name of safety. Fatalistic negativity pervades. Naysayers outnumber yea-sayers. Within this world, authoritarianism breeds dependence and resistance that frequently end in destruction.

Fortunately, the film idea had one key supporter, the deputy governor, a progressive who understood the prison culture and exactly what we were up against and supported it anyway. He wanted us to include in our film prisoners who were not otherwise participating in any educational or work programmes. This challenge created its own difficulties as the security department in the prison were resistant to the idea of grouping the 'bad boys' together and rewarding them by making them into movie stars.

Synopsis

In our version of *Macbeth*, *Mickey B*, the setting is a fictional private prison called Burnam, where gangs run the wings with violence and drugs as their common currency. Duncan is the number one drug dealer who is about to be released. Mickey B is his muscle collecting on his behalf. The three witches are three bookies, fixing the odds for their own ends. Lady Macbeth is Ladyboy – Mickey B's bitch – the queen of hate. She schemes to reach the number one slot, only to realise later the price she was to pay. Over-come with guilt after Mickey B has Duffer's family murdered, Ladyboy hangs herself from the bars of her cell.

Mickey B's world implodes when the walls of C wing collapse, echoing Birnam wood moving towards Dunsinane. Duffer and Malcolm join the enemy forces of the prison staff to lay siege to Mickey B's cell, eventually breaking through his cell walls with a sledgehammer. Malcolm claims the victory. He's the new number one in the jail. However, the price of his victory is that the buckets (screws) are back controlling the wings.

The obstacles we faced in making this film adaptation were numerous. Some staff thought we had too many Catholics and not enough Protestants in the cast. Others hated the script – citing the swearing, the drug references and the murders as problematic. In particular, Lady Macbeth's suicide was a problem because of recent suicides in the prison.[2] The fact that it was set in a prison at all gave rise to the fear that some people would view the film as a slice of life in Maghaberry prison itself. The plot, prisoners controlling the jail, was too close for comfort given the recent memory of the Maze Prison where prisoners did run their own wings.[3]

In response to these concerns, we undertook to recruit more Protestants and set the film in a fictional private prison called Burnam. We also toned down the swearing and cut the drug references, and promised to emulate Hitchcock and suggest, rather than actually portray, any violence. The prisoners naturally, felt censored, and arguments ensued. However, we ultimately convinced them that quitting the project would only make the prison naysayers happy. To their credit, they pushed forward.

Then there were logistics to contend with. Jason, our Ladyboy (Lady Macbeth) was being released from prison within the year. We had to decide whether to re-cast or move into production ahead of schedule. Eventually we opted to move into production eight weeks early, leaving the director and cast with only five days to rehearse.

We could not shoot in the prison proper without disrupting the other inmates and posing major security risks. Fortunately, John Davies, the officer in charge of overseeing the cast and crew during production, suggested shooting in the prison workshops, where prisoners learn trades and skills like Braille, painting, woodwork and bricklaying. The beauty of the space was that it came ready-made with painters and builders (whom we needed to build our cell and jail hallway sets), lots of available extras, and a canteen for feeding and housing cast members.

Once shooting actually commenced, with a few notable exceptions, prison staff reacted to the film and to our presence with suspicion and inflexibility, appearing either blatantly apathetic or downright hostile. They seemed terrified that our production would cause them to lose their 'authority' over the prisoners. Several staff members who had promised to play small roles in the film dropped out. The film crew were treated like prisoners as well and their possessions were confiscated – props, DVDs and cameras. The crew were also subjected to long, interminable and unnecessary delays, while dogs were brought onto the set to search for drugs and weapons.

Yet, despite these many provocations, which included prisoners' cells being overturned, staff pouring talcum powder over the prisoners' cell floors, and denying the men obligatory gym visits and 'out of cell' time, not one of the prisoners retaliated or took the bait. In four weeks of shooting, there was not one major incident with any prisoner on our film. Not one.

Our film crew went into the prison expecting to learn a lot about prisoners. Instead, we learned a great deal that scared us about the people who care for them, the people we put in charge of our most vulnerable, our most violent, our most damaged.

This is not to imply that the prisoners behaved like choirboys. They sometimes came onto set high on drugs. They didn't always know their lines. They insisted on wearing their own clothes, which presented a film continuity nightmare. They resented having to be quiet during shooting. A few imagined we were slighting them and walked out. They complained constantly about the food and the lack of pay. Meanwhile the crew was suffering from the stress of working under such unusually tense conditions, and our make-up girl was developing a serious flirtation with a lifer convicted of murder.

We had no idea that the worst was yet to come.

In the months after the shoot ended, an important cast member failed to return to the prison after being sent home on compassionate leave; the horrific details of his original crime were all over the press and the prison took an embarrassing public beating. Fears that his (and others') involvement in our 'violent' film might be publicised could trigger a massive public outcry resulted in the cancellation of a BBC feature about the film, and very nearly prevented the first public screening of the film in Belfast.[4]

Meanwhile, the gutter press ran sensationalist stories saying that our make-up girl was impregnated, that we had brought guns and ammunition into the prison with us, and that we had made a sick, twisted 'Driller Killer' flick with murderers playing murderers. We eventually had to strike a deal with the prison not to show the film at all in Northern Ireland. The drama group itself was disbanded for fear that the prisoners would begin to feel they had too much personal power. The actor who played Ladyboy, who had been out of jail for several months, was arrested and sent back to prison. Mickey B, Duffer and others rebelled against prison authorities and were separated from other prisoners under Rule 32 which provides for good order and discipline within the prison.

Why we use film with prisoners

The Educational Shakespeare Company (ESC) has been making films in Maghaberry Prison since 2003, yet some drama practitioners still want to know why we filmed *Macbeth* in lieu of staging it 'properly.' For one, the prison does not have a functional, dedicated stage. Whilst prisoners generally know very little about theatre and Shakespeare, they can and do spend up to twenty-three hours a day locked inside cells with televisions. So they know a lot about films. They watch films, they like films, they discuss films. Their thoughts and observations are frequently insightful.

Staging *Macbeth* would also have required an exceptionally high, unrealistic level of stamina and skill for these particular men. Making the film, which involved several short bursts of work over several days and included long breaks for new camera set-ups, helped to balance out the prisoners' less-developed concentration and listening skills, as well as memorisation/literacy problems.

Filming also allowed us to accommodate all the ongoing and unavoidable interruptions and delays (legal and family visits, court dates, alarms, prison jobs, other classes, etc.) and provided opportunities for those who did not want to appear onscreen; those men ran cameras, held microphones, interviewed documentary subjects, assisted with make-up and composed music.

We have also found that while funders are interested in all the 'soft skills' that stage acting provides (confidence, cooperation and teamwork), they are exceptionally keen to provide prisoners with the information technology and multimedia skills acquired in filmmaker training. Additionally, our films and documentary 'makings of' provide the hard physical evidence we need in order to provide prisoners with learning and literacy problems with accredited qualifications, such as Active Citizenship awards.[5] In addition, films with high-quality production values typically have a longer shelf life than videotaped drama; this shelf life is critical to gaining exposure for the work and providing visual evidence of the need for the work.

Finally, we have learned that film is an extraordinary self-evaluation tool. People will watch their onscreen behaviour (either as actors in narratives, or as themselves in a documentary), and learn from this 'objective' third party vantage point in a way that cannot be replicated in any other medium. We call this the 'video feedback loop'. It is particularly helpful in working with groups in conflict, as film can allow groups to virtually meet each other before any actual face-to-face meetings occur. Through our cross-community work with young people we realised the power of video feedback in encouraging people to improve their own performance after watching themselves on screen. This is the most effective method we have witnessed for enabling people to modify their own behaviour at their own pace and on their own terms.

The methodology

Augusto Boal speaks of the distinction between education and pedagogy – essentially between the accrual of information and the process of discovery. As an alternative to traditional didactic education we also use the Socratic Method; that is, teaching by asking instead of by telling (Boal, 1998: 128). We find this method works more effectively with prisoners, especially those labelled 'high risk' and those that have an attitude problem with authority. We encourage prisoners to become independent and to choose their own level of responsibility through the role they play in the film. We try to play to people's strengths in order to develop their confidence and abilities. This in turn strengthens their internal motivations to attend and participate in the project. Self-discipline turns into self-respect (McLaren, 2000: 79).

Why *Mickey B*?

It became clearer in retrospect why we made *Mickey B*. Taking part in the film enabled non-conforming life-sentence prisoners to act out and understand the implications of their violent crimes. For those prisoners who are not prepared to address their own crimes, it provided a stepping-stone towards examining and understanding their own motivations and relationship with violence.

Tommy, an ex-lifer with whom we are working on a short film project in another programme explains: 'I carried this story around with me for 17 years. It's only now that I am able to tell it.' The story is about the day he murdered another man. He is telling that story now through film and it is a release for him. He tells us he feels lighter after telling it. More at peace with himself then he has ever been. I knew that was the case. I could see him relax.

I asked why he couldn't have told that story in prison. He told me, 'I did tell the story of what I did. But I never told the truth about how I felt about what I'd done. I wore a mask to protect myself.' 'Could you not use the Offender Behaviour Programmes to tell the story?', I asked? 'No. You had to keep the mask on. The other prisoners would see it as a weakness if you told the truth', he replied. Prison peer group pressure to take drugs, escape and live in denial behind the mask of misplaced pride that 'doesn't give a fuck', makes it difficult for prisoners like Tommy to come to terms with their crimes, in order to make the internal journey from understanding to acceptance and forgiveness that is necessary for them to move on.

Fifty per cent of the men we work with will return to prison within a year after release; 70 per cent of adult male offenders have literacy/numeracy deficiencies; 66 per cent have substance abuse problems; 51 per cent are unemployed on committal; 50 per cent of prisoners had experienced problems within their community because of their offending behaviour, which was manifested in punishment beatings, sectarian attacks and intimidation; 50 per cent of prisoners will have accommodation problems on release; 49 per cent have financial difficulties; 40 per cent have been diagnosed as suffering with mental health problems. In addition, 34 per cent were in care as a child (*Promoting Healthy Prisons*, 2006).

Prisoners also label themselves, and this process can have an even more detrimental effect on their self-esteem and well-being than being labelled by others. Before we began production the men we worked with on *Mickey B* also referred to themselves as 'empty heads, scumbags, hoods'. When questioned further they said they believed they were stupid and incapable of producing anything of worth. The majority had failed within the traditional education system. Their lack of qualifications and literacy skills produced a lack of self-belief, confidence and ability to communicate, especially within a group setting.

Prisoners bottle up those feelings of guilt and remorse. Unexpressed feelings create anger, frustration, regret, resentment, hatred, and violence. Drugs provide an escape from those feelings. But it is only a temporary release. Then the cycle starts again. Peer group pressure stops prisoners from dealing with the guilt and remorse they feel about their crimes within Offender Behaviour Programmes.

That's one of the main reasons why we felt that *Mickey B* was the right thing to do in a prison setting. The moral of *Macbeth* is that crime doesn't pay. The means do not justify the ends. Ill-gotten gains have a brief period of enjoyment. Involvement in the film *Mickey B* became a peer-group acceptable way of addressing violent offending behaviour through fiction.

Drama and filmmaking are premised on teamwork. Drama has a transformative power that has the potential to take prisoners on a journey from shame to pride. Using classical fiction like *Macbeth* can create the necessary distance for prisoners to understand the implications of their crimes in safety. It can create empathy, particularly in relation to victims, even fictional victims. We experienced that prisoners can come to understand the relationship between cause and effect that can, in turn, lead to transformation.

Creativity also comes easily to prisoners. Crime and creativity are linked. They both share the invention of an original way of doing things. One is legal the other is not. Crime is an impulse to create something out of nothing. Creativity is a similar impulse. However, there is a fundamental difference. Crime is based on taking; creativity is based on giving. In crime, we can take a life or take what does not belong to us. In creativity, we take what is ours and give it away. This process of giving puts us back in control as the author of our actions. It gives us choice – the choice to change – from being a taker to being a giver.

Victims rarely see or hear prisoner remorse. The portrayal of true remorse through fiction is one way to begin that process. Our experience of making films with victims has shown that victims can leave the ghosts of their perpetrators behind when they express and record their stories on film. The question then remains, can perpetrators leave the ghosts of their victims behind, after expressing true remorse, albeit through fiction?

Tommy told his story just as it happened. But that was after carrying it for 17 years. Not everyone is so ripe for telling their story. Telling it through fiction, through the mask of a character is a step towards addressing the motivations and implications of their crime. Either way, I believe it is a cathartic process that is ultimately healing. Empowering violent criminals to transform and heal themselves will hopefully reduce recidivism and consequently, the number of victims.

To be a prisoner is to be defined by the worst thing you have ever done. It is a great loss that the public in Northern Ireland will never see what these men and this work can actually accomplish.

Over and over again people ask, 'Why do criminals get to make a movie? What do their victims get? How does this make sense?' We suspect that the questions would not be asked if we were 'only' putting on a play, but the potential for public exposure and acknowledgement of the prisoners' efforts, as the result of creating a film, evokes outright fury. It is a question with which we as an organisation and as individuals are now seriously wrestling: What *about* the victims? How can we serve both, in a way that helps both? We have already begun working with victims; *Two Sides of the Coin* filmed the stories of medically retired prison officers and widows serving during the Troubles. They chose to tell their stories of being held hostage and tortured in the prison where these atrocities actually happened, and afterwards told us that this process helped them 'leave their ghosts behind them'.

In the months before we went into production, we saw that the prisoners were not able to talk about their violent pasts (in or out of therapy), so we chose a play about violence and the repercussions of violence, by an author we believed would excite and impress prison staff and funders. Unfortunately, we no longer have access to these men because the group has been disbanded by the prison authorities.

Postscript

We think back to those four weeks. Those four long difficult weeks of shooting, when the prisoners were operating as a productive, responsible, committed team, a team that made an amazing piece of art. They were four weeks when none of the prisoners got into trouble or were sent to the punishment block. Four weeks of risks taken and new skills learned.

This brings to mind Win Wenger's Law of Effect: 'You get more of what you reinforce'.[6]

Within the prison system, what is normally reinforced for these prisoners is fear and distrust. A lack of expectation in relation to their abilities and potential coupled with an overwhelming sense of negativity.

For four weeks in Maghaberry Prison during November/December 2006 we challenged these values and instead reinforced respect, trust, choice and responsibility. We gave the cast a safe space to recreate themselves through the fiction of *Mickey B*, learning the lessons from the characters within the film. We give them the opportunity to apply these lessons to their own daily lives and provide them with the tools, should they choose to use them, to shape and decide their own futures (McDonnell, 2008).

Notes

1 www.esc-film.com
2 www.nuzhound.com/articles/irish_news/arts2007/jun14_Wright_witnesses_-deaths_similarities.php
3 http://news.bbc.co.uk/1/hi/uk/44750.stm
4 http://www.culturenorthernireland.org/article.aspx?art_id=87
5 www.asdan.co.uk/about_asdan.php
6 www.winwenger.com

References

Boal, Augusto (1998) *Legislative Theatre: Using Performance to Make Politics* (trans. Adrian Jackson), p. 128, London: Routledge.

Freire, Paulo (2004) *Pedagogy of Indignation* (Series in Critical Narrative), p. 5, Boulder, CO: Paradigm Publishers.

McDonnell, Bill (2008) 'Only Catholics Combine: Loyalism and Theatre', in *Theatres of the Troubles*, pp. 112–25, Exeter: University of Exeter Press.

McLaren, Peter (2000) *Che Guevara, Paulo Freire, and the Pedagogy of Revolution* (Culture and Education Series), p. 79, Maryland: Rowman & Littlefield Publishers.

Promoting Healthy Prisons (2006) *A Conference Report Joint Initiative between the Health Promotion Agency and the Northern Ireland Prison Service*, September 2006.

10 Making, breaking, and making again

Theatre in search of healing in India

Aanand Chabukswar

A group of young people make a circular formation in a village square singing and enacting. The audience are squatting, standing, sometimes clapping along, nodding, laughing, some leave. What is going on? What is it doing to the audience? What is it doing to the young people?

Any record of the dynamic between theatre and healing in India is a mere snapshot of the ongoing weaving and unravelling. If we start in ancient times, the above group could be performing a ritual. If we fast-forward to today, it could be a street-theatre piece on politics, gender equality or health. Even today, it could be a religious or secular celebration. To put forth the experience shaping healing theatre in India is an act of balancing the traditional and the contemporary, the vivid colourful and the unexpressed, the felt cosmic and the experienced concrete.

The push-start for my personal search for a meaningful contemporary theatre was:

- dissatisfaction with the cultural, educational, political systems;
- the need and search for a way to evolve, to be functional and contributing;
- feeling the power of theatre medium, its depth and possibilities.

Where to go with a rebellion, a mission, and a method? My theatrical and performance activities were initiated in Marathi language theatre from the state of Maharashtra. Theatre activities in India share the backdrop of Sanskrit poetics, rural and folk traditions, and the influence of the West during and after the colonial period. Contemporary 'theatres' of India are multi-regional, multilingual and multi-centred. There is no 'one' national theatre, but theatres that bear some distinguishing features, elucidated in 'a stream of plays . . . widely differing in method and approach, but bearing common hallmarks' (Masud 1976). They form the body of contemporary Indian theatre. As Dharwadkar (2005) in a thorough discourse on post-independence urban Indian theatre states, 'the quest is not so much for a "national theatre" as for a significant theatre *in* and *of* the nation, linked intra-nationally by complex commonalities and mutual self differentiations' (p. 24). This is the modern Indian theatre.

The Marathi theatre feeds the National theatre as a foremost contributor. The recorded history of Marathi theatre shows a mixture of influences from Sanskrit classics, folk forms and British theatre (Mehta 1995). Marathi theatre passed a glorious era in *Sangeet natak* musical plays, and struggled for survival through the 1940s. With independence, the 1950s witnessed the dawn of new thought and a young generation – many of them recognised today as stalwarts of Indian drama. A theatre that expresses the struggles, issues, concerns and dreams of post-independence Indian life, for mostly an urban, middle-class audience, is the new Marathi theatre of past 50 odd years. This movement is described as 'experimental' or 'amateur' theatre, and its essential features can be summarised as follows:

- *Playwright at the centre*:   The survey of 150 years of Marathi theatre is titled 'Playwright at the Centre' (Gokhale 2000). The post-independence Marathi theatre is held together by playwrights. Translations or adaptations from other regional languages and British/European playwrights add to the canon.
- *Styles*:   Most original plays in Marathi are in the realistic vein, plying the naturalistic style. The second trend is the merging of the folk forms or historical, mythological content with the contemporary. Only a few plays inch close to the expressionist, or absurd and existentialist styles.
- *High quality of performers and practitioners*:   Theatre directors and actors in Marathi theatre have shaped and met the audience's expectation of high quality performances. Many practitioners owe their beginnings to a trend of strongly contested inter-college and state competitions (Gokhale 1989). These competitions have a place of respect in serious theatre, and they have yielded ready theatre talents, writers, directors, and actors to the new Marathi drama.
- *Experimental vs commercial*:   Experimental theatre is distinguished from commercial theatre in terms of purpose, organisation, reach, ideological/artistic commitment, and risk-taking. To sustain the spirit of enquiry and experimentation in a financially uncontaminated and free atmosphere is the great challenge of experimental theatre.
- *Splits*:   A curious feature of post-independence Marathi theatre is that most theatre organisations are born from each other. It is for numerous reasons, but almost all experimental theatre groups have split off from other groups. Richmond *et al.* (1993) read these groups as built around a committed individual, usually the director of the group, who has 'power and responsibility . . . unless an equally strong personality emerges . . . When that happens the result is likely to be the formation of a separate theatre group' (p. 408).

Each of these features has a bearing on anyone growing up in this milieu. Even as children, we were admonished to have 'correct' enunciation because 'Marathi theatre is a spoken theatre' and the playwright's words are paramount. We were influenced by the nurturing but harsh theatre competitions. One of them required us to make a theatre piece using multiple art forms. For our generation of urban youth, unfamiliar with folk forms, this was the first challenge on composite use of the arts in theatre. Another influence was the theme-theatre (*prasang-natya darshan*) done way back in high-school. In this form, the play had to be improvised within an hour. The presentations were followed by a critique done by peer teams, which had to be heard out, and answered. The emphasis was on developing ability to work in groups, expressing ideas dramatically and verbally, exploring multiple meanings theatrically, and learning to face questions and assert within a forum (Palande and Bapat 1990). For me, this was a vital training that seeded the idea of theatre as more than the play-text and stage, rehearsal and production.

For those of us who were on the threshold of experimental theatre in the early 1990s, its features were a given strength, but they also felt like an inescapable heaviness. The 1990s in India marked the explosion of television networks, Internet, and economic liberalisation. It was not easy to sustain theatre, and there was no resilience built in to absorb experiments that did not belong to the playwriting tradition. The struggle for survival claimed practitioners for television soaps. The audience in general became fewer. Reflective people, as if having a premonition, had raised questions of the theatre movement:

> Somewhere we have fallen short of the demands of the experimental theatre. And although it is going to be uncomfortable we have to ask ourselves the question: how truly experimental we are? . . . Have we failed to realise that real experimentation goes much deeper and much beyond than merely a new form and/or novel content. It is a light that illuminates one's work from within. And this light in the spirit of quest – not only aesthetic quest – it is an amalgam of so many quests – intellectual aesthetic, but most of all, spiritual quest.
>
> (Elkunchwar 1995: 29–30)

Is this a tall order for theatre? I was still at college, but also worked as a part-time teacher. As a volunteer, I was also part of literacy projects for tribal and slum children. The difficult social, economic and political realities directly contrasted with the 'unreality' of the theatre we were attempting. But how could theatre be authentic? Isn't that an oxymoron? It was an unbearable cliché to think in terms of merely 'writing a play' on these conditions. For me, the inevitable osmosis meant that I carried theatre to my teaching projects, and within the theatre space issue was taken about 'what are we doing?' and 'why should we do this? Not do that?'

Many people I encountered were working with a fierce commitment to transformation. To follow their example meant taking risks – be it uncomfortable nights in tribal huts or being labelled 'idealistic/dreamy', or cleaning public toilets in slums to understand what Gandhi meant. Influences from very near and far, like the feminist theatre *At the Foot of the Mountain of Minneapolis* (1976) were inspiring 'to relinquish traditions such as linear plays, proscenium theatre, non-participatory ritual and seek to reveal theatre that is circular, intuitive, personal, involving'. The idiom of street-theatre leant itself to the first step in this search. Street-theatre does not essentially need a playwright of high capacity or great acting skills. What it needs is a commitment to the 'message' and readiness to carry it to the streets. To practise street-theatre was thus meaningfully closer, and artistically more accessible. I could share this form in schools and projects. To be the theatre 'director' was not useful anymore. A way to inspire performers to convey the message as part of one's own life was needed. In the school street-theatre troupes, we examined why we needed to go onto the streets to say something. Each issue was discussed, its personal relevance sought. The theme would then be narrated through an episodic structure filled in with attention-grabbing satires, songs, and attractive spices for the road. The street-theatre with themes from education reflected the students' own experiences, perceptions and feelings.

It is difficult to gauge if these street-plays made any big difference to the crowds that gathered and laughed, stayed or moved on. But they definitely affected all who participated in making them. At a school in Pune city we got a call from a 'green' group with a request for help in the protests against cutting down ancient trees on the main street. The students of the theatre troupe decided that it was relevant, so we jumped into the fray, building up impromptu lyrics and improvisations. We campaigned after school hours singing songs, asking questions, and playing the road contractors, politicians, victims:

> Today we shall get a road widened,
> But, for tomorrow's breath, who will worry???
> Please, for the sake of trees,
> Please, for the sake of our city!
> (Translated from Marathi)

The Court order in favour of the tree-cutting ejected us from the roads. We went back to our routine, but not before an intense discussion: 'If this is how things are to be, then why should we ever care?' 'Why don't the adults and the government see what we see?' 'How is it that this ended like this?' No, it was not the end. Under the pain and anger were portals of seeing, not permissible in our 'average' education – the spirit of questioning, effort to understand things, placing actions in the context of a larger whole, and examining our choices. The commitment to bring a message to people on roads brought us humility and some courage to 'walk the talk'. It opened the space and voice to examine the world around us and ourselves.

We were not engaged with theatre for mere aesthetic pleasure. It was joyful in its playing with images, roles, songs and dance, but it also had a direct thematic connection with those who participated. A variety of groups – rural women in a health project, management postgraduates, village teachers – engaged with this art-making without feeling out of place. The artistic choices made by these groups paved the way into seeing the deeper potential of theatre. One such group was a bunch of bored students at a residential school. We paced through theatre games and groupwork to get the students involved and familiar with expressing ideas through images. The 'fun' and ease of theatre brought them close to what they wanted to say. The piece that we eventually made was not a street-play. It was a story of a boy who longs for a deeper connection with his parents, but instead gets lots of material choices, unsympathetic education, and a disturbed family. It was about his search for love and authentic friendships. The group picked things from their own lives, often discussing them openly. It was a delicate task – to allow the exploration, and yet to let the drama shape and contain it. The final piece was a comment on experience of childhood neglect, uninvolved parenting, uninspired education and the hope/despair of growing up in such a world. During the process of making this piece, a personal transformation for many of the players had happened, I realised it only later. Teachers and parents talked about these changes in the students. The surliness of their stance was gone; it was replaced with initiative and camaraderie. This, then, was their real accomplishment. Such explorations progressively veered away from 'performing' for an audience. Sessions simply became artistic playing. Another teenage group made their own version of *Romeo and Juliet* – a bold study of love and romance, changes in body and feelings. Their play had several invented characters who 'investigated' the suicides of Romeo and Juliet. The exploration uncovered the way conditioning affects our under-standing and motives, and how decisions in life are thus shaped. Explaining what prompted his suicide, Romeo declared that it was inspired by 'ideas about love, glamour in death' but confessed that 'I might feel differently about love and loved one at a different time' (Redstone 1998).

What is this theatre? There is no audience in the modern sense, or a 'place for viewing' (Latin – *theatum*, Greek – *theatron*) of the old. Theatre as defined by Nātyaśāstra is the special world created and 'depicted by means of representation' (Tarlekar 1975). The actions are representative, not common-place in life. Yet there is no longer a boundary between the performer and the audience. Participants are creators and recipients of their own work. This representation acquires meanings within the context of the participants' life, needs, and issues. This has a resonance with a theatre 'at beginning of 1990s' described by another practitioner from another part of the world as:

less self-centred and was ready to become an instrument of social action through laboratories, workshops, and performances with a goal of healing and of heightening the quality of social interactions. It was a theatre that linked the experience within the group to the sociocultural, economic, and historical context the group emerged from and remained a part of. This was and is called Social Theatre.

(Schininà 2004: 22)

Social theatre comes out of the prosceniums and, in moving away from traditional performance spaces, it finds first and foremost, spaces that need it the most. This journey in reinventing theatre's identity and functions of old and new is like the transformation of the woman who is obese with many untold stories. The woman abandons her village, journeys through jungles, tells the stories to walls in a ruin. The walls crumble under the weight of her pain, and she regains her original shapely self (Ramanujan 1993).

A group at an alcohol and drug rehabilitation centre, mostly men, make this story of untold stories their own. Through a series of exercises, they have re-connected to their capacity to play with theatre. Beginnings and rituals ensure that the group has ground rules; warm-ups ensure that there is enough skill and no inhibition to use body and voice theatrically. The group absorbs the characters, scenes and landscapes of the story. Because the woman is obese, three men co-join to depict her, and they playfully wrap a *sari*. Space is divided into village, jungle, house in ruins. Chairs and props are assigned places in the 'set' as road, trees, walls. The participants embody the story; they mostly use movement and sounds. The story is known to everyone so the focus is not on the action. The focus is on the personal meanings of the tale in this particular representation. Since everyone shares the context, the individual or collective meanings are readily accessible. The men trapped in one sari struggle to move through the jungle of scary sounds with the burden of untold stories and acquired selves. Finding the ruins, the disconcerted woman starts a monologue of screams and wails addressed to the walls – men shaped as walls wait for a dramatic crescendo when they feel the intense pain and crumble. With the walls crashing, many layers of clothing and confusion are abandoned. The woman finds her original self. In reflection, after clearing up the 'set', the men talk about their own difficult journeys, with addiction as the unwanted constant companion. They talk about the aptness of the ruined home as the rehabilitation centre – metaphorically and literally. Some men are deeply silent. Most report feeling light. The participants are surprised to find clues and connections with their life in this seemingly 'unreal' exercise. This is the beginning of the manifestation of theatre's therapeutic value. A theatre that can be claimed by people has to be brought forth:

1   *Come to people with theatre*:   No judgement! A little enthusiasm goes a long way in brushing off inhibitions.
2   *Mark the space*:   Through rituals, co-creations, and discussions the groups must choose and state their purpose and mark the boundaries (dos and don'ts) and stand by them.

3 *Shared convention builds theatre*:   The agreement by everyone to play and play along manifests this theatre. It is the facilitator's charge to bring enough initial energy to make (and later dismantle) this special time and space. No matter what place – a temporary school for children affected by a tsunami, a psychiatric ward, a settlement of Burmese refugees in Delhi or Roma youngsters in an open field in a Romania – shared convention instantly makes theatre possible.

4 *Life situations assign meanings*:   As group members establish a personal connection with the art materials, inner meanings are automatically assigned in this metaphor-world.

In these conditions, the healing properties of theatre can begin to emerge and manifest.

A group of adults with multiple cognitive and physical disabilities living together in a community home had numerous difficulties – prejudice, discrimination, high need for physical care, emotional outbursts, mood swings, fights, and the pressure of leading life from one day to another with such physical, financial, social, medical and emotional needs. This was the situation when my colleagues and I started the arts-based therapies at this home (WCCLF 2004). The group had many self-defeating complexes and immense sadness within. In our sessions, they played rhythms, moved to music, and told and retold stories. Unwanted experiences took shape as objects and metaphors. The baggage of negative self-perceptions and emotions became the mountains we climbed and descended as we journeyed. Having the support of colleagues working on the same agenda with various art forms helped tremendously (Kashyap 2005). In the drama group, we had a flower song that mentioned each person in the group with actions that they had made. It was a favourite song, and the way the creative process makes its way into life situations can be seen in this conversation:

When singing the flower song, seeing that a couple of group members did not fully participate, Shyam asked:

Shyam:	What to do to those who do not sing?
Facilitator:	(*Repeated the question and asked the group for responses*)
Era:	Hit them
Shyam:	Tie to the chair
Anupa:	Give no food
Shanti:	No food, no food
Deva:	Lock in the room
Shyam:	Send them to God . . .
Facilitator:	How does it feel if food is not given?
Anupa:	Feel like crying
Deva:	I cry

Facilitator:	How does it feel when hit?
Era and Kala:	Like crying . . .
Facilitator:	What when tied to chair . . .?
Shyam:	Feel as if I am mad (crazy) . . .
Anupa, Kala, Deva:	Very sad. . .
Era:	What if the rope (with which one is tied) is loosened?
Anupa:	Will be free . . .
Shyam:	Those who do not sing, no food for them, but also not to celebrate their birthday!
Anupa:	(*to Shyam*) No one will celebrate your birthday. My birthday will be celebrated. . .
Facilitator:	Let us decide what happens inside the session, if someone is not singing. . .
Shyam:	Those who will not sing the song of the flower, their flower will not bloom!

This solution was supported by almost everyone, and we resumed the song!

(Translated from Marathi)

This conversation is not a reflection of the punishments at the community home. They came from a different time, much of which we had no clue about. For a group like this, the pace and ways required to access the creative power are different from the usual, but the essence of the creative process is the same. Blocked emotions flow through the playful and the symbolic. Creative engagement with embodiment, projective play, role explorations (Jennings 1998) reveal, release and bring new openings. The group got in touch with the creative parts of themselves, taking small strides to come forth as a 'person'. Each had a shining quality of being, which gradually emerged in the sessions. Deva was a good joker; Jose a giant with a gentle heart. Anupa, who seemed deeply self-absorbed, had a streak of unconditional care for Kala; Shanti would fall ten times, cry, and immediately resume dancing. Each one a celebration! Most of the group members felt it too, maybe for the first time ever. The access to one of the highest pursuits – the arts – brought equal opportunity, listening, turn-taking, acceptance, inclusion and mutual respect for each one's uniqueness and identity. Violent altercations all but stopped and caregivers were more at ease. Idle time in front of television reduced. The changes were initiated in the artistic spaces, but without the managers, care givers and volunteers, who carried the spirit of the sessions into the routine day, it would not have resulted in any transformation.

This group reconfirmed that theatre and life share a tenacious interconnection. Practitioners have discussed the essential qualities and processes that show life itself as dramatic in structure and drama as healing (Jennings *et al.* 1994). Augusto Boal (1992) defines theatre in its archaic sense as the uniquely human 'capacity . . . to observe themselves in action' (p. xxxvi). This theatre, then, is the spiritual quest that permeates eastern thinking and practices – to witness and lead life from that plane of awareness. In the Indian context, this re/search is beginning to beckon:

- *Release and heal*: Emotions, perceptions and actions are the play-material in the theatre space. One can come out of it and say 'that was just playing'. One may also learn to develop the ability to see from the vantage point of the observer–witness. The choice and safety of the former and the opportunity and possibility of the latter, both are accessible at all times.
- *Whole*: Creative processes in healing theatre make contact with the person as a whole. Expression in this space is an act of creation, no matter how impaired that person seems to be. When a person makes contact with an experience of completeness, it can push boundaries and make openings quite beyond the mere 'possible'.
- *Holy*? At a certain moment, a person can recognise layers of meanings made by action–interactions and relationships. Imagination followed by action, the invisible becomes manifest. Life is enriched by this power to see and to act.

It is important to emphasise that the facilitator, the practitioner, as the 'frontiersperson' (Jennings 1990: 129) has tremendous responsibility in practising this form of theatre. Ensuring training, developing the ability to perceive and articulate, to live life itself as a practice of self-evolution, are the inevitable and compulsory challenges. The practitioner's competence determines how deep this search can go.

Equipped with the experience of how theatre works as a healing force, I revisited the performing theatre. This experiment had a 'developmental approach' that needed 'self-discovery in the performer as the inevitable prelude to self-transcendence' (Hindman 1976: 75). A bunch of actors explored poetry on trees in the context of life, and brought life to the tree metaphors. As part of the process, we partnered with an environment group to work on the reforestation of hills, kept notes on trees, shared tree-memories, thought about people significant in our lives as trees, got actors' families involved in play-sessions. We traversed through exercises that let us express our patterns and reflected on their use in (or damage to) our life. We looked for the theatre within – as close to authentic expression and witnessing as possible – an unfulfilled high quest! When the piece was ready, it felt embedded in our lives, not a mere performance. We did have a long run and handsome reviews, though. The strength of the piece is that it flowed from the actual through the metaphoric, which we experienced first and then shared with others. Yet after all, the piece is limited by the systems of production and circulation, performance spaces, and finance (or the lack of it!).

The piece indicated once again that the attention and energy in theatre can enrich the performance as well as life. The awareness that explodes on the performer is the same as when one is mindful and attentive in living. Is that not so . . .? This question is the current guidepost. Even though dramatherapy is not yet formally recognised in India, what matters is that we invest sincere effort in bringing the healing power of the arts to various groups and places. The journey is to go on, search and simplify.

Bibliography

At the Foot of the Mountain of Minneapolis (1976) Feminist ensemble, *Brochure*.

Boal, A. (1992) *Games for Actors and Non-actors* (trans. Adrian Jackson), London/ New York: Routledge.

Chabukswar, A. (2003) 'Birth of a Story', *The Prompt, The Magazine of the British Association of Dramatherapists*, Summer: 9–10.

Chabukswar, A. (2004) 'Story-circles in De-addiction', *Healingstory Alliance*, Winter, *12*: 10–11.

Chabukswar, A. (2006) *Bridging the Worlds: A Case of Brief One-to-one Dramatherapy*, Aaina, Pune: Centre for Advocacy in Mental Health.

Dharwadkar, A. (2005) *Theatres of Independence: Drama, Theory, and Urban Performance in India Since 1947*, Delhi: Oxford University Press.

Elkunchwar, M. (1995) 'Experimentation in Marathi Theatre', in *Marathi Theatre*, pp. 19–30, New Delhi: Maharashtra Information Centre.

Gokhale, S. (1989) 'Interview of Vijaya Mehta', in *Contemporary Indian Theatre: Interviews with Playwrights and Directors*, pp. 179–184, New Delhi: Sangeet Natak Academy.

Gokhale, S. (2000) *Playwright at the Centre: Marathi Drama from 1843 to the Present*, Calcutta: Seagull.

Hindman, J. (1976) 'Developmental Approaches to Theatre', *The Drama Review, 20*, 1: 75–8.

Jain, N. (1992) *Indian Theatre: Tradition, Continuity and Change*, New Delhi: Vikas Publishing House.

Jennings, S. (1990) *Dramatherapy with Families, Groups and Individuals*, London: Jessica Kingsley Publishers.

Jennings, S. (1998) *Introduction to Dramatherapy*, London: Jessica Kingsley Publishers.

Jennings, S., Cattnatch, A., Mitchell, S., Chesner, A. and Meldrum, B. (eds) (1994) *The Handbook of Dramatherapy*, London: Routledge.

Kashyap, T. (2005) *My Body, My Wisdom*, New Delhi: Penguin.

Masud, I. (1976) 'The Savage God', *Enact, 116–17*, Delhi.

Mehta, V. (1995) 'Review of Marathi Theatre', in *Marathi Theatre*, pp. 35–43, New Delhi: Maharashtra Information Centre.

Palande, V. and Bapat, V. (1990) *Prasanganatya – Pathanatya*, [*Theme-theatre – Street-theatre*], Management for Teachers, Part 10, Pune: Atul Book Agency.

Ramanujan, A. (1993) *Folktales from India*, New Delhi: Penguin Books.

Ranganekar, M. (1968) 'Marathi Theatre: Age 125 Years', *Natyabhumi, 8*, Mumbai.

Redstone (1998) *Redtheatre: Street and Theatre*, Year-end Report, Panchgani: Redstone Farm Home School.

Richmond, F., Swann, D. and Zarrilli, P. (eds) (1993) *Indian Theatre: Traditions of Performance*, New Delhi: Motilal Banarsidass.

Schininà, G. (2004) 'Here We Are: Social Theatre and Some Open Questions about Its Developments', *The Drama Review*, *48*, 3: 17–31.

Schutzman, M. and Cohen-Cruz, J. (eds) (1994) *Playing Boal: Theatre, Therapy, Activism*, London/New York: Routledge.

Sircar, B. (1978) *The Third Theatre*, Calcutta: Badal Sircar.

Tarlekar, G. (1975, 1991) *Studies in the Nātyaśāstra*, Delhi: Motilal Banarsidass.

WCCLF (2004) *Wellsprings: Music, Drama, and Dance Therapies at Sadhana Village*, Pune: World Centre for Creative Learning Foundation.

Part III

Social theatre, politics and change

A development of cross-cultural perspectives

Introduction

In one sense most of the chapters have addressed issues of cross-cultural work and most authors address themes that are culturally specific. However in this section we have an acknowledgement of both the politics and the cross-cultural context.

Andy Hickson (Chapter 11) looks at the phenomenon of bullying and intimidation in schools and the current rise in incidence even though there is a greater awareness of bullying and there are many anti-bullying initiatives. He suggests that social theatre is an ideal intervention both in confronting behaviours as well as in teaching new skills and strategies. He emphasises the importance of young people's involvement in the pro-grammes, just like Schutzman (Chapter 6) in Part II. Above all there should be a climate of respect towards young people and the opportunity for them not only to have a voice, but also to lead workshops and performances that they have written and devised.

Marina Barham is a Palestinian who works at the forefront of social theatre intervention through the El-Harah Theatre Group. In Chapter 12 she comments on the number of theatre initiatives that have not survived, with the additional difficulties of military intervention on the one hand and the issues from traditional Muslim society on the other. By and large women do not participate in theatre. However in 2000 she describes how there were two revolutions happening in Palestine: a revolution against the occupation and a revolution of arts and culture. The occupation became a source of artistic and theatre creation rather than violent demonstrations. Schools began to request performances, including exercises to help children overcome their fears. It was reported that the performances and workshops provided a more positive atmosphere for the children, and helped them regain their awareness of their childhood.

The work of the GGAV Institute in Slovenia has stimulated the develop-ment of new theatre forms and techniques and a whole system of training termed the AV method, described in Chapter 13 by a social theatre practitioner, Alenka Vidrih. One aspect of the training is 'Team Tuning' where participants commit themselves to a six-month process of training that is then applied in their workplace. Participants 'learn through insight', where people learn about their own patterns of interaction and the possibility of change. Vidrih emphasises the supportive nature of this specific theatre model, and in her description it probably comes nearest to a form of 'therapy through action'. The culmination of her work has been the evolving of workshops based on non-violent communication. Social theatre thus becomes a harbinger of the culture of peace.

Rather like Vidrih, Lucilia Valente (Chapter 14) describes a personal quest that has led her through creative education in the arts, theatre, drama with children with special needs, dramatherapy and finally a form of applied social theatre that is integrated into the university syllabus at Evora in Portugal. Many of the chapters have focused on personal experience bringing about a profound insight into processes inherent in all forms of theatre practice. The self has been the starting point, and Valente is no exception here. It would seem that introspection in the creative process is necessary before externalization leading to the social process.

Terrence Brathwaite (Chapter 15) describes the Trinidad *Camboulay* as a 'mind–body–spirit' healing celebration of creativity, change and excitement. Like Tselikas in Chapter 1, he draws on neurological theory to support the notion of mental, physical and social sovereignty in the positive affect engendered by this carnival 'social theatre'. He discusses the improvised nature of some of the responses, the 'trance music', and suggests that there is a revitalising of revellers' bodies that contributes to greater mental health. He reminds the reader of the stresses brought about by 'post-traumatic slave syndrome', where generations of the populations have been oppressed and denied access to socio-economic benefits.

All the chapters in this section discuss the potential for therapeutic change that can happen through social theatre, although we need to widen our concept of therapeutic change to include an increased awareness of the self, opportunities to challenge the status quo, an understanding of the political processes inherent to much of social theatre practice. Are we beginning to describe something that could be called 'Social Therapy'?

11 Social theatre

A theatre of empowerment to address bullying in schools

Andy Hickson

Introduction

This chapter is concerned with the prevalence of bullying in UK schools (and probably elsewhere) and the lack of pupil-led strategies to address the issue. Most anti-bullying initiatives are led by adults for children.

My own work has been influenced by the writings of Foucault (2000) and Freire (1972). My contact with the pioneering work of Augusto Boal and his 'Theatre of the Oppressed' (1979) has expanded my own thinking and practice.

I have developed a pupil-led approach to bullying (as well as other issues such as racism) in which theatre is a means of empowerment both for participants as well as witnesses. I see a theatre of empowerment as one of the most potent forces for addressing issues of bullying.

The theme of 'theatre' and 'performance' is addressed elsewhere in this book (Chapters 2 and 3 respectively) and I highlight the issues as ones that need further definition.

Meanwhile, my own approach to social theatre can be summarised by Schninà (2004) when he says:

> at the beginning of the 1990s, a new form of theatre – taking inspiration and methodologies from animation and community-based theatre, new theatre, and therapy – found its way into direct interaction with the problems of individuals and groups in specific areas. It was a theatre based upon the body and relationships, but distanced from purely therapeutic approaches and without solely aesthetic and artistic goals. It was, in fact, less self-centred and was ready to become an instrument of social action through laboratories, workshops and performances with a goal of healing and of heightening the quality of social interaction. It was a theatre that linked the experience within the group to the social, cultural, economic, and historical context the group emerged and remained a part of. This was and is called Social Theatre.
>
> (Schininà 2004, p. 22)

Bullying in schools

With an increase in bullying in our schools, adults appear not to have been tackling bullying effectively. It is hard to find statistics on levels, but bullying and violence appear to be on the increase in our society. The charity Childline reported that 22,000 children rang them about bullying in the year 2000 (Furniss 2000, p. 11), rising to 31,000 in 2004, and to 34,000 by 2006 (Esther Rantzen personal communications 2004 and 2006). 'School bullying has become recognised as a very serious issue for schools . . . and more than half of all British schoolchildren have been bullied . . . the problem is pervasive; it's happening everywhere' (Sullivan 2006, pp. 9, 11 and 12).

The government states now that 'all UK state schools need to have bullying policies by law' (Bullying Online June 2007). We can see 'helplines, national and school wide initiatives adopting a zero tolerance approach to the problem, and many schools are taking it upon themselves to teach the message of respect, tolerance, understanding and fair play' (Sullivan 2006, p. 12), along with an inclusive atmosphere which 'encourages pupil involvement' (Furniss 2000, p. 13). And yet 'many children indicate quite clearly that they feel oppressed . . . they are ignored . . . and are not recognised as a person, not counted, being meaningless and overlooked' (John 2003, p. 57).

Franklin suggests that children are denied rights because they are seen to be incapable of making informed decisions, lack the wisdom of experience and are prone to make mistakes (in Wyse 2001, p. 209). This may be one of the reasons why 'many peer mediation schemes in schools seem to fold within the first couple of years' (Cremin 2002, p. 138).

Adults often believe they know what is best for young people and will usually be the ones who design, implement and deliver the programmes of work to young people, whether through normal education channels such as school, or other mediums such as local authority Special Units or local authority run Student Councils. During my work over the last 20 years with young people across the UK and abroad, young people have consistently voiced the opinion that they have no real power to challenge and tackle issues that affect them.

My previous work in this area has included designing and delivering peer support projects throughout the UK and abroad, through to producing the first ever national anti-bullying conference for young people in the UK, an event that now takes place annually.

Young people 'want to play an active role in creating change' (Cairns 2001, p. 355) and many adults voice a similar message. For example Annan (2003) states that 'it is crucial that we ensure that children's voices are heard loud and clear'. In 2002 the Commonwealth's Heads of Government identified 'youth participation' as critical to democratic nation building (CHOGM 2002). In the same year the British Prime Minister, Tony Blair, stated that young people were our future and that cross-Commonwealth initiatives would allow us all to learn from each other. The government Green Paper 'Every Child Matters', published in 2003, shows a commitment to 'find out what works best for children and young people . . . to involve children and young people in this process . . . [and] listen especially to the views of children and young people themselves.' In March 2005, the first Children's Commissioner for England was appointed, to give children and young people a voice in government and in public life (www.childrenscommissioner.org/young/index.cfm August 2007).

Despite these calls for young people to participate in issues that affect them, governments around the world are often criticised as paying no more than lip service to this notion. They fail to:

> recognise the significant obstacles that young people currently experience when trying to participate socially, economically and politically, and both the conceptualisation and operationalisation of official youth participation policies reveal an agenda that is seriously at odds with the rhetoric of democratic participation. This raises questions about whose voice is actually being heard and to what effect.
>
> (Bessant: 2004, p. 387)

Youth participation and empowerment

Matthews suggests that when youth forums are created they are often flawed and are inappropriate participatory devices that hide the voices of young people from actual decision making (2001). Cairns goes on to say that 10 years after the United Nations Convention on the Rights of the Child was ratified in Britain 'it would be difficult to find many children and young people who could describe how things had changed for them' (2001, p. 347).

However; advocates of youth participation would challenge this view and suggest that it is possible to find programmes that involve and empower young people in dealing with issues of bullying. In the UK these include the Peer Support Forum, Childline, Mental Health Foundation, Actionwork, Peer Mediation Network, UK Observatory, Young Voice, and a number of Local Authority schemes.

Bullying

One of the problematic definitions in this area is the word 'bullying'. We do not see just one definition of bullying or violence in the literature. The word bullying not only means different things to different people in England, it also means different things to different people around the world. 'Agreed definitions of bullying are hard to find' (Randall 1996, p. 2).

Current examples in defining bullying include:

- Cruel, abusive behaviour which is persistent and pervasive and causes suffering to individuals which is severe and sustained (Rigby 1996 cited in Fitzgerald 1999, p. 1).
- Being exposed repeatedly and over time, to negative actions on the part of one or more other [people] (Olweus 1993, p. 9).
- A systematic abuse of power (Smith and Sharp 1994, p. 2).
- Repeated aggression, verbal, psychological or physical, conducted by an individual or group against others (Primary school guidelines in Randall 1996, p. 4).
- Aggressive behaviour arising from the deliberate intent to cause physical or psychological distress to others (Randall 1996, p. 5).
- Anything which one or more people do to another person to hurt or upset them. Also, bullying does not happen once – it happens again and again (Hunter and Boyle 2002, p. 326).
- A continuum of behaviour that involves the attempt to gain power and dominance over another (Askew, quoted in Tattum and Herbert 1997, p. 53).

The above definitions hold many similarities but can also be seen as quite different. For example, Askew (1997), Smith and Sharp (1994) talk about the power relationships underlying bullying, whereas Hunter and Boyle (2002) exclude it from their definition. Randall (1996) is the only one of the above who talks about the 'intentionality' of bullying behaviour.

Bullying is also not solely a UK-based issue. Bully/victim problems were first explored in Sweden in the 1960s under the title of 'mobbning or mobbing' (Heinemann in Smith *et al.* 1999, p. 8).

Power

My role – and that is too emphatic a word – is to show people that they are much freer than they feel, that people accept as truth, as evidence, some themes which have been built up at a certain moment during history, and that this so-called evidence can be criticized and destroyed.

(Foucault in Martin 1988, p. 10)

The concept of power is central to a discussion on bullying. Bullying can be seen to be an abuse of power (Smith and Sharp 1994, p. 2), and a lack of power can lead to high risks of bullying (Randall 1996, p. 109). In my work with young people I generally use Randall's definition of bullying (above) as it can be difficult to tell a young person that bullying is a 'systematic abuse of power', not least because power is not a thing or a 'fixed entity or institution, but is incarnated in historical social practices' (Foucault in Dreyfus 2004, p. 2). Nevertheless, power is an important underlying issue in bullying behavior that needs to be give proper consideration.

Foucault tells us that power can be more than a repressive concept (such as that exercised by the state or the sovereign).

> What makes power hold good, what makes it accepted, is simply the fact that it doesn't only weigh on us as a force that says no, but that it traverses and produces things, it induces pleasure, forms knowledge, produces discourse.
>
> (in Rabinow 1984, p. 61)

Indeed Foucault goes further by saying that 'power is a positive, productive phenomenon which produces and incites effects in the social realm rather than simply repressing and denying' (McNay 1992, p. 148). It is the abuse of power that is the negative aspect, such as in bullying and oppression, whereas the use of power can be empowering, motivating and positive.

> Power relations are extremely widespread in human relationships. Now this does not mean that political power is everywhere, but that there is in human relationships a whole range of power relations that may come in to play among individuals, within families, in pedagogical relationships, political life etc . . . Liberation is sometimes the political or historical condition for a practice of freedom.
>
> (Foucault in Lotringer 1996)

'Power also traverses and drives other powers' (Foucault 2000, p. 83), power moves between us like smoke in the wind, dancing between people, objects, ideas and knowledge in visible and invisible ways. Power can be invested in symbols such as a national flag, the police, the constitution or churches.

Peer support

Peer support is embedded in naturalistic relationships and is arguably a natural part of everyday life in a 'civilised' society because it is based on interaction with others and sharing ideas of identity. Young people involved in peer support learn by 'doing and action'. They 'do' things rather than just talk or be talked to about them. Peer support involves learning about identity, relationships and safety through an interactive process. The process of peer support also enables young people to take action on issues that they feel strongly about. It is a living process, as Dewey might talk about education as a process of living and that education is part of life. He also indicated that children learn from 'doing', and that education should involve real-life material and experiences should encourage experimentation and independent thinking (Dewey 1966 and 1969).

Peer support was first formally recognised in the UK over 20 years ago (Tyrell 2002). It is made up of a variety of approaches that allow, among other things, young people to help other young people. These include peer mentoring, peer advocacy, circle time, peer tutoring, peer listening, circle of friends, peer befriending, buddies, mini-buds, and peer counselling. Peer support also includes certain conflict resolution practices such as peer restorative justice, peer anti-bullying workshops, peer leadership training, and peer counselling. Some of the key peer-led anti-bullying programmes are: The Olweus bullying prevention programme, the No-blame approach, Shared concern, R-time, Bully Courts, peer support schemes and Circle time (Sullivan 2006).

Cowie and Hutson (2005, p. 40) suggests that the main features of peer support are that young people are trained to work together, are given opportunities to learn good communication skills, share ideas and reflect on their own feelings. In addition young people should be trained to deal with conflict and help other young people relate to each other in a non-violent and constructive way.

Social theatre and empowerment

Recognising, tapping into and negotiating our way through all this power can be difficult. There have been distinctions made between 'invested power and divested power' (Lukes in John 2003, p. 50).

How we locate this power and harness it for ourselves can be problematic. Morrow and Richards advocate using creative methods in exploring power with children (in John 2003, p. 70). Boal would agree and suggests that the Theatre of the Oppressed creates a dialogue between the audience and the actors so that the actors through the performance can try to change the audience's thoughts and feelings, and the audience can try to change the action and direction of the show (Boal 1995, p. 42). We can search for and challenge all kinds of oppressions using these creative techniques. For example Boal suggests that in England we do not need all our Police to carry guns like they do in Brazil, as English people carry 'cops in their heads' (Augusto Boal personal communication 1994). We can locate these 'cops' through the use of creative action and techniques of the theatre.

Theatre and creativity are action techniques useful for people with a range of abilities and are important in dealing with situations of bullying and other issues:

> Conflict resolution through active participation in drama and role play is an important approach for working with young people with learning difficulties. Peer mediation methods are developed through peer training to deal with situations of ridicule and bullying, together with appropriate role-modelling from staff. I refer to this type of work as 'Social Theatre' or 'Applied Theatre'.
>
> (Jennings 2007 personal communication)

There are many writers who help us to understand learning through creative action, performance and role. I often draw on Boal's ideas that 'we can observe ourselves in action and study alternatives' (1995, p. 13) to explore how we can transform the power that prevents us from achieving our goals into power that can help empower us to achieve them. Theatre techniques are also very useful tools in helping us to take away people's inhibitors and leave them with creative liberation (Grotowski in Kumiega 1987, p. 113).

> Theatre is physical, it engages the body and the voice; it returns the energy to the world in the form of a performance, as a creative, interactive force, rather than in the form of disconnected destructive discharge.
>
> (Reisner 2002, p. 16)

Reisner shows us how theatre may help us create positive and creative experiences in the process of interaction. Most useful of all is that in the context of social theatre, as suggested by Sternberg (and others) is that 'theatre can be done anywhere by anyone' (1998, p. xv).

It is important that the participants feel safe, physically and emotionally, during creative workshop sessions, particularly when we are exploring the difficult subject of bullying. Using performance is a safe option as 'performance genres are outside of ordinary life but at the same time being totally absorbing' (Schechner 1988, p. 11). Boal suggests that theatre and performance:

> is the capacity possessed by humans – not animals – to observe themselves in action. Humans are capable of seeing themselves in the act of seeing, of thinking their emotions, of being moved by their thoughts. They can see themselves here and imagine themselves there; they can see themselves today and imagine themselves tomorrow.
>
> (Boal 1992, p. xxvi)

Although funding has recently been announced by the government for 'cultural' projects, the funding of youth projects, youth cultural projects in particular, is notoriously difficult to find. Social theatre projects have the advantage of being able to operate on minimal funding.

I was recently involved in a social theatre project to tackle bullying in schools. I worked with four teenagers over a period of two months. On average we were together for 12 hours per week. During this time we played a lot of creative games, including trust games and games that explored power and how we felt about bullying and what it meant to us. The teenage group, under my guidance, designed their own creative workshop programme. During this period I raised funds to take them to Japan where they delivered their creative workshop sessions to young people in Japanese schools. In addition, on return to the UK, they gave their sessions to students in schools around England. This social theatre experiment was primarily concerned with 'process'. The young people I worked with went through a concentrated programme of learning and sharing skills in a safe space without adult interference or fear of ridicule or retribution.

The young people and the programme all received excellent feedback from both teachers and students. Success in my eyes was that the young people were able to create and deliver the programme and feel good about what they had done. Through social theatre methods they were empowered to build confidence and gain knowledge. This formed the basis of their own creativity and experience that enabled them to form and deliver a young people's programme for young people.

Social theatre in this example provided a framework that helped young people engage with each other and with the subject they were exploring. The process they experienced gave them both a set of skills and a way to utilise these skills. The recipients of their workshop programme – that is, the young people they delivered to – also experienced a valuable lesson. Social theatre helped empower young people to deal with bullying from the perspective of young people. As one of the participants said when asked how they knew their workshops were a success: 'I knew because I felt good afterwards'.

Conclusion

Social theatre projects are happening in a variety of forms throughout the world. It could be argued that social theatre is part of many people's everyday lives. Social theatre can be seen as creating a community to help explore issues that affect us. In a society where we have witnessed the disintegration of the extended family and where people appear to have a lack of meaningful rituals to bring them together, social theatre can help bridge those gaps. Using the techniques of social theatre we can create rituals, and bring people together, where they can share, explore, challenge, learn, educate and have fun.

With the urgent issues of bullying and violence in our schools it is essential that we find new means that are effective in bringing about change in behaviours. The young people in the project discovered that they could develop confidence and skills through their social theatre experience. As we know, most young people who bully are individuals who lack confidence and skills, and social theatre could prove to be a way to empower them appropriately. As I said earlier, young people want action, not words; they want to do something about themselves and their lives.

Social theatre is proving to be a potent method for bringing about change at a fundamental level in schools and the community for children and young people.

References and further reading

Annan, K. (2003) Quoted in http://ceecis.org/child_protection/word/UzbC Parliament.doc, accessed 31 January 2006.

Askew, S. (1997) Quoted in D. Tattum and D. Herbert (eds), *Bullying: Home, School and Community*, London: David Fulton.

Bessant, J. (2004) 'Mixed Messages: Youth Participation and Democratic Practice', *Australian Journal of Political Science*, *39*, 2: 387–404.

Boal, A. (1979) *Theatre of the Oppressed*, New York: Urizen Books. (Reprinted 1982, New York/London: Routledge)

Boal, C. (1992) *Games for Actors and Non Actors*, London: Routledge.

Boal, C. (1995) *The Rainbow of Desire*, London: Routledge.

Cairns, L. (2001) 'Investing in Children: Learning How to Promote Rights of All Children', *Children and Society*, *15*: 247–360.

CHOGM (2002) Quote from Commonwealth Secretary-General Don McKinnon at Fifth Commonwealth Youth Ministers Meeting, Gabarone, Botswana, available at www.catatax.org/upiloads/NLJune2003.

Cowie, H. and Hutson, N. (2005) 'Peer Support: A Strategy to Help Bystanders Challenge School Bullying', *Pastoral Care in Education*, *23*: 40–44.

Cowie, H., Naylor, P., Talamelli, L., Smith, P.K. and Chauhan, P. (2002) 'Knowledge, Use of and Attitudes Towards Peer Support', *Journal of Adolescence*, *25*, 5: 453–67.

Cremin, H. (2002) 'Pupils Resolving Disputes: Successful Peer Mediation Schemes Share their Secrets', *Support for Learning*, *17*, 3: 138–44.

Dewey, J. (1966) In F.W. Garforth (ed.), *John Dewey: Selected Educational Writings*, London: Heinemann.

Dewey, J. (1969) *Interest and Effort in Education*, Bath: Chivers.

Dreyfus, H. (2004) Quoted in http://ist-socrates.berkeley.edu/~hdreyfus/html/paper_being.html.

Fitzgerald, D. (1999) *Bullying in Our Schools*, Dublin: Blackwell.

Foucault, M (2000) 'Truth and Judicial Forms', in J. Faubion (ed.), *Power*, New York: New York Press.

Freire, P. (1972) *Pedagogy of the Oppressed*, Harmondsworth: Penguin.

Furniss, C. (2000) 'Bullying in Schools: It's Not a Crime – Is It?', *Education and the Law*, *12*, 1: 9–29.

Hunter, S.C. and Boyle, M.E. (2002) 'Perceptions of Control in the Victims of School Bullying: The Importance of Early Intervention', *Educational Research*, *44*, 3: 355–68.

Jennings, S. (1995) *Theatre, Ritual and Transformation. The Senoi Temiars*, London: Routledge.

John, M. (2003) *Children's Rights and Power*, London: Jessica Kingsley.

Kaufman, R. and Burden, R. (2004) 'Peer Tutoring between Young Adults with Severe and Complex Learning Difficulties', *European Journal of Psychology of Education*, *19*, 1: 107–17.

Kumiega, J. (1987) *The Theatre of Grotowski*, London: Methuen.

Lotringer, S. (ed.) (1996) 'The Ethics of the Concern for Self as a Practice of Freedom', in *Foucault Live (Interviews 1961–1984)* (trans. Lysa Hoch), New York: Semiotext(e). (Original work published 1984)

McNay, L. (1992) *Foucault and Feminism*, Cambridge: Polity Press.

Martin, R. (1988) 'Truth, Power, Self: An Interview with Michel Foucault, October 25, 1982', in L.H. Martin, H. Gutman and P.H. Hutton (eds), *Technologies of the Self: A Seminar with Michel Foucault*, pp. 9–15, Amherst: University of Massachusetts Press.

Matthews, H. (2001) 'Citizenship, Youth Councils and Young People's Participation', *Journal of Youth Studies*, 4, 3: 299–318.

Olweus, D. (1993) *Bullying at School*, Oxford: Blackwell.

Paterson, B. (2001) 'Myth of Empowerment in Chronic Illness', *Journal of Advanced Nursing*, 34, 5: 574–81.

Rabinow, P. (1984) *The Foucault Reader*, Harmondsworth: Penguin.

Randall, P. (1996) *A Community Approach to Bullying*, Stoke-on-Trent: Trentham Books.

Reisner, S. (2002) 'Staging the Unspeakable: A Report on the Collaboration between Theater Arts against Political Violence', in M. Losi, S. Reisner and S. Silvatacci (eds), *Psychosocial Notebook*, Vol. 3, pp. 9–30, Geneva: IOM.

Schechner, R. (1988) *Performance Theory*, London: Routledge.

Schininà, G. (2004) 'Here We Are: Social Theatre and Some Open Questions about Its Development', *The Drama Review*, 48, 3: 17–31.

Smith, P.K., Morita, Y., Junger-Tas, J., Olweus, R., Catalano, R. and Slee, P. (eds) (1999) *The Nature of School Bullying: A Cross National Perspective*, London: Routledge.

Smith, P.K. and Sharp, S. (eds) (1994) *School Bullying*, London: Routledge.

Sternberg, R.J. (1998) *In Search of the Human Mind*, 2nd ed., Orlando, FL: Harcourt Brace College Publishers.

Sullivan, K. (2006) *Bullying: How to Spot It, How to Stop It*, London: Rodale.

Tattum, D. and Herbert, G. (eds) (1997) *Bullying: Home, School and Community*, London: David Fulton.

Temiar Web www.temiar.com/punan.html, accessed January 2007.

Tyrell, J. (2002) *Peer Mediation: A Process for Primary Schools*, London: Souvenir Press,

Wyse, D. (2001) 'Felt Tip Pens and Schools Councils: Children's Participation Rights in Four English Schools', *Children and Society*, 15: 209–18.

12 Social theatre in Palestine

Marina Barham

Social Theatre may be defined as theatre with specific social agendas: theatre where aesthetics is not the ruling objective: theatre outside the realm of commerce, which drives Broadway/the West End, and the cult of the new, which dominates the avant-garde.

(Special Edition of *The Drama Review*, co-edited by James Thompson and Richard Schechner, 2004, p. 12)

The theatre movement in Palestine was not given the attention of any other literary forms. There was no single book written about theatre in Palestine. No research has ever been done scientifically on the theatre movement in Palestine until the last couple of years (Mohamad, 1979).

After reviewing articles, archive materials and some books on theatre in Palestine, I discovered that there were attempts in the 1900s in the Arab world and also in Palestine at school and university levels to produce theatre and imitate whatever was happening in Europe. There were some experiences of Shakespeare and Chekhov plays at an amateur level. These attempts failed dramatically.

Theories agree that nothing is born out of nothing, and so is the Palestinian theatre. The Palestinian theatre, like other forms of theatre in crisis or social theatre, started after the 1948 war. Then it flourished after 1967 to express the social and ideological issues of its people. It is a way of resistance.

There was no city or village in Palestine where some theatrical form was not created; through story-telling, singing and then through experimental European theatre.

At the beginning of the 1970s new ideological and political factions started presenting themselves in the Palestinian community and so new and different artistic and literary forms were created. The writers and artists started taking their place in the resistance.

The first theatre groups started getting established as a form of resistance. New playwrights such as Mohammed Kamal Taher and Dr Abdullatif Aqel and others started writing.

New theatre groups started working as a way to express their reality in a new form, the form of resistance each from his or her position.

The goals of these groups that were formed in the 1970s were summarized as (ibid.):

1   Resisting the occupation and creating a theatre of resistance.
2   Creating awareness among the people towards the oppression of the occupation.
3   Creating a basis for theatre to develop the Palestinian culture.

So the Palestinian theatre movement started as a movement that follows what goes on in the area and relates to the audiences and expresses their needs. The movement succeeded in reaching a huge number of people and having an affect on them.

The main theatre groups were established mainly in Jerusalem and Ramallah, but other areas lacked any form of theatre until 15 years ago.

No archive records were found for several theatre groups that were formed in the 1970s. Many of these groups disappeared after their first shows. Several of them were also prohibited from performing by the Israeli military authorities. In the 1980s several new groups were founded but also disappeared after their first performances.

According to writer Mohammed Mahameed, these groups were divided into the following categories (Al-Mallah, 2002):

- *The first groups*:   These were theatre groups that tried to hold theatre activities in Palestine after the Israeli Occupation of the West Banks, such as Al Hilal, which did not continue for too long.
- *The theatre developers*:   This category included three theatre groups, Dababis, Balalin, and Be la Lin. These groups were the first attempts to develop theatre movement in the West Bank. These groups also disappeared quickly.
- *Professional attempts*:   Two new groups started working in theatre at a professional level, Al Hakawaty and the Box of Wonders, but they also failed.
- *The New Born groups*:   These were groups that were established after the above and also divided very quickly.
- Then new theatre organizations that developed slowly but surely such as Ashtar, Al Kasaba, Palestinian National Theatre and other smaller groups, which were mainly in Jerusalem.

Most of the above mentioned groups disappeared for the following reasons (ibid.).

First, the political situation in Palestine, meaning the Israeli Military Occupation, has been one of the main reasons for theatre groups to disappear quickly because of the following:

- Prohibition of the theatre groups from performing in different spaces, by the military occupation.
- Arrests of theatre workers by the Israeli military, as they feel threatened by the power of theatre performances on the people.
- Deportation of several theatre artists because of their role in resisting the occupation.
- Horrifying audiences during shows by the Israeli military invasions of theatre halls and closing them down as a collective punishment.
- Imposing curfews and closures on areas, thus prohibiting any theatre activity during the evening hours.
- The difficult economic situation as a result of the restrictions and regulations imposed by the occupation on the Palestinian economy.
- Not allowing theatre artists to travel outside the country for security reasons.
- Imposing new regulations on the Palestinian people, such as no public gatherings, so no performances were allowed.
- Freedom of expression that Israel claims as part of its democracy is a right prohibited for Palestinians.
- More obstacles imposed on the movement of the Palestinian people and so affecting Palestinian theatre groups.

The second factor is the traditional Society in Palestine. Palestinian society is like other Arab communities, still traditional with its positiveness or negativeness, which affects the lives of Palestinians and so affects the theatre movement heavily (Bernardi *et al.*, 2002).

1 Many members of the Palestinian community still think of theatre as an outsider field which is not accepted easily.
2 Some theatre groups faced a lot of objection and criticism, and accusations of being immoral and impolite. This has affected several theatre groups and caused their isolation.
3 Several fanatics have even attacked theatre and cinema halls and even vehicles of theatre artists.
4 Several families also stopped their children from being involved in any theatre activities that they considered immoral.
5 Many also refuse to allow their children to stay late outside and so they cannot see theatre performances that usually take place in the evening hours.
6 Some families also refused to marry their daughters to theatre artists or men from other arts fields.
7 Educational and academic institutions still look at theatre as a talent or a hobby and consider it secondary, so until today there are no institutions for teaching theatre.
8 Wives of theatre artists looked at their husbands' theatre work as secondary and on the side and not a real job.

9　Schools in Palestine until the beginning of the 1980s stayed separated for girls and for boys and so did not accept the gathering of actors and actresses on stage together.

10　Because of the traditionalistic society no theatre books were made available in public libraries even at the university level.

11　The difficult economic conditions made it difficult for theatre artists to travel outside the country and learn more about theatre movements in other countries, so the theatre development stayed slow.

All the above have not made it impossible for audiences to attend theatre performances. Audiences still attended shows, especially the educated and politically active persons.

The traditional community also made it extremely difficult for women to participate in the theatre movement. Very few women participate in theatre work. These women faced a lot of objection from their families and also from the community. Some were considered politically involved and so were taking part in political plays against the occupation.

In the first intifada uprising, theatre was rejected by the community because the traditional society refused to accept any kind of entertainment when people were being killed or injured (ibid.).

There were attempts by some theatre groups to perform in church halls and community halls only political plays that talked about the oppression of the Israeli Occupation. As in other Arab communities, when death happens in the family or the community then people should mourn and not even put on the TV or have any kind of celebration. So during the first intifada, the theatre movement was put on hold for several years.

Movement was becoming more difficult and more collective punishments were imposed on the Palestinian people.

In the 1990s new theatre groups started to be established by young people, and other groups that were formed in the 1980s continued developing their work.

Theatre work started to take new forms and new styles through theatre companies like Al-Kasaba, Ashtar, the Palestinian National Theatre, Theatre Days Production and Inad Theatre, at the time, which changed its name in 2004 to Al-Harah Theatre.

In the year 2000 a new era started for Palestinian theatre and arts in general. There were two revolutions happening in Palestine: a revolution of people against the occupation, and a revolution of culture and arts. As mentioned above during the first intifada, theatre and all other forms of cultural and artistic activity were totally rejected by the society. The community did not consider them suitable for what the country was going through at the time. In October 2000 all this was turned around. Cultural organizations and theatres were in great demand by the schools, the community, and the leaders of the country.

The protest against the Occupation started taking a different route of expression. Instead of demonstrations and stone throwing there were artistic marches, using musical instruments and street performances to tell the Occupation that we will continue living and producing arts, because it is our way of sending our voice to the world (ibid.).

In 2000, two weeks after the beginning of the second intifada, several theatres started organizing activities and performances as a way of challenging the Israeli Occupation in their invasion of Palestinian towns and villages, which included bombing them. Schools that previously refused to have performances during school hours were now asking for our help. Our initial response was to consider the way we could help. The answer was a performance that involved the children. At Inad Theatre we devised a performance with songs and dances to help the children deal with the state they were in. We approached a specialist, Amira Barham, MSW, to help us understand how we could add to the performance to help the children. She suggested including some exercises that could help the children overcome their fears, by shaking their bodies or screaming out their fears. She also suggested we talk about the violence that was happening around them, so they could express themselves.

The first performance was for children aged four to ten years old. The children, the teachers and the principal of the school were very happy about the performance and demanded we come back to do more with the other children. We created different performances for the various age groups. We began by visiting all the schools in the Bethlehem area, before moving on to the schools in the Hebron area. We offered a set of five different performances with workshops after each of them, for the different age groups for each school. We performed for a whole week in each school. The results were amazing. We wanted to understand how the performances helped the children. According to Ms Barham:

> The performances and workshops provided a more positive atmosphere for the children and helped them regain their awareness of their childhood out of the crises they keep witnessing on the street and on television. The activity touched on issues relevant to the children. This gave an atmosphere of temporary safety for the children. This time gave them space to discharge their thoughts, fears, emotions, and to be heard by each other and by adults, which is something they lack in such a situation where the people around them are preoccupied with their own distress with the current events. Furthermore, being with and listening to other children's issues, fears, and emotions gave each one of them a sense of unity and safety with the others, broke their isolation, and gave them the idea of 'I am not alone.'

Notwithstanding the achievements accomplished in the field of culture and media in Palestine, there still existed extremely complicated problems blocking the development towards creating cultural and media environmental conditions capable of carrying out our duties properly. This can be mainly attributed to the ongoing Israeli occupation of over 70 per cent of the Palestinian West Bank and Gaza Strip and the consequent enforcement of military law over the occupied territories where over half of the Palestinian population live. The arbitrary Israeli actions included, for example, restrictions imposed over radio and television transmission, the jamming of public and private Palestinian radio and television stations, barring Palestinian journalists from entering Jerusalem and some areas under the military control of the Israeli army, and withholding information, in addition to attacking Arab journalists and photographers and breaking their camera equipment.

In 2005 after five years of the second intifada, again there was a new political development when Palestine for the first time after the Madrid agreement held democratic elections in January 2006. The Palestinian people elected Hamas to form a new government in the Palestinian territories.

As a result of this election the Israeli authority together with the powerful countries of the world punished the Palestinian people by stopping any funding to the newly elected Palestinian authority.

Since the beginning of 2006, no salaries have been paid to Palestinian teachers, and employees of the government ministries. Any funding coming to the Palestinian NGOs is controlled and takes a long time to reach those organizations. As a result several NGOs are closing down because of financial difficulties.

As Al-Harah Theatre we had to make a decision to continue despite all problems to work even for very little income (Marina Barham, General Director of Al-Harah Theatre).

Al-Harah Theatre was established in January 2005. The group stayed together to form a new Theatre company called Al-Harah, which means 'The Neighbourhood'. A place full of relationships between young and old, men and women. A place where real stories happen to real people.

Al-Harah emerged as a collaborative effort of seven young Palestinians: a theatre director, a technician, a producer and four actors. The whole group has extensive knowledge of and experience in both establishing and working in theatre over the last 15 years. And this knowledge and experience is now being used to create a new body with new aims and objectives.

Members of Al-Harah have participated in several Arab and International Theatre Festivals and tours over the past six years.

Al-Harah Theatre is a non-profit organization, based in Beit Jala, Palestine, which aims to produce theatre that is well crafted but moving, challenging but accessible and, essentially, honest. Theatre that has the potential to change the lives of those who make it and those who watch it. We believe in promoting a high dramatic standard while remaining accessible, and through both our performances and our educational work we bring compelling stories to audiences throughout Palestine, the Arab world and beyond in one of the last uncensored spaces.

Al-Harah Theatre is working towards creating the first drama school in Palestine. By promoting theatre arts in Palestine we are assisting in building and maintaining a civil society that emphasizes human rights, democracy and pluralism.

Al-Harah members have been working in the community and concentrating on marginalized areas of Palestine. Over the last ten years, through hard work, downright stubbornness and a continued belief in our ability to make a positive change in society, we have performed throughout the West Bank. Over 400 performances were staged in Hebron and its surrounding villages and refugee camps over the last five years. We also introduced the teaching of drama in various schools in the Bethlehem and Hebron area. Young people who had never even considered doing drama are now applying in increasing numbers to study theatre at university. We have taken great strides towards reconciling the community with artistic performance. It is no longer immediately considered inappropriate but is increasingly recognized as a legitimate means of expression and of assertion of individuality and identity, a goal that is at the heart of the Palestinian cause. Our work is part of the development of a new generation of Palestinians, a generation who with the help of artistic expression, with the weight of knowledge that they can take from the drama they are involved in, will be self-confident and strong.

And it is not only young people who we are involved with. Over the last five years we have worked with social workers, therapists, physiotherapists, occupational therapy students, volunteers who work with children and young people, workers with women and teachers.

The Palestinian youth has been a cruelly neglected part of the community for the last ten years. Al-Harah emphasizes working with young people to help fulfil their artistic need and curiosities. Al-Harah sees theatre as a medium through which they can explore diversities of culture and opinion otherwise unavailable to them, and as an essential alternative means of expression. It is a step on the road to empowerment, a step towards life in a civil society that respects human rights and democratic principles.

By touring and participating in international festivals we also aim to communicate with audiences from all over the world.

Drama training is a very important part of Al-Harah Theatre work. We train young people and adults on how to use drama in their lives and also in their work.

The big dream for Al-Harah Theatre is to establish the first theatre college in Palestine to give an opportunity for young people to study theatre and to assist their community in developing and in creating more spaces for creation and expression.

There are new challenges facing us as artists and as people by the continuation of the building of the 'Segregation wall' built by the Israeli Occupation. The Berlin wall was destroyed to give birth to the only wall imprisoning Palestinians in a huge prison. Our role as artists is to use the language of theatre in reaching out to the whole world asking for justice.

To conclude I have to affirm the power of theatre in changing the lives of the people who work in theatre and those who attend theatre. By promoting theatre arts in Palestine we are assisting in building and maintaining a civil society that emphasizes human rights, democracy and pluralism.

Social theatre is the powerful tool for Palestinians to continue challenging injustices and human rights violation by reaching out to the world for support in developing this tool, '*Theatre*'.

References

Al-Mallah, Dr Yaser (2002) *Folded Pages from the History of the Palestinian Theatre*, 1st edn, Hebron, Palestine: Al-'Anqa' Publishing House.

Bernardi, C., Dragone, M. and Schininà, G. (eds) (2002) *War Theatres and Actions for Peace*, Community-based Dramaturgy and the Conflict Scene, Milan: Euresis Edizioni.

Mohamad, Anees (1979) *The Palestinian Theatrical Movement in the Occupied Territories*, Jerusalem: Galileo Publishing House.

Thompson, J. and Schechner, R. (2004) 'Why Social Theatre?', *The Drama Review* (special edition), *48*, 3, 11–16.

13 'The only thing better than playing on stage is playing at the heart of life'

Alenka Vidrih

Our involvement in European projects made us aware of the diversity of experiences and premises relating to the term 'Social Theatre'. Allow me to focus on our understanding of this term and the various forms of this phenomenon that contribute to the wider European space. As someone who is responsible for these practices I will try to limit myself to an overview of those within our institution, the GGAV Institute.[1] The *Komunikativa* movement (a movement for open, unhindered communication), which started as a consequence of our activities, only enriches our other work.

I am bound now and again to stray into thoughts about and idealisation of some of the general positive effects of social theatre on both individuals and society, although I really intended to bypass them here. They are defined in writings about applied theatrical forms and methods. Let me use the term 'the profession' to encompass and welcome all those individuals from various vocations and with different profiles who, in making use of one of the applied theatrical forms (or to put it simply, theatrical activities), are united in their endeavours to move society and the individuals in it towards a greater and fuller awareness of themselves and the environment they inhabit. I am referring to those who wish to preserve the alertness of individuals and society so that acting and the theatre remain at the centre of life itself. Not only when we take our first steps in life, but long after, until we depart from it. I am referring to those who through their theatrical experience enjoy the sensation of freedom that embraces their whole person and is thus the source of what is good. I am referring to those who wish to share this with others, enriching them with the experience, be it in theoretical discourse or in practice.

By founding the GGAV Institute we have also provided a formal framework for social theatre activities involving the organisation of numerous workshops for business people, for educational institutions and for the institutions that finance the formal training of those working in education, of those involved in amateur cultural activities, as well as of the informal education of young people and adults. The existing activities are thus part of social theatre, covering institutional life. With communication training using the AV^2 method (09/07)^3 we have even reached the public administration, the reason for which, in my opinion, lies in the fact that the society around us is, as I see it, functioning at 'high speed'. Education, too, where our training and workshops have already been present for some time, has become more open to what are seen as 'unusual' methods and forms of communication. Rhythm and dynamics are far removed from routine and balance, and thus the established methods cannot cope with the complex development of society. The latter is increasingly looking for something that enables the more complete development of the personality. Alongside the attention given to professional integrity and development (and endless possibilities of improvement and promotion) an open interest has arisen out of what was merely an awareness of the importance of more integrated approaches. Within this interest there is now openness and willingness, and thus an opportunity to look at one's own communication patterns.

It is at this point that we appear with various forms of activity based on theatrical practice, and which as such retain the main qualities of the theatrical process.

Let me thus start with one of our programmes that is called 'Team Tuning (TT) Training', where participants agree to a more long-term process (2 hours a week for approximately 6 months), with activities that take place more or less *in medias res* within their working hours and at their workplace. This enables the participants to directly use the experiences they have gained in their work and within the group participating in the process.

As the programme involves the active and well-rounded acquisition of practical knowledge on interpersonal communication, the programme is implemented in the economic sector, in public administration and in education. A special feature of Team Tuning is that in an indirect manner it balances and neutralises relationships within a specific team. There is also a spontaneous redefinition of values and the formulation of rules within the team, which are in line with the hierarchy of the system of values as structured by the team. We are talking here about 'dramatic/theatrical supervision'.

Like all our other activities, Team Tuning is conducted using the pronouncedly 'soft' AV 'method', which involves 'learning through insight'. This facilitates the process of the analysis of individual and social patterns of behaviour, based on the detailed analysis and formulation of a theatrical part. It functions at a number of levels as its effects are those of re-socialisation; it de-emphasises the individualism and alienation of the socially indifferent individual; it enables the recognition and alleviation of stress; it supports the individual in examining and facing up to his or her own patterns of communication and behaviour and in the creation of new patterns; and it offers support in the transfer of theoretical content into practice.

It is clear that with the formulation of the AV method (irrespective of the already existing forms of theatrical art and the many already established applied forms) I focused on creating a specific supportive theatrical model. Using the method of 'learning through acting' it leads an individual and supports him or her in the process of tackling issues such as: How and to what extent do encumbering impulses from the environment affect me in my working environment? How is this reflected in my psycho-physical structure and how does this influence other areas in my life with respect to the structure of my personality? How do I influence others and how do others influence me? What is my personal feeling of freedom like and what is my tolerance level of the freedom of others? What are the obstacles to my being relaxed, creative and innovative? Why do I not exude personal happiness?

I see an individual as, on the one hand, fragile and vulnerable material looking for safety and the realistic support that would enable him or her to respond to relationships and situations in an appropriate manner, while on the other hand seeing and counting on the as yet undiscovered potential of the primordial strength of this individual, which is gradually revealed and released through our activities. What I have in mind here is 'creative potential'. The individual realises that the strength required for maintaining balance, stability and flexibility, as well as for the preservation of his or her own integrity, comes from within and not from some external crutch.

At the same time, we are drawing 'potential from theatrical art', involving a wider process at the crossroads of art, science and education. With the AV method, and by exploring and developing the theatrical forms and derivations thereof, we are trying to discover new forms of theatrical creative process, as well as using the existing forms and tying them into existing teaching and existential processes within institutions.

Creativity and acting may be among the essential components of theatrical art, but this does not mean that they are reserved only for artists involved in theatre. They can become a constituent part of our everyday work or education.

However, connectibility is only one of the very noticeable current trends in this particular environment, which demand from society that the purpose and meaning of various areas of human life and work should be revised. Social theatre offers to all theatrical practices an opportunity for self-reflection and an incentive for development, not only in a theoretical sense but also with regard to future action. The level of engagement and the type of response is shaped by the individuals involved in theatrical and applied theatrical practices.

Thus, my understanding of social theatre is that it is a reaction to new social needs in the here and now. From my viewpoint, it is related to all the existing applied forms of theatre, which are mutually linked by a new aspect of socialisation. Social theatre poses questions about how theatrical forms are included in society, it assesses the definition of its role and importance to the individual and to society and in general places its social function at the forefront.

Because of its fundamental nature, artistic theatre, in contrast to many other activities, does not have to evaluate itself and coordinate with the environment. It is enough for it to react through artistic expression. It is worth mentioning here that artistic theatre in its many institutional and alternative forms is to a certain extent, and increasingly, merely an object of fascination and, as such, distanced and alienated from the individual and society. It offers the audience an even more passive role, thus establishing a superficial relationship. If theatre audiences follow and experience what they are seeing with increasing passivity, it is even easier to understand the renewed initiative of what is known as social theatre. If artistic theatre is progressively moving away from the function of catharsis, then we can perhaps say that this function is fulfilled by the flourishing of social theatre. This wishes to draw individuals into its process so that they fully experience it, expressing themselves and thus participating interactively. In this sense, social threatre is closer to Aristotle's original definition of theatre. The presence of another in this process and inter-connectedness – that were both lost somewhere along the line, some time before the start of the information technology era – are those qualities of social theatre that have been newly brought to our attention.

I personally experience social theatre as an appeal that, in contrast to the predominantly rigid and rational European performance orientation and to consumerism, challenges society with its playful content and methods. It draws attention to the fact that, albeit in a specific but tested way that is 'right under our nose', it can effectively work through many issues; it can breathe new life into the parameters of the quality of an individual's life; it returns in a genuine way that which was taken away from us by rapid development, thus humanising us again; it can refresh the memory of forgotten mutual relationships and co-dependence, which can offer great fulfilment.

Social theatre thus, under a new flag, blows new wind into the sails of the already existing forms. At the same time, there is still enough room for new forms, derivations and uses, as long as they do not forget to be aware of or make a specific contribution towards the socialisation and sociability of the individual in society.

Through our work at the GGAV Institute we are trying to provide an answer to the question of what new possibilities are offered by theatre.

In addition to the already mentioned TT, let me mention also the slightly older 'Personal Presentation Programme' (PPP), which supports groups of individuals in the same sections of society as TT. It is clear from the title of the programme that it focuses on the individual's expression and action. It takes place outside work, that is at weekend workshops, as is otherwise customary for training activities.

Both TT and PPP, in addition to the forms mentioned below, function in the desired manner only in connection with the AV method mentioned above.

'Theatre Lab' is a workshop that introduces the AV method and the principles of dramatherapy into amateur theatre. Members of amateur theatre groups and their mentors thus come across opportunities for extending the positive effects theatre has on the participant as a person and on the quality of the activities of the group as a whole. Thus it could be seen as a kind of socialisation of amateur theatre.

Those teaching the 'AV' method are themselves trained within a small group and are mostly also 'actors in social theatre', appearing in 'Theatrical AV Interventions'.

A theatrical AV intervention is a derivative of communicative theatre, in which there is no fourth wall. A group of actors enters a professional congress, conference or consultation unannounced. This group of social theatre improvisers helps to throw a different light on a certain subject within the context of adult training. In this way they lead their audience to an active approach. The professional sees the subject from a different perspective. At the same time, any tensions appearing as a result of intellectual effort are neutralised by such an improvised treatment of the central theme. The participants of the gathering find themselves in the middle of a performance and are animated by its performers. This consciously provocative method contains elements of many theatrical forms and applications, and yet it is a specific form, defined by the profile of actors with a specific knowledge, as well as by the target audience, purpose, time and space.

'Drama AV Support' and 'Drama AV Mediation' are two forms of individual encounter that serve as a supplement to and continuation of the above mentioned forms of training and workshops in education, business and public administration. They are an independent theatrical form with elements of counselling and mediation, which include aspects of psychodrama, artistic therapy and of traditional theatrical processes, but which are not any of those forms.

Workshop participant groups have always been wonderfully different and remain so. I could roughly divide them into managers and employees in the commercial sector (corporate culture), civil servants, public relations employees, educators (trainers, mentors, teachers, therapists, psychologists), those shaping educational systems, social workers, students, pensioners and theatre enthusiasts.

As the AV method is an important connecting link among the programmes (some of them are merely a derivation of the method), let me return to its origins. Creating it, I made use of the knowledge and experience gained in my parallel acting and singing career in the most tangible and concrete way possible. My professional experience, however, was a good starting point: in addition, there were years of study and experience in non-theatrical learning environments and theory (pedagogy, psychology, supervision and therapy) which is indispensable in working with people. There was also the knowledge and experience I gained from the teachers and masters of various skills (martial arts and voice exploration), which result in a symbiosis of art, science and psychosocial health and which appear to me to have no limits. Above all, I gained from the groups I have led. Trainees are my constant, my alpha and omega, the feedback to my endeavours and expectations. I grew in tandem with their development.

The process of an actor's research, the internalisation and then re-socialisation of the actor and the role, the physical and oral expression served as more than just a good starting point, but the major part of my learning took place in the overlapping of my acting and singing career, in self-exploration and in the transfer of my experiences to others. Wonderful insights occurred. Later, on the basis of my own experiences, I engineered the right circumstances for workshop participants to be able to experience them, too. Their insights were expected by me, but to them they were still their own and brand new. The model as it is envisaged offers to an individual and a group much of what it offers to an actor or a singer in their work – that which is most constructive for their personal development. It is an exploration of already existing or consciously provoked feelings and thoughts, emotions and experiences, as well as of physical structure and expression. It is based on the idea that convincing presentation and constructively oriented communication demands certain synchronisation between body, thinking and breathing patterns. This kind of learning through playing is strongly connected with important issues such as rhythm, awareness, intuition, sensibility, empathy, the sensitivity of the senses, responsiveness and spontaneity. Actors, however, are also craftsmen and have at their disposal, if required, certain techniques and methods that enable them not to have to discover the procedures over and over again. But it is not necessary for actors to have a system or to be very deeply involved in their work. Sometimes they remain on the surface, at a purely formal level and their success does not depend on any of this. But one thing is certain: if actors/singers are active in their profession, they are training their instrument, their psychophysical structure, thus becoming professional experts in transitions from one to another emotional state, in the finessing of expression, in preserving their inner child as a 'professional duty', and although equipped with past experiences they are aware every time of the zero point from which they are starting when creating a new role. And I could go on describing the actor's professional advantages and skills obtained through training and experience.

To what extent and in what way individual actors explore depends on their personal structure. Also to what extent and in what way they deal with dramatic circumstances, as well as if, and what, they change or discard from within in the name of exploring a character, in order to function totally differently from what their nature would demand. Usually, actors turn within (the asocial phase), observe and explore themselves and their psychophysical structure, testing how they influence others and how others influence them. Only when they feel at home in their own skin and in the fictitious dramatic circumstances does there follow a phase during which they open up again and re-socialise. Undoubtedly, they enter the process of creating a role or interpreting a poem with the goal of appearing authentically and convincingly within the dramatic circumstances and to respond in a way that is appropriate for these circumstances.

It was necessary to systematise this process in order to work with workshop participants, making notes throughout and analysing the effects in order to develop it further. The differences among the participant groups confirmed the effectiveness of the model. Each time there is a different background and different individuals, who with some of their contextual questions and problems only confirm the model that, in spite of some adjustments, remains the same.

With a desire to preserve the curiosity and openness so typical of the child within us and with a commitment to the values that in communication give priority to love, I found myself on the path of a peace seeker, linking our workshops with non-violent communication. Social theatre thus becomes a harbinger of the culture of peace.

Notes

1 The short version of the name is legally correct, but it is sourced from, and connected with, the author's first profession: Glasbeno Gledališče Alenke Vidrih (in translation: Music Theatre of Alenka Vidrih). The long form has not been changed, out of respect for the history of our Institute, but at the same time, it is not used because it has historical connotations.
2 The author's initials are AV, and at the same time, and more important, these initials are strongly connected with the essence and aim of our work/activity, to improve the Art Vitae (the Art of Living).
3 These numbers are dates of registration of the practical method at the National Agency (which was only the step to get more safety). This does not mean the method has National Evaluation status, but it is a practical method/module for working with people. It refers more to the qualifications of the trainers – who use a particular methodology that will safely bring users through our education programmes.

References

Brocher, T. (1972) *Skupinska dinamika in izobraževanje odraslih* [*The Dynamic of the Groups*], Ljubljana: Državna založba Slovenije.

Čehov, Mihail (1999) *Igralska umetnost* [*The Art of Acting*], Ljubljana: MGL.

Dolar, Mladen (2003) *O glasu* [*About Voice*], Ljubljana: Analecta.

Efros, Anatolij (1979) *Gledališka vaja – ljubezen moja* [*The Acting Rehearsal – My Love*], Ljubljana: MGL.

Gippius, Vasiljevič Sergej (1980) *Gimnastika čutil* [*The Gymnastic of Senses*], Ljubljana: MGL.

Jennings, Sue (1992) *Dramatherapy. Theory and Practice*, London: Routledge.

Jennings, Sue (1998) *Introduction to Dramatherapy. Theatre and Healing*, London: Jessica Kingsley Publishers.

Lenee, Raphael (1983) *Strah. Analiza i terapija* [*The Fear, Analysis, Therapy*], Zagreb: Biblioteka popularne psihologije.

Levine, Peter A. (1997) *Waking the Tiger: Healing Trauma, The Innate Capacity to Transform Overwhelming Experiences*, Berkeley, CA: North Atlantic Books.

Lionel. F. (2006) *Individuals, Groups and Organizations beneath the Surface*, London: Karnac.

Makarovič, J. (1986) *Sla po neskončnosti. Človek kot ustvarjalec* [*The Human Being as the Creator*], Maribor: Obzorja.

Moreno Levy, Jakob and Moreno Teoman, Zerka (2000) *Skupine, njihova dinamika in psihodrama [Groups, their Dynamics and Psychodrama*], Ljubljana: Inštititut Antona Trstenjaka.

Musek, J. (1990) *Simboli, kultura, ljudje* [*Symbols, Culture, People*], Ljubljana: Znanstveni inštitut filozofske fakultete.

Ravnjak, Vili (1991) *Umetnost igre* [*The Art of Acting*], Ljubljana: ZKO Slovenije.

Ravnjak, Vili (2005) *Gledališče kot stvarnost in iluzija [The Theatre as Reality and as Illusion*], Maribor: Slovensko narodno gledališče.

Stapley, F. Lionel (2006) *Individuals, Groups and Organizations Beneath the Surface*, London: Karnac.

Strehovec, Janez (ed.) (2003) *Teorije igre pri Johanu Huizingi, Rogerju Cailloisu in Eugenu Finku* [*The Theories of the Play*], Ljubljana: tudentska založba.

Toth, Cvetka (1998) *Metafizika čutnosti* [*The Metaphysics of Sensuality*], Ljubljana: Znanstveno in publicistično središče.

14 Social theatre: An integration of education and theatre arts

The Portuguese Experience

Lucilia Valente

Introduction: A journey of discovery

My own journey during the past 30 years has mirrored what I see as the development of what is now known as social theatre in Portugal. This journey has taken place against a backdrop of a major revolution and changes in all areas of Portuguese society; yet areas of change in relation to the arts and health has been gradual. Despite pioneering work by Portuguese artists and clinicians, and overseas practitioners, it was only in 2007 that the Portuguese Association of Integrative Dramatherapy was established.

The journey started with a pilot experiment in 1977 in 'Education through Art' that was held at the National Conservatoire in Lisbon, which completely changed my thinking on artistic experience and change.

I travelled to England to do Masters research followed by a doctorate in The Theory and Practice of Dramatherapy (Valente 1991; Valente and Fontana 1991, 1992).

On my return to Portugal I created a new association in 1994 that was heavily influenced by the early 'Education through Art' experience and I became president of the 'Portuguese Movement of Artistic Intervention and Education through Art'.

I was due for a sabbatical and I travelled to Brazil to carry out a systematic research project on theatre a community in Latin America. I spent 12 months gathering data through interviews, 'life story' and participant observation. I continued to be drawn towards an integrative methodology. I conceptualized these meaningful influences as 'people, places and experiences'.

I moved to the University of Evora as director of the Theatre Studies course, which then changed to a new scientific subject, 'Theatre and Community'; it enabled the staff team and myself to scientifically consider, 'What is Arts and Community?'

Restlessness towards knowledge

This was the impact of my attending the 'Education through Art' programme, that was a development of Herbert Read's ideas, albeit in an idiosyncratic fashion. During the first year, although it was not called therapy, the aim was to develop self-knowledge. It was inspired by a poet and medical doctor, Dr Arquimedes da Silva Santos, who created a theoretical framework for the course called 'Psychopedagogy of Artistic Expression' (Santos 1977). It was an interdisciplinary approach to the arts that aimed at psycho-social development. Santos used the term 'globalization of artistic expressions' to name these bio-psychological integrative arts practices.

This 'globalization of creative arts' was for us a real quest. We all had to experiment and discover how to do globalization of the arts. Our lecturers (most of them very prestigious artists, actors and pedagogues) were themselves seekers of how this integration could be done. We worked with all the creative expressions: creative drama, musical expression, creative movement, voice and visual arts.

Special education – the touching experience

Crinabel is an institution in Lisbon created in the late 1970s by a group of parents who had special needs children. There were a number of specialists in different areas, among them a creative arts teacher, and that was how I was contracted to work in special education in the 1980s. Intuitively I discovered ways of promoting an atmosphere of communication through creative expression, which brought changes in behaviour.

Important discoveries emerged from an experiment that I set up at the time with a team of teachers and therapists who worked with the more disabled classes. We ran weekly sessions, working together promoting simultaneously one-to-one work within a group context. Each week a specialist in turn conducted the session. An important fact is that drama became the prompting activity for all sessions; it was a kind of pivotal activity. Since then I have nurtured the idea of training and research into what I imagine would be the therapeutic use of creative expressions.

My encounter with dramatherapy

The opportunity to go out searching for new knowledge happened as a consequence of my entrance into higher education in 1985, when I entered as a lecturer of drama at the Polytechnic of Oporto. As I had to pursue postgraduate studies for career purposes and, as the area of arts postgraduate studies was almost non-existent in Portugal, I embarked on the adventure of flying to Great Britain to study for a Masters degree. It was in 1991 that I obtained my PhD in 'Theory and Practice of Dramatherapy' (see Valente 1991; Valente and Fontana 1991, 1992).

Community theatre – South American experience

In 2002 I travelled to Brazil as part of a year long sabbatical leave of absence to carry out systematic research on theatre and community in Latin America. It was in Brazil that the largest data collection was done, but I also collected data in Argentina and Chile. The research tool used was interviews, emphasizing 'story life', observations, and participatory observation. As the research developed, a set of new questions arose, which made me devise an integrative methodology for research inspired by an ethnographic approach. The methodology developed was in line with my interest in human development and transformation, and fitted in with my interest as a psychologist, dramatherapist and artistic educationalist. Subjects interviewed were responsible for meaningful projects on 'theatre for development', both as researchers and as practitioners, or were course leaders in leading universities. The narratives of the interviewees allowed the construction of a very complete picture of how each one built an approach to theatre for development from their own biographical process. I identified three sets of references for meaningful influences that determine the nature of their narratives: 'people', 'places' and 'experiences'.

In Brazil I identified many examples of good practice termed theatre for development. There is relevant work that is a result either of university projects like project CRIA, at S. Salvador da Bahia, Teatro Transito at Forianopolis run by Beatriz Cabral, or that comes from a tradition of community work, largely carried out by NGOs in poor areas of Brazil denominated *favelas*. Some of these projects are interventions inspired by the ideals of such individuals as Paulo Freire and Augusto Boal. In Buenos Ayres (Argentina) the Group Catalinas Sur was for me the most striking experience.

The Portuguese context

Since the enormous changes starting at that time, and for the last 30 years, we have assisted in various kinds of development in some areas, which we call 'Social Cultural Animation' (Animação Socio Cultural). There was the creation of various 'social cultural animation courses' in some polytechnics in the country, along with the creation of associations in the areas like APDASC, Associação Portuguesesa de Animadores Socio Culturais.

One of the problems in the area named 'Social Cultural Animation' was that most of the time it does not have an artistic dimension. However, studies carried out in Portugal show the interest of researchers in popular performances has an impact on the construction of new artistic objects in theatre and dance, with anthropological approaches as well as in the conceptualization of new methodologies of artistic creation (Barba and Savarese 1999; Brook 2002). What kind of contributions can these areas make to social theatre? I don't have an answer yet, but the members of our research team (NECAA – Nucleo De Cultura Educação e Artes Aplicadas), as I mention later, are carrying out a research project in this area, and we hope to be able to give some answers to that question.

From 'theatre and community' to 'social theatre'

When we mention intervention in the community, from my perspective we can consider three different focuses:

1   Theatre FOR the community
2   Theatre IN the community
3   Theatre WITH the community

I have some assumptions about the perspectives of social theatre that we are building into our training of 'Theatre in Education' teachers at the University of Évora:

1   Theatre has a social function and a role to play in the mobilization of a community and concrete intervention in society.
2   'Theatre in Education' today is not confined to school and the way it occurs in informal settings can be a form of social theatre.
3   Thus 'theatre in education' and social theatre in the first stages share common strategies and objectives.
4   It is a social function of a 'theatre in education' teacher to use the transforming power of theatre in other spaces beyond school and for that we must train professionals prepared for these new roles.

The experience showed me that from this perspective, social theatre is a privileged way to include the community in a dynamic and participatory way in its own growth and emancipation. What we aim in this work is to generate and articulate new relationships between theatre in education and theatre in the community in an inventive, participatory and dialectical way.

Thus the training experience aims to develop a student's empowerment, critical thinking and autonomy in three dimensions: (1) training, (2) intervention and (3) research.

Dimensions 1 and 2 are aimed essentially at expanding a student's repertoire of technical, personal and interpersonal competencies. Dimension 3's research is connected with 1 and 2, but is focused on identifying the strategies that more efficiently promote the basic conditions that we consider the essence of our approach to social theatre, namely encounter and *communication*.

Participatory theatre and community research projects at the University of Évora

The project 'Imagery Fair' (Bezelga *et al.* 2006), which ran for 3 years, integrated various local partners in the region of Évora such as theatre companies, schools and students in training, aiming to work in schools with a connection to the community. The construction of an imaginary object with a story, using theatre and arts, which would be 'sold' in the imaginary fair built in town, allowed a good link between school and community. The project was initially devised within the work with gipsy children whose families live by selling in fairs, but was transformed in later years into a larger project for various children and schools. It really allowed the involvement of school teachers, artists and families, making bridges and facilitating dialogues among all these 'actors'. This kind of project helped the team to gain expertise not only in approaching multicultural situations but also in establishing partnerships.

In another project *Odemira in action*, I travelled to another region in the south of the country (Odemira), with the students attending the theatre studies course, a big region lacking work of this kind. During a whole week all members engaged in the practical work inspired by 'teaching in role' techniques, in a modified form. Students observed me and the local partner responsible for a local theatre group (3 em pipa) working directly in three different settings (a unit for adults with special needs, a centre for the elderly and a local primary school). Gradually students were introduced to the different groups as leaders and developed small group work. There were two interventions in each setting in order to address issues such as:

- approaching a new group;
- building group confidence;
- using creative language to communicate to the group;
- building stories and performing them using basic dramatic techniques.

In this way we adapted the techniques of 'teaching in role' and team teaching to approach special populations, in this case special needs adults, elderly people and small children. In the first stage, the integrative model of globalization was used, which at the second stage developed a performative product arising from the first stage. In our strategies of approach with the institution, we first work with caring professionals and then with the special groups, integrating everybody in the construction of the performative product; that is, social theatre.

Contributions to social theatre from our research group NECAA

In 2003, as a way of dealing with our research conundrum, I set up a small research unit (NECAA – Nucleo de Educação Cultura e Artes Aplicadas), which I coordinate and which belongs to the CIEP – Centro de Investigação em Educação e Psicologia of the University of Évora.

This small research team (NECAA) is a team of trainers in the area of art education who use integration of the arts and creativity as our working tool. The rationale of the work I develop is inspired by the perspective of 'Education through Art' developed in Portugal during the 1970s that, as I explained earlier, is based on the integration of creative arts for personal and social development. In our approach, theatre is the dominating creative area of our work, but some of us develop further with visual arts education. Part of the research on methodologies is based on group interaction techniques and that's how we create a dimension of our research and practice that we call *creative partnerships*.

The projects referred to above involve members of this team illustrating the contribution of the interdisciplinary approach within which we are developing the area of theatre and community as an academic subject and as a field of social intervention through creative partnerships and team teaching. Another trend of the team-work tends to preserve theatre traditions, to understand theatre's functions: that is, as a ritual, as a celebration, as socialization; and to identify – the universal axis of theatre – common principles present in different contexts and social groups.

According to the interests of the group, we feel we are developing a dimension that seeks to enlarge the contexts of application of social theatre and cultural co-education, through the analysis of cultural mediation processes (Proença 2006; Fontes and Macedo 2001), in the construction of knowledge and didactic-artistic competencies, as a result of the interactions between the museum staff, teachers and students and exploration of the relationships between education and culture, and the aspects that have their origins in situations of cultural co-education.

My approach to social theatre

These interventions for the team involved a precious laboratory for our discussions and our experiments. At the moment we feel that a new stage of more rigorous research is needed. Nevertheless, based on our experiences, I am proposing a definition and description of our participatory action research projects (Kemmis and Mactaggart 2005), taking into account the description of principles, objectives and strategies of our interventions.

I propose the approach to social theatre is inclusive, affective and social. Its development is based on working in partnership and it aims to have multiplying effects by creating networks of new, autonomous, organized groups in communities. I believe that it requires particular ways of training qualified professionals for this work, someone between a drama teacher, a cultural animator and a dramatherapist; a theatre professional with a profile that is simultaneously artistic, educative and healing, but mainly humanistic, I have proposed a term for this professional: *'professor motor'*. This is someone who can:

1   Seek the foundations for a collective pedagogy and new forms of culture related to daily life, namely through the development of citizenship, as a practice starting in theatre contexts (microcosms) and developed in other fields of life (macrocosms).
2   Enrich social and cultural perspectives.
3   Look for alternative ways of healthy intervening, significant in trans-forming lives.
4   Involve the community in cultural dynamics, giving to social theatre a privileged way towards communication and transformation, and towards a sustainable development of communities.

Conclusion

I would say that social theatre is a social construction with its own epistemological principles and its own complexity as it brings together many different fields combining artistic, ethical and ideological concerns. In order to resize and structure, to obtain a plus effect, it will be necessary to adopt new strategies, with redefinitions based on historical contributions such as those by Paulo Freire (1981, 1984) and Augusto Boal (1979, 1990), or the ones of theatre in education such as Koudela (1984), Spolin (1963), and Barret and Landier (1994); and socio-cultural practices that promote situations generating creativity and freedom in a holistic and humanizing perspective (Basadre 1995; Ander-Egg 1997; Ucar 1992).

In the last few years we have been building a repertory of creative techniques inspired by my work in dramatherapy (Valente 1991, 1993; Fontana and Valente 1993); expressive education and integrated arts (Valente and Melo 1997; Cruz *et al.* 1998) and educational drama. More recently I have enriched my approach with a holistic perspective. By expressive education I mean the globalization of music, movement, drama and arts used towards the global development of the person. I was not alone in this journey; different teams of colleagues and artistic 'friends' have been with me in this search (see Valente *et al.* 2003).

My belief is that the perspective of personal and social transformation through integrated expressive arts is a challenge that involves new practices and new training techniques. The experiences I refer to involve an inter-active and communicational work for both trainers and trainees and local partners. The research is giving us evidence of the importance of linking therapeutic processes with performative presentations that are an outcome of the group interactive processes.

I would like to claim that social theatre of the future is a gradual path for social transformation, where creative partnerships have a fundamental role to play. The approach we are devising can be used with groups without previous artistic training.

Through creative and expressive work, we hope to help build more interactive and interventive communities. Within the 'state of the art' I have presented, our research team is making endeavours to contribute academically towards the definition of a perspective of social theatre. Currently one of the members is developing a project at Odemira, in the south of Portugal, and we hope it will help to define social theatre in Portuguese contexts in the light of European established practices (Chafirovitch 2007).

I defend a perspective of social theatre largely based in the area of education; that is, the *use of theatre as a method of expression, communication, encountering and development* (Courtney 1987, 1995; Bolton 1979; Spolin 1963; Landy 1982; Koudela 1999).

Portugal had a political revolution, but it is still in the process of undergoing a cultural revolution. I hope that social theatre will play a role in the Portuguese formal and informal system as an educationally significant tool for building a liberating and empowering citizenship within a cultural democracy.

References

Ander-Egg, E. (1997) *Metodologias de Acción Social*, Madrid: Instituto de Ciências Sociales Aplicadas.

Barba, E. and Savarese, N. (1999) *The Secret Art of the Performer*, London: Routledge.

Barret, G. and Landier, J.C. (1994) *Expressão Dramática e Teatro*, Porto: Edições Asa.

Basadre, C.C. (1995) *Teatro y dramatización. Didáctica de la creación colectiva*, Archidona: Aljibe.

Bezelga, I., Espiridião, A. and Carvalho, I. (2006) 'Imaginary Fair: A Community Work in the Field of Arts', in Associação de Professores de Expressão e Comunicação Visual (ed.), *Proceedings of the International INSEA Congress: Interdisciplinary Dialogues in Arts Education*, CD-ROM.

Boal, A. (1979) *Theatre of the Oppressed*, New York: Urizen Books.

Boal, A. (1990) *L'Arc en Ciel du Désir: Méthode Boal de Théâtre et de Thérapie*, Paris: Ramsay.

Bolton, G. (1979) *Towards a Theory of Drama in Education*, London: Longman.

Brook, P. (2002) *A Porta Aberta: Reflexões sobre a Interpretação e o Teatro*, Rio de Janeiro: Civilização brasileira.

Chafirovitch, C. (2007) 'Emergência de Estratégias em Teatro Social: A Experiência do 3 em Pipa no Conselho de Odemira', paper presented at the Conferencia Nacional de Educação Artística, Casa da Música, Porto.

Courtney, R. (1987) 'On Dramatic Instructions: Towards a Taxonomy of Methods', *Youth Theatre Journal*, 2, 1: 3–7

Courtney, R. (1995) *Drama and Feeling: An Aesthetic Theory*, Montreal: McGill/ Queen's University Press.

Cruz, J.Z., Valente, L. and Charréau, L. (1998) 'A integração das Artes: Uma resposta educativa aos problemos do nosso tempo', in *Actas III Jornades D'História de LÉducació Artística*, Barcelona: Universitat de Belles Arts, Facultat de Barcelona.

Fontana, D. and Valente, L. (1993) 'Dramatherapy and the Theory of Psychological Reversals', *The Arts in Psychotherapy*, 20: 133–42.

Fontes, P.J. and Macedo, A.P. (eds) (2001) *Cultural Mediation between School and Museums*, Proceedings of the 58th Annual Convention of the International Council of Psychologists.

Freire, P. (1981) *Conscientização: Teoria e Prática da Libertação*, São Paulo: Cortez & Moraes.

Freire, P. (1984) *Acção Cultural para a Liberdade e outros Escritosi*, Rio de Janeiro: Paz e terra.

Kemmis, S. and Mactaggart, R. (2005) 'Participatory Action Research: Communicative Action and the Public Sphere', in N.K. Denzin and Y.S. Lincoln (eds), *Qualitative Research*, London: Sage.

Koudela, I. (1984) *Jogos Teatrais*, São Paulo: Ed. Perspectiva.

Koudela, I (1999) *Texto e Jogo*, São Paulo: Ed. Perspectiva.

Landy, R. (1982) *Handbook of Educational Drama and Theatre*, London: Greenwood Press.

Proença, A.P. (2006) 'Formas de Mediação Cultural entre Escolas e Museus', *Itinerários, revista de Educação do ISCE*, 2nd series, 3: 75–85.

Santos, A. (1977) *Perspectivas Psicopedagógicas*, Lisbon: Livros Horizonte.

Spolin, V. (1963) *Improvisation for the Theatre*, Evanston IL: North Western University Press.

Ucar, X. (1992) *El teatro en la animación sociocultural. Técnicas de intervención*, Madrid: Diagrama.

Valente, L. (1991) *Therapeutic Drama and Psychological Health: An Examination of Theory and Practice in Dramatherapy*, unpublished PhD thesis, University of Cardiff.

Valente, L. (1993) 'Dramaterapia Aspectos Relevantes na Formação de Professores e Educadores', in *Actas do II° Congresso da Sociedade Portuguesa de Ciências da Educação*, Braga.

Valente, L. and Fontana, D. (1991) 'Dramatherapy and Psychological Change', in G. Wilson (ed.), *Psychology and the Performing Arts*, Amsterdam: Swets & Zeitlinger.

Valente, L. and Fontana, D. (1992) 'Research into Dramatherapy Theory and Practice: Some Implications for Training', in H. Payne (ed.), *One River, Many Currents: A Handbook of Inquiry in the Arts Therapies*, London: Jessica Kingsley.

Valente, L. and Melo, M.C. (1997) 'A formação Artística dos Educadores e Professores do 1° Ciclo', *Revista da escola Superior de Educação de Castelo Branco*, Ano II, Número Especial, Actas do Encontro: Culturas de Aprendizagem: 449–55.

Valente, L., Peixoto, A. and Lopes, M.J. (2003) 'Re-encantar a Formação de Professores através das Expressões Artísticas', in António Neto *et al.*, *Didácticas e Metodologias de Educação*, Vol. II, Évora: Departamento de Pedagogia da Universidade de Évora.

15 Trinidad's *Camboulay* Street Dance-Play and the carnivalesque placebo

A neurotheological interface between social theatre and post-traumatic slave syndrome

Terrence Wendell Brathwaite

Mother Molly Ayhe (Iyalorisha of Opa Orisha Shango) analysed the present-day Carnival using a system of biochemistry based on Kessler's system of holons. She sees the Carnival as a great organism, a living entity. She sees the band as the cells in the body. She sees the component parts in Carnival as organisers energising the cell and she sees the female masqueraders as the mitochondria.

(John, 1999: 19)

Everything in nature is interrelated.
(George Washington Carver in Adair, 1989: 52)

Introduction

Like nature, all the live arts of the Trinidad *Camboulay*[1] Street Dance-Play are interrelated, and when studied in depth, they reveal how a holarchy of natural processes – biochemical and psychosocial – come into play and interact to produce and nurture a social theatre of Afro-Caribbean resistance. While emphasising a cross-fertilising of the scientific (symptomatic) with the folkloric or metaphysical (symbolic), this chapter limits itself to:

1 Determining how and why the participation and enjoyment of the *Camboulay* Street Dance-Play (through the mind and emotions) can have a neuro-immuno-modulatory (NIM) healing impact on the human body.
2 Signifying the future of *Camboulay* in a transnational era as a neurotheological remedy,[2] not only for bodily disorders and bio-psycho-social-spiritual effects of post-traumatic slave syndrome[3] but for an imagined cultural emptiness at the heart of global modernity (or the 'new world order').

Within this context, a brief overview of the impressive scholarship on the history and educational agenda of the festival's adaptive live arts experiences is apropos here. But before doing so, I wish to set the stage. This is not done by recycling any tangential evidence of politico-economic or socio-cultural dynamics[4] within the Trinidad community, which some sceptics may advance to digress from the 'joy triumphs over stress' picture of the Carnival tradition. Instead, I begin by providing some clarification about the solution-focused nature of the people's mythological themes, which are intuitively applied to the interpretation of such politico-economic and socio-cultural issues in an oil-rich nation, where the *Camboulay* rituals of communal responsibility were 'forged from the love of liberty', into a holarchicaly operating, transgenerational forum for tension management and resistance to imperialistic oppression. In my examples, I draw from African-Egyptian cosmology[5] (see Figure 15.1) as is often done in archetypal psychology (Hillman, 1983), because of its seminal role in the African diasporic Carnival culture, which continues to serve as a functional safety-valve in a plantation economy, instigated by European slave-owning societies in the West Indies.

Ab ovo . . .

Geographically, Trinidad is 1,864 square miles in area, and as the southern-most island in the Caribbean archipelago, it is situated approximately 7 miles from Venezuela, on the northeast coast of South America. Encountered by Christopher Columbus in 1498 and maintaining a population today of 1.4 million, Trinidad, more than any other Caribbean island (including its sister isle Tobago, which is 116 square miles in area and based 21 miles to the northeast) can be described as a 'palette of peoples', who come from every single ethnic group, except Eskimos. As I clarified in an earlier publication (see Jennings, 1997: 332):

> African descendants and East Indians, each comprising approximately 42% of the population, form the base of the multiethnic stew, while smaller groups sprinkle their own flavour to taste. These groups include the mixed races (14%), whites (1.2%), Chinese (0.86%), Syrian/Lebanese (0.11%) and others (1.83%).

It is not odd, then, for a visitor to Trinidad to be introduced to a resident whose racial ancestry is a cultural kaleidoscope. The lyrics of a bouncy calypso ballad adequately signify this phenomenon, portraying an attractive female Trinidadian 'reveller' on a Carnival day as 'So Cosmopolitan . . . A Negro girl with Chinese eyes, Red Indian, Spanish and Portuguese . . . A Syrian, Scot and Lebanese who is English French and German too . . . mix up just like Callaloo'[6] (ibid.: 332). Therefore, with a plurogeneous society characterised in the past by racial tension, cultural bias, religious bigotry,

(a)

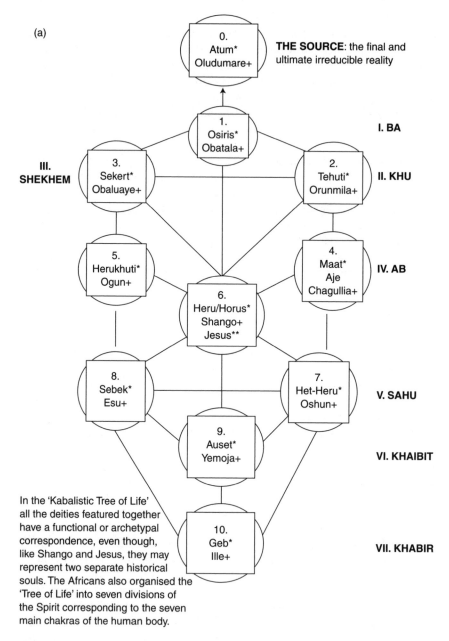

THE SOURCE: the final and ultimate irreducible reality

0.
Atum*
Oludumare+

I. BA

1.
Osiris*
Obatala+

**III.
SHEKHEM**

3.
Sekert*
Obaluaye+

2.
Tehuti*
Orunmila+

II. KHU

5.
Herukhuti*
Ogun+

4.
Maat*
Aje
Chagullia+

IV. AB

6.
Heru/Horus*
Shango+
Jesus**

8.
Sebek*
Esu+

7.
Het-Heru*
Oshun+

V. SAHU

9.
Auset*
Yemoja+

VI. KHAIBIT

In the 'Kabalistic Tree of Life'
all the deities featured together
have a functional or archetypal
correspondence, even though,
like Shango and Jesus, they may
represent two separate historical
souls. The Africans also organised the
'Tree of Life' into seven divisions of
the Spirit corresponding to the seven
main chakras of the human body.

10.
Geb*
Ille+

VII. KHABIR

Notes:
* Egyptian deity; + Yoruba deity; ** Christian counterpart.

(b)

African-Egyptian concept of chakras	Western translation
I. BA	The crown chakra
II. KHU	The third eye of chakra
III. SHEKHEM	The throat chakra
IV. AB	The heart chakra
V. SAHU	Solar plexus chakra
VI. KHAIBIT	Navel chakra
VII. KHABIR	Root chakra

Figure 15.1 Chakras in African-Egyptian cosmology

and a recursive master–slave relationship of *conflict–accommodation–change–conflict–accommodation*,[7] Trinidad's modern-day insecurities are seen to be tempered by cross-fertilisation and a rich cultural expression.

This is an expression which originated not from the traditional West, but from Trinidad's street culture and its melange of immigrants. These settlers, historically speaking, are still perceived by themselves and others as appendages of Europe, while they continually seek to reconcile their humiliating inward tensions between a Caribbean cultural identity and Eurocentrism (Nettleford, 1978). Nettleford (ibid.: 30) further interprets the essence of the Trinidadians' personal struggle on Eurocentrism within the wider Caribbean, when he contends that:

> Their actions are seen as 'responses' or reactions to the initiatives of Europe. Columbus is still supposed to have 'discovered' America; indigenous Amerindian civilisations are said to have a pre-Columbian history . . . We are yet to decide among ourselves whether not being able to quote from Shakespeare or hum Shostakovich should debar us

from membership in the human race. There is no doubt in my mind that failure to recognise a phrase of music from the composition of Bob Marley, or a line from the poetry of Derek Walcott would not render such an 'unexposed' Englishman or Russian less whole.

Predictably, this internalisation of the authority relationships that sustained Trinidad's socio-cultural systems was further compounded by an over-dependence on foreign-controlled petrochemical/natural resources, agricultural production and unsustainable tourism, with the ensuing resource transfer from north to south being echoed throughout other sectoral patterns of national production. Within this context, it thus became easier to understand how the European (and later the American) colonial powers, via their monopoly on the politico-economy and literacy, maintained a stabilising affinity between petit bourgeois ruling interests and the realm of cultural ideas in the twin-island Republic. Of the post-World War II American ravagers for example, Raymond Quevedo (1983: 72) who was both calypsonian (sobriquet: *Atilla the Hun*) and politician was scathing in his commentary:

> The Yankees launched a real social invasion
> They did as they pleased in my native land
> They had a lot of money and spent lavishly
> And they broke down the pillars of our aristocracy
> I must confess they helped us financially
> But they played hell with our morality
> They took all our girls and had a glorious time
> And left us blue-eyed babies to mind.

From this cause, as both Trinidad and Tobago (aka 'Trinbago') moved for self-government between 1921 and 1956 and beyond, it was the post-World War II generation of 'black-skinned blue-eyed babies' who procreated and floated in the communal mainstream of what can be characterised as a Carnivalesque 'immune system'. Such a symbolic 'immune system' signified the African diasporic optimism and volition for survival life-view (or 'the will to live') with a fiery resistance to western domination and its inherent stresses. Khan (in *The Trinidad Guardian*, 2003: 15) attests to this when he writes:

> Trinidad is a great example of what England will be. I always say that, politically, America is ten years behind Britain, but Britain is probably ten years behind Trinidad in the sense of its integration. By no means is Trinidad perfect, but there's a lot of stuff that's happened that makes Trinidad an exemplary model worldwide. It's not surprising that so much has emerged from Trinidad because of that.

However, while the Roman, French and later on some American influences are evident in the annual presentations of the Trinidad Carnival, the scientific verdict on the foundation of this pre-Lenten festival dictates that it lies in Africa where, paradoxically, it had nothing at all to do with the Lenten season. Thus, in an official bid to do away with any further controversy on the advent of the Carnival issue, Dr Hollis Liverpool, Director of Culture for the nation's government stated:

> All the evidence supports the view that Trinidad Carnival originated with the Africans who were enslaved on the sugar plantations of the island; that the majority of customs associated with the festival are African in form and function; that the whites' Mardi Gras also has African roots, Egypt being the ultimate source . . .
>
> (cited in Riggio, 1998: 37)

His confirmation of the Carnival's African-Egyptian origin and the Afro-centric way the festival's live arts activities have been developed and practised in Trinidad over the years, has also been passionately reinforced by other devoted scholars of the Caribbean celebrations (see Blake, 1995; Smart and Nehusi, 2000). They have all noted in ancient Egypt or Kemet and many parts of the African continent, the recursive circling of villages was believed to bring good fortune, to heal communal problems, and chill out angry relatives who had died and passed into the next world (see Crosley, 2000; Hanna, 1978 and Some, 1998). During their scientific enquiries these researchers have acknowledged that the Egyptians engaged in a variety of festivals, including the commemoration of the change of seasons, the dawning and closing of crop season, initiation and funerary rites.

Most notable among the varied Egyptian calendrical festivals the scholars paid particular attention to was the 'Passion' festival dedicated to the god Ausar/Osiris[8] and described by the nineteenth-century curator of the British Museum E.A. Willis-Budge (cited in Smart and Nehusi, 2000: 84–5):

> A procession formed of priests and the ordinary people. Appuat walked in front, next came the boat containing the figure of the god and a company of priests of 'followers' of the god, and the rear was brought up by a crowd of people . . . The boat of the god was then attacked by a crowd of men who represented the foes of Osiris . . . A solemn service was performed in the temple before the body was carried from it, and offerings were eaten sacramentally, and then the procession set out for the tomb. When it reached the door of the temple it was received by a mighty crowd of men and women who raised the death-wail, and uttered piercing shrieks and lamentations, and the women beat their breasts. Many of them in the crowd were armed with sticks and staves, and some of them pressed forward toward the procession with the view of helping the god, whilst others strove to

prevent them. Thus a sham fight took place, which, owing to the excitement of the combatants, often degenerated into a serious one . . . This fight was, of course, intended to represent the great battle which took place in prehistoric times between Set[9] and Osiris, when Osiris was killed.

Today, the essence of the diasporic Carnival presentations still involves the basic elements of this sacred process, as we recognise the stickfighting or kalinda,[10] the use of floats[11] and the crowds in street-processions who fall in behind their band leaders of various sections. In Willis-Budge's description of the 'Passion Play' one can even distinguish the mimed combats, which summon forth sacred memories for a Trinbagonian of the traditional mock battles – and actual ones – once staged by the steel band orchestras, whose male members fought over 'territorial imperatives' and their women folk in the 1950s. It is against this ancient Afrocentric backdrop that the history of Carnival began.

The *Camboulay* as restorative justice

Subsequently the collision of the three Old World cultures: 'the Spanish and French, each of a powerful white minority, and those of the African masses, an enslaved decultured black majority' (Dettmers, 1996: 6) created a disruption that culminated in the *Camboulay*. After 1834, when chattel slavery was abolished, the ex-slaves turned out dancing en masse and took to the streets in jubilant though systematic processions. When emancipation became effective on 1 August 1834, the ex-slaves, who had been forbidden to strike and had no trade unions, chose to celebrate their newly acquired freedom. They annually reproduced and reinstated the former *Camboulay* festival as an auto-therapeutic collective experience, a multi-faceted educational forum, and an anniversary symbol of mind/body/spirit liberation from the shackles of colonialism.

Thus, in a roundabout manner, the *Camboulay* allowed further possibilities for tribal and (as time went by) mass communal mobilisation involving a mode of 'free association'. This method can be juxtaposed to the original Jungian technique in which patients undergoing psychoanalysis are encouraged to articulate freely all the thoughts and images that come into their minds, devoid of constraints, reservations, intellectual control or concentration and without guidance from a therapist.

Since its inception, it can be argued that the *Camboulay* evolved as a contextual life model parallel to verbal psychoanalytic therapy. It has been personalised by subsequent generations of African diasporic people, who made use of the 'free associations' as eclectic channels to their collective or racial unconscious, which was not related to any personal or individual characteristics, but originated in the evolution of their brain over centuries (see Henry, 2003). Inspired by the collective vibrational energy of their bodies, the revellers/spect-actors projected their mythic imaginations into the *Camboulay* ritualistic oral traditions, by borrowing from the African heritage of assembling natural objects such as bones, grasses, beads, shells, fabric, feathers[12] and copper to create a piece of sculpture, a mask, or a costume. Each object or combination of objects represented a certain idea or spiritual force that manifested as a gift of wholeness within the revolutionary social theatre (see Boal, 1979; Cowley, 1996; Smart and Nehusi, 2000).

Nowadays, with over 200,000 multi-racial participants appearing in what many western observers believe may be the greatest annual theatrical spectacle of all time (Hill, 1983), we can clearly see how African healing trance dances and music traditions progressively transformed the early *Camboulay* celebrations via the embodiment of folk tales (for entertainment) and myths (for spiritual instruction) in the Americas. Remarkably, for all its frenzied quality, the *voodoo* religion's 'spirit possession' infused in the trance dances was by no means undisciplined. Therefore, as African drum rhythms, large puppets, stick fighters, and stilt dancers began to make their appearances in these festivities of symbolism and civil disobedience, the *Camboulay* Street-Dance Play also metamorphosised into a 'safe environment' cum 'sanctified bliss station'[13] for exploring the collective human psyche as a neurotheological experience of auto diagnosis and auto-therapy towards social change.

This is a holarchical development that is essentially the same in all human beings, with the same organs, the same instincts, the same impulses, the same conflicts, the same fears. Furthermore, it is a phenomenon out of which have come what Jung, during his journeys in Africa, described as the biological archetypes (or common mythical constructs) of the unconscious (see Burleson, 2005).

The neurotheology of *Camboulay*: Spiritual opiate for the oppressed

The auto-therapeutic value of such a communal inward journey towards spiritual transformation is aptly described by Trinidadian cultural scholar Bukka Rennie (2002 [online]). He wrote:

> Carnival is our theatre of the streets. Carnival is both parody and catharsis at one and the same time as our current lives are exposed to be examined in the raw. Calypso is our current editorial in song, timely in lyrical content and rhythm and relevant to said time and place. Steelpan is the specially crafted instrument through which the 'editorial' and the 'theatre' come together in a most dynamic and explosive mix of movement and art. Everything fits, all the parts go together to make the whole; the three handmaidens of our art cannot and should not be separated in any way.

What's more, when Afrocentric trance dances are explored within the Trinidad *Camboulay's* 'sanctified bliss station', where the participants are released from oppressive roles, such a ritualistic ceremonial experience becomes the 'structural nexus' at which 'healers' or 'shamans' (*mas' designers, drummers, steelpannists, calypsonians*), patients (*revellers/spect-actors*) and ancestral spirits (*Carnival holographic memory*) meet to neurotheologically interface with the community's post-traumatic slave syndrome. The old colonial communal war zone thus becomes a post-colonial 'level-playing field', where the lingering biopsychosocial impact of enslavement on Africans, can and will be healed, as the 'Carnivalesque Placebo'[14] becomes manifest.

In other words, the inspiration for the *Camboulay* rituals comes from the unconscious. And since the collective or racial unconscious minds of the people of any single small society have a lot in common, what the Carnival 'shamans' do is take a personal journey into their individual unconscious. Then, on their return, they stimulate a cathartic interaction between them-selves (as seers), the revellers/spect-actors and the ancestral spirits by bringing forth a 'story/myth' that is waiting to be brought forth in everyone (past and present) within the current symbolic field or Carnival holomovement.

Thus, when people visit the mas' camps to view the costumes or listen to the calypsos, drum chants and steelpan arrangements from these 'shamans', they respond 'Aha! That is my story. This is something that I had always wanted to say but wasn't able to say it. I can now say and "do it" without fear on the streets of Carnival'. The more popular Carnival 'shamans'/ 'seers' are the ones the people want to hear, while those who are ineffective will be wiped out during the various competitions. This is because the myths are so intimately bound to the culture, time and place, that unless the symbols and metaphors are effectively kept alive by constant recreation through the *Camboulay* live arts, Trinbago society feel that their life will slip away from them, and be replaced by the emotional damage they continue to suffer as descendants of the mentally enslaved. Thus many Carnival scholars are able to predict that if the festival is ever discontinued, post-traumatic slave syndrome will lead to major riots in Trinbago (see Regis, 1999 and Leary, 2005).

Dilthey (1985: 226) reminds us that a 'structural nexus' draws phenom-ena within its presence, as it organises the 'qualitatively determined reality that constitutes lived experience'. During the *Camboulay* Street Dance-Play, we observe the manifestation of such phenomena with the sound of skinned drums and steelpans invoking the rhythmic mode particular to African ancestral spirits (e.g. Legba Orisha[15]), the singers clapping with *call and response* calypso singing, the sound of trance street-dancing, the jingle-jangle of tin cans adorning a masquerader's costume and the 'likety-tang' of the old car iron rims in the steelband's 'engine room'.[16]

These, according to Dilthey (ibid.), 'would not be epiphenomena – something that merely accompanies other more important ritualistic activities'. Within the sheer intensity of the *Camboulay* Street-Dance experience or 'structural nexus', such events would instead become the very substance of a sacred clinical reality or 'carnivalesque placebo', where ancient African performance art and medicine reunite. This is because they are parts of the same energy of healing that manifests itself during the positively stimulating *Camboulay*, when the left and right brain hemispheres of each reveller/spect-actor are synchronised so as to induce a (w)holistic state of mind, and the theta brainwaves are initiated indicating the deep state of trance synonymous with deep meditation or visionary mystical states (see Friedson, 1996).

It is at this point that the personal and collective healing takes place both on a physical level (because the body is cleansed of toxins and tensions) and on an emotional level (with the whole body–mind being activated and thus releasing locked emotions and repressed traumas). There is also collective healing on a mental level because the incessant chatter of the mind is transcended, and there is healing on the spiritual level because there is communion with the Source or 'Spirit of Carnival'. The creative process of 'hardwiring' the mental/emotional of the revellers/spect-actors through breath, body and rhythm thus serves as a fast track to transcendence (see Crosley, 2000).

Conclusions

Therefore, I argue that tapping into this life force through a social theatre of *civil disobedience, joyful engagement,* and *free association* within the 'carnivalesque placebo' process, results in a 'hardwiring' of the mental/ emotional states of the individual revellers/spect-actors. Such mental/ emotional 'hardwiring' impacts on each person's entire human organism while helping to heal the community as an animated collective participating in the sanctification of their local landscape.

I also subscribe to the view that especially within the context of the *Camboulay* live arts indulgences as social theatre, joy confronts and triumphs over the stresses of post-traumatic slave syndrome (colonial/post-colonial ills) when 'health emerges from hope, optimism, laughter, connectedness, support, commitment, self-worth, a sense of control, and perhaps something more: the perception that life has meaning . . . and what enriches our lives is also good for our health' (Poole cited in Butler, 1993: 11).

Acknowledgement

This chapter is dedicated to my beloved sister-in-law Keri-Ann Marcella Blake.

Notes

1 *Camboulay* is derived from the French words *Cannes Brulees* meaning 'burning cane', performed in celebration of resistance and emancipation of enslaved Africans.

2 In this chapter, the neurotheological remedy refers to the neural basis of religious experiences and spirit-world evolution in the *Camboulay* Street-Dance Play, which provides a spiritual opiate for the people that is of psychobiological therapeutic benefit.

3 A testable model developed by multicultural social work consultant Dr Joy Degruy Leary (2005), that explicates the aetiology of the diverse adaptive survival behaviours to the multigenerational trauma of the Atlantic Slave Trade, employed particularly by African-Americans, but which extends globally to Africans and African diasporic communities in general. Dr Leary contends that a systematic re-evaluation of those adaptive behaviors that have been passed from generations to generations is critical for communal healing, so that where necessary, modern maladaptive behaviours can be interchanged with positive ones that will advance, guarantee and extend the healing and development of African/African diasporic culture.

4 See for example Bettelheim and Nunley (1988); Cowley (1996); Smart and Nehusi (2000) for an excellent detailed analysis of the Carnival's historical, generic organisational, socio-cultural and theatrical (entertainment) activity issues, which this chapter ignores.

5 The ancient cosmology being referred to throughout this study is that of the forgotten *Baladi* Egyptians, many of whom fled the foreign invasions and religious oppression, and rebuilt the Ancient Egyptian model system in Yorubaland, Nigeria and other parts of Africa. Since the instigation of the Atlantic slave trade, descendants of the Yoruba people have formed the largest and most widely dispersed group of Africans in Trinidad and Tobago, and are known to make no distinction between a metaphysical state of being and one with a material body, since they believed that such a distinction is a mental illusion and that wo/men exist on a number of different levels at once, from the most physical to the most metaphysical. Notably, this school of thought is now much more acceptable to modern quantum physicists beginning with Wolgang Pauli, who concurred with Carl Jung that metaphysics begins where physics ends. The Austrian physicist Erwin Schrodinger, a pioneer of quantum mechanics and originator of the quantum theory 'Schrodinger's Cat', further validated the African-Egyptian cosmological construct in the 1920s. (See Davidson, 2001; Gadalla, 1997; Gribbin, 1998; Meier, 2001 and Some, 1998.)

6 Callaloo is a metaphor for the diverse racial heritage of the island.

7 By using the term *conflict–accommodation–change–conflict–accommodation* I am arguing that the advent of the Carnival street celebrations was not always well received by the British colonial authorities in Trinidad and indeed many riots (conflicts) originating from street parades occurred, from the nineteenth century to the steel band wars of the 1950s through to the Carnival courts of the 1970s, 1980s and 1990s. For example, dancing, singing and the use of drums were restricted or forbidden. The resultant accommodating response was a change from the use of drums to the use of the tamboo bamboo – a musical instrument that originated in Ghana and is made from various lengths and diameters of bamboo. When this type of instrument was found to be inadequate, in terms of longevity, the ultimate change – the steel drum was developed (see Bacchus, 1983).

8 The Greeks interpreted the Egyptian God Ausar as *Osiris*, brother and husband of the Egyptian Goddess *Auset* or *Isis* (Greek variation) – the original Black

Madonna or Virgin Mary. Egyptologists also aver Osiris was known as 'El' (Semitic) and represented in the word Is-ra-el, with 'Is' being taken from Isis and 'Ra' meaning the Egyptian sun/son of God (*Heru/Horus*). Thus, we can see the essence of the name 'Is-ra-el' being indicative of the African-Egyptian 'divine trinity' – *Isis, Horus* and *Osiris* (see Davidson, 2001).

9 The Egyptian deity *Set* represents the universal role of opposition (the archetype of the shadow) in all aspects of life – physically and metaphysically. In human psychological terms, Set therefore represented the opposition powers within, and so, the objective during Carnival is to learn about aspects of one's self by embracing one's shadow and understanding how to control and manage these types of *Set* energies, thus striking a balance between the opposing forces, while seeking the 'divine within' and evolving like the sun-God *Heru or Horus* (born of *Osiris* and *Isis*) – whose name means *He Who Is Above* (see Gadalla, 1997).

10 Derived from a mock-combat dance of African-Egyptian origin that became a popular form of entertainment on plantations throughout the Caribbean islands. The kalinda is the dance referred to by French planters as the origin of *Camboulay*.

11 These 'floats' (symbolic of those which sailed along the river Nile) or sacred boat litters have even survived in the New Orleans (USA), Rio de Janeiro (Brazil) and other carnival celebrations around the world, where they are pulled along the streets.

12 Interestingly, feathers are still frequently used by Africans in their motherland on masks and headdresses as a symbol of our human ability to rise above problems, pains, heartbreaks, and illness – to travel to another world to be reborn and to grow spiritually (Some, 1998; Gadalla, 1997 and Riggio, 1998).

13 The 'hardwiring' of the mental/emotional states of the Carnival participants and the healing impact that results from this creative process must be understood within the context of the streets of Carnival providing a 'safe space' where the people can allow their vulnerability to come to the surface. Thus, all those mundane things that they may think about when they go about their daily 'busy-ness' can be dropped and they can reveal a little more about who they really are – their true nature (see Gerber, 2001).

14 From a psychobiological perspective, the carnivalesque placebo involves the therapeutic effect of the *Camboulay* as an institutionalised medium, which provides psycho-energetic equilibrium by offering a socially sanctioned cathartic vent to instinctual drives usually limited by the cultural system of Trinbago society.

15 Legba is the divine trickster described in Yoruba mythology as the guardian of the gate between the spiritual (sacred) and material (profane) world, who communicates with the other deities. The epitome of what the *Sankofa* symbol represents, Legba is believed to have great wisdom and knowledge of both the past and future. Therefore invoking Legba at the beginning of every ritual/ ceremony was not only done to fend off invading African tribes in pre-colonial times, but the deity was also activated in 'Plantation America' to counter modern slavery via rebellion and nonconformity. As a guardian of the sun, Legba's colour is 'black'. S/he is both male (sympathetic nervous system) and female (para-sympathetic nervous system), and when a ceremony is held for Legba, the elements are sexually suggestive in content, as is evident in the Carnival where s/he is the owner of the profound life forces of sexual energy and *kundalini*.

16 The percussion section of a steelband consisting of drums, tambourines, bells, brake drums, scrapers, and rattles. The engine room, like that of a ship, drives the steelband and is considered the heart of the band (see Martin, in Riggio, 1998).

References

Adair, G. (1989) *George Washington Carver*, New York: Chelsea House Publishers.

Bacchus, C. (1983) 'Mas of Carnival.' *The Social and Economic Impact of the Carnival*, Trinidad: University of the West Indies.

Bettelheim, J. and Nunley, J. (1988) *Caribbean Festival Arts*, Seattle: University of Washington Press.

Blake, F. (1995) *The History and Evolution of the Trinidad and Tobago Steelpan*, Spain: Grafiques 85.

Boal, A. (1979) *Theatre of the Oppressed*, London: Pluto Press.

Burleson, B. (2005) *Jung in Africa*, London: Continuum International Publishing Company.

Cowley, J. (1996) *Carnival, Camboulay and Calypso*, London: Cambridge University Press.

Crosley, R. (2000) *The Vodou Quantum Leap: Alternate Realities, Power and Mysticism*, St Paul, MN: Llewellyn Publications.

Davidson, B. (2001) *African Civilisation Revisited*, Trenton, NJ: Africa World Press Publishers.

Dettmers, P. (1996) *In Celebration of Carnival*, London: The Arts Council of England.

Dilthey, W. (1985), 'Poetry and Experience', in R. Makkreel and R. Frithjof (eds), *Selected Works*, Vol. 5, Princeton, NJ: Princeton University Press.

Friedson, S. (1996) *Dancing Prophets: Musical Experience in Tumbuka Healing*, Chicago: University of Chicago Press.

Gadalla, M. (1997) *Egyptian Cosmology: The Absolute Harmony*, Greensboro, NC: Tehuti Research Foundation.

Gerber, R. (2001) *Vibrational Medicine*, Rochester, VT: Bear & Company Publishers.

Gribbin, J. (1998) *In Search of Schrodinger's Cat: Quantum Physics and Reality*, London: Transworld Publishers.

Hanna, J.L. (1978) 'African Dance: Some Implications for Dance Therapy', *American Journal of Dance Therapy*, 2, 1: 3–15.

Henry, F. (2003) *Reclaiming African Religions in Trinidad*, Trinidad & Tobago: University of the West Indies Press.

Hill, E. (1983) 'History of the Carnival', in *Proceedings of the Conference on the Social and Economic Impact of Carnival*, 1983, Trinidad: University of the West Indies.

Hillman, J. (1983) *Archetypal Psychology: A Brief Account*, Dallas, TX: Spring Publications.

Jennings, S. (ed.) (1997) *Dramatherapy, Theory and Practice 3*, London: Routledge.

John, D. (1999) 'African Influences in T & T Carnival', paper retrieved 20 February 2007 from www.trinisoca.com/features/270699.html

Khan, K. (2003) 'BC Question and Answers' [online], interviewed at *The Trinidad Guardian*, retrieved 8 June 2003 from www.guardian.co.tt/news12.html

Leary, J.D. (2005) *Post-traumatic Slave Syndrome: America's Legacy of Enduring Injury and Healing*, Baltimore, MD: Uptown Press.

Meier, C.A. (2001) *Atom and Archetype: The Pauli/Jung Letters 1932–1958*, London: Routledge.

Nettleford, R. (1978) *Caribbean Cultural Identity: The Case of Jamaica*, Kingston, Jamaica: The Institute of Jamaica Press.

Poole, W. (1993) Quoted in K. Butler (ed.), *The Heart of Healing*, Atlanta, GA: The Institute of Noetic Sciences/Turner Publishing.

Quevedo, R. (1983) *Atilla's Kaiso*, Trinidad: University of the West Indies Press.

Regis, L. (1999) *The Political Calypso*, Gainesville, FL: University Press of Florida.

Rennie, B. (2002) *Exploding the Myths Pt 3 Coming under 'Bap'*, paper retrieved 20 May 2003 from www.trinicenter.com/BukkaRennie/2002/Nov/162002.html

Riggio, M. (ed.) (1998) 'Resistance and Identity: Carnival in Trinidad and Tobago', *The Drama Review: The Journal of Performance Studies*, *42*, 3: 6–23.

Smart, I. and Nehusi, K. (2000) *Ah Come Back Home: Perspective on the Trinidad and Tobago Carnival*, Washington, DC: Original World Press.

Some, M. (1998) *The Healing Wisdom of Africa*, New York: Tarcher/Putnam Books.

Winkleman, M. (2000) *Shamanism: The Neural Ecology of Consciousness and Healing*, Westport, CT: Bergin & Garvey Press.

Part IV

Dramatherapy and social theatre in practice

What we actually do

Introduction

This final section brings together the experiences of many skilled practitioners both in theatre and therapy and looks at the various ways in which people are touched by the process of theatre. We have a recurring theme of theatre for peace and the first chapter from Japan by Kyoko Okumoto (Chapter 16) considers a formal script 'Ho'o Pono Pono: Pax Pacifica' that was performed for peace, reconciliation and closure. The model has five phases: establish the facts, explore why it happened (emphasizing acts of commission and omission), sharing responsibilities, apologizing, constructing a future orientated programme, closing the conflict with symbolic burning of records. The author feels that people are moving forward, although as yet there is no complete solution to the conflicts in Asia.

John Somers (Chapter 17) looks at aspects of the therapeutic role of applied theatre. He uses and describes a methodology of 'interactive theatre' in which a specially trained theatre group explore the issue of teenage psychosis in a 17-year-old boy. He draws our attention to 'a morally implicated audience' and aims to bring about attitude change in particular audiences and client groups. He discusses how an interactive theatre programme is researched, developed, delivered and evaluated. He is the only author to place his methodology in relation to more intentional therapeutic uses of psychodrama and dramatherapy.

Joan Moore, dramatherapist (Chapter 18), describes her own practice through creating theatre performances with children who are being adopted. In a type of 'living life story' she creates an ambience for both child and parents where they can take part in a fictionalized narrative of the child's traumatic past. As she says, 'Encapsulating intensely personal experience dramatically, allows us to confront painful emotions in the process of discovering our prevailing inner strengths.' She emphasizes the importance of witnessing of the child's history, which removes the self-blame, and how parents and children can move forward to greater confidence and mutuality. By the use of fairy stories and fables, adapted to the child's particular circumstances, a certain distance is established that para-doxically can enable a child to encounter their own story.

Lilia Raileanu's chapter (Chapter 19) describes her social theatre work with lesbian, gay, bisexual and transsexual people (LGBT) in the Republic of Moldova. The participating group work with forum theatre, image theatre, autobiography and puppet theatre in order to create a safe environment for them to express themselves. Emphasis is placed on developing self-confidence and positive self-image. This leads to the development of non-violent dialogue with other members of the community, the promotion of human rights, and a mutual understanding. She describes how social theatre crosses interdisciplinary borders of other professionals and considers her own hypothesis for this diversity and empowerment.

Finally in this section, David Evans, Sandy Akerman and John Tripp (Chapter 20) describe the RAP (Respect and Protect) project that is concerned with sexual health of young people. Just as Hickson in Chapter 11 describes the increased incidence of bullying of young people, despite new laws and policies, the authors point out that the UK has the worst sexual health in Europe, the highest teenage conception rate and a soaring rate of sexually transmitted infections, despite increased public education. The project trained 'peer-educators' to work with scripted role plays with learners in pupil referral units, mother and baby units or similar institutions. The peer-educators were themselves from disrupted educational settings and they became apprenticed as professional theatre facilitators. The authors emphasize the point that because there were similarities in background between the peers and the learners, more could be achieved through role-modelling and identification.

This final section brings together the range of diversity in dramatherapy and social theatre. It does not answer the question of whether social theatre as a term is useful to describe the 'portmanteau' of methods discussed by Seymour in Part I (Chapter 2). Indeed it introduces yet more terms such as applied theatre, interactive theatre, theatre facilitators. And perhaps this is to be welcomed. Just as no generation has been able to pin down an exact definition of theatre, neither are we able to define an exact meaning for the myriad of theatre forms and practices from direct therapy through drama-therapy to community theatre for 'the common good'.

16 Using an art form for mutual understanding and reconciliation in East Asia

A drama project, 'Ho'o Pono Pono: Pax Pacifica'

Kyoko Okumoto

Introduction: TRANSCEND-Japan's drama project, 'Ho'o Pono Pono: Pax Pacifica'

In order to transform serious conflict in East (North-East) Asia, Dr Johan Galtung, the Director of the TRANSCEND International Network, has written a text titled 'Epilogue: Pax Pacifica in Yokohama Harbor', which I interpret as a recitation play.[1] In the play, conflict is treated as a mutual issue for everyone involved in the region, and it starts where all actors look into the past history, and then a place gradually develops where all members can dialogue. The concept of the play emerged from Galtung's challenge of a dialogue-based reconciliation role-playing session in a TRANSCEND workshop held in Yokohama in 2002. I explain briefly what it is about, and try to analyse it from my own perspective. Three of the members of TRANSCEND-Japan including myself translated the script into Japanese (another member worked on a Korean translation too) for future occasions of performances in Japan. The project is now called, 'Ho'o Pono Pono: Pax Pacifica' (peace for Asia-Pacific, or more specifically, for North-East Asia).[2]

Galtung's script is inspired by a Hawaiian community-based reconciliation ceremony called 'ho'o pono pono', a Polynesian word meaning 'setting right'. In Galtung's theory, reconciliation consists of both factors of closure and healing that ho'o pono pono may be most likely to achieve. 'Pax Pacifica in Yokohama Harbor' is written in the form of a recitation play in which 13 actors basically read out their lines, and the audience listens. The 'Wise Person' opens, directs and closes the whole process, and the other 12 actors, divided into four groups of three, follow in the drama. The first group of three people are from Japan: a Japanese politician, a Japanese zero bomber, and a Japanese *hibakusha* (atom bomb survivor) woman. The next three are a US politician, a US Hiroshima bomber, and a US Hawaiian. The third group is from the Korean peninsula: a Korean politician, a Korean 'comfort woman' (sexual slave for the Japanese military), and a Korean *zainichi* (Korean resident in Japan). The last group consists of a Chinese politician, a Chinese Nanjing victim, and a Chinese Taiwanese.

The drama starts with the first act where each person states what she/he experienced and thinks about what happened during the Pacific War (the Fifteen-Year War) and after. They all look back at the past, and describe the situation in the way they looked at it, their 'act of commission'. The second act brings another aspect where each person looks at the past and confesses what she/he did not do even if they could have, and apologizes for their 'act of omission'. The third act is when everybody looks forward to the future of the regional community. If all the characters desire to live in a peaceful world, then they need to commit themselves to something positive and creative. Thus comes the idea of an East Asian Community based on non-violence, empathy and creativity – the three pillars of the conflict transformation method.

'Ho'o Pono Pono: Pax Pacifica' has five phases:[3]

1   Establishing the facts, *what* happened in the community of nations.
2   Exploring *why* it happened, emphasizing acts of commission and omission.
3   Sharing responsibility, also for acts of omission, apologizing.
4   *A constructive, future-oriented programme*, based on (1), (2), (3).
5   Declaring the conflict closed, symbolic burning of records.

Galtung (2005, p. 76) explains, in order to reconcile, we need truth and confession, hopefully done in a public manner. I believe the drama theatre will enable us to create such an environment in numerous ways. By combining different forms of art into the drama, such as music, photography, painting, dance, poetry, and more, the script will be effective in giving people good opportunities at least to start thinking about the possibilities of mutual understanding, or if pursued further, reconciliation in the region. Therefore, I would like to suggest this project on the conflict transformation in East Asia will give chances for 'Ho'o pono pono: Pax Pacifica'. TRANSCEND-Japan has been exploring opportunities to use it in Japan to deepen understanding of the regional conflict, and also performed it as a show in public once in Vancouver, the other end of the Pacific, at the World Peace Forum. We have also started to expand the project in cooperation with Korean and Chinese friends. We expect to use the play in a series of workshops in different places in East Asia (we have done so outside Japan, at Jeju international conference in memory of the 3 April incident[4]), or we could ask a group of actors to actually perform it on stage. In this chapter, I explore the theoretical analysis of the drama based on our experiences in workshops and performance. In order to do so, first, let us prepare ourselves by grasping what the conflict in East Asia looks like.

The untransformed conflict in East Asia

Unfortunately, more than 60 years after the Second World War (the Pacific War or the Fifteen-Year War), Asia and the Pacific have failed to confront conflict sincerely. As for Japan, it has not done enough to compensate for its colonialist past and for what it did before and during those wars. The post-imperial government has not yet given its 'proper' apology to the 'invaded' and the 'victimized' parties. For example, people in China, Korea or other Asian countries still have deep hostility toward Imperial Japan and post-war Japan's attitude, often labelled as 'anti-Japan sentiments'. There are many reasons for the phenomena, but I do not pursue them here. It cannot be denied that the media are adding fuel to these issues to make the news look more shocking and scandalous, and it makes it appear that all people in China or in Korea hate Japan, which is not true. Obviously and unfortunately, the roots of the conflict have not been resolved, or transformed yet.

Let me explain one of the major factors of the conflict in the region. Justified by state Shintoism, Imperial Japan (particularly during 1931–45, but even before that period) practised an aggressive foreign policy and invaded other countries. One of the basic concepts that supported this foreign policy and that represents celebration at the Yasukuni Shrine and state Shintoism is called *kokutai*, which apparently glorifies the emperor system and patriotism altogether.[5] People in Japan before and after the wars are not innocent of the *kokutai* mentality either, and this has sustained the emperor system embedded in deep-culture, rarely being questioned or criticized before and during the wars, and as a result, even after the period, people and the government failed to clearly cut the war-related past out of their structure and culture. People in Japan have allowed a nationalist movement to grow, and this has enabled a widespread belief that Japan is superior to others.

This type of belief goes hand in hand with the tendency to ignore outside pressures to stop politicians' nationalist behaviours. Priority is not placed on other Asian countries; instead, because of the mutual cooperation and security treaty with the US, AMPO, since the 1960s (strictly speaking, right after the Second World War), the Japanese rely on the military umbrella of the US and thus feel a sense of 'security'. This, unfortunately, results in a somewhat arrogant attitude towards other Asian countries. This disproportionate point of view that lacks proper understanding of the neighbourhood should be changed because this way of viewing the world only isolates Japan from its neighbours. It is in the interests of the US to maintain this setup since it prevents Japan from joining the East Asian Community (EAC), now discussed at all levels, where economic, political and security issues will become the main concern of this group of nations, thereby excluding the participation of the US.[6]

When we discuss the conflict in East Asia, we need to see the whole picture. People, especially the media or the governments, tend to simplify things by picking on one segment of the big picture, such as the Yasukuni visit of the prime minister, one particular historical textbook, or territorial issues. In order to disentangle the conflict, we need to learn that there is a huge gap between Japan and other Asian countries regarding recognition of the past history, and this is a major factor of the 'anti-Japan sentiment'. The holistic picture of East Asia should be focused, and we should consider that all the issues are intertwined with one another as a big conflict in the region. Conflict should be transformed by peaceful means, not by violent means. Before it is too late, East Asia as a society needs to work on the conflict together with all its people, because people cannot live with each other while carrying on a conflict in the same society forever.

Is dialogue possible at all? An experimental experience at the World Peace Forum, June 2006

This drama project has much potential to create dialogue, challenging citizens to constantly think positively but critically. The TRANSCEND method emphasizes 'empathy' as an attitude, 'non-violence' as a way of behaviour, and 'creativity' as an approach to resolve contradictions. Listening to others and having dialogue are the basic elements for empathy and non-violence, and with creativity we can build 'peace-spaces' in our society. We expect that the drama itself can be a circuit or a tool for creating such 'peace-spaces'. The content of peace work is crucial, but the means, in this case, the drama form, an art form, are nonetheless as important as the content.

It was a tremendously interesting experience for the TRANSCEND-Japan members to give a workshop session at the World Peace Forum (WPF) in Vancouver, Canada, on 25 June 2006.[7] The session lasted three hours, and was titled 'Ho'o pono pono: Pax Pacifica'. We made use of the recitation drama as an introduction to the issues of East Asia of today to think about the roots of the big conflict. Three of us performed the first act of the recitation, and asked some of the participants to read lines for the second and third acts, and had a dialogue session involving all people in the venue.

During the dialogue session, some participants showed their great appreciation, while some showed honest resistance to the performance. Most of the resistance came from the fact that we, the presenters, are from a country of the former perpetrators. Japan cannot even suggest that all the actors should apologize in the second act, they said. Some of them felt as if the actors were forced to apologize, and found the idea unacceptable. This was understandable, and we appreciated their sincere honesty. To recognize one's own 'act of omission' is far more difficult and painful than the 'act of commission'. In order to do this, we need to expose ourselves at a deeper level and to a greater extent whether we like it or not. At the same time, we have to have a deep insight into the idea of an 'act of omission', which is to realize that we did not do enough to prevent the violence in the past. It is comparatively easy to consider this from the perpetrators' point of view, and is hard to grasp for the 'victims', but it is still necessary for better mutual understanding. Dialogue is most important in order for participants of the drama workshops to be able to expose themselves in a secure environment, and we need to create trust and friendship among everyone. That is again, I must insist, a major part of the whole process of the drama project. To address the audience's resistance, there is further analysis in the next section.

Transcending dichotomized concepts

The resistance was based on dichotomized concepts. 'Bad people' are responsible for war violence, and 'innocent ones' are 'good ones' and have no responsibility at all. Dualistic ways of thinking are very easy and sometimes quite comfortable because you can avoid critical thinking. You have the ultimate answer to the question by judgement. Although empathetically I understood the reaction, the participants who showed resistance judged Japan as a former perpetrator and as a lazy nation-state that does not work for a proper apology, and did not allow any space to discuss it.[8]

However, I dare to question; is Japan a perpetrator and nothing else? It is easy and simple to categorize oneself as a 'perpetrator'. Saburo Ienaga (1985) points out that there are various different types of people who are responsible for the war crimes, including the establishment at the time, the military who worked for them, the media, artists, and even ordinary citizens.[9] Ienaga himself fought against his own 'crime of omission', which he believed he had committed. Not only within 'perpetrators' is the variation of quality and quantity, but also within Japan as a 'perpetrator' there were 'victims'. Needless to mention Hiroshima and Nagasaki, Japan was not only a perpetrator, but at the same time, it was a victim of the Pacific War. People in the Okinawa islands were victims not only of the US, the then 'enemies', but of the Japanese military as well. Also, uncountable citizens were victims of the *kokutai* mentality, being brainwashed that the emperor was a god and Japan was established under him.

It is unfair to mention only the victimhood on Japan's side. Obviously, there were other people outside and inside Japanese islands who suffered even more, including 'non-Japanese' victims of Imperial Japan, and even Japanese descendants outside the islands. However, when it comes to 'victims', do we not tend to unconditionally decide that 'victims' are not to be blamed at all? They can be labelled as 'innocent' people and are not to be questioned about their responsibility. The concept of Hawaiian ho'o pono pono questions this dichotomy, and the idea is used also by Galtung in the play. We need to look closely into the side of 'victims' more carefully because we tend to avoid it as it is such a delicate and emotional work. We need to discuss what the responsibility of the 'victims' was, if there is any. Even so-called 'victims' have some responsibility, maybe indirectly, for what they have not done.

Theoretically, there is no perfect 'victim'. There is neither 100 per cent victim, nor 100 per cent victor. However, it is extremely difficult for me to say so, only because I am Japanese, who is a descendant of the 'perpetrators'. It is painful for me to point this out as a person who lives in Japan and has a Japanese passport, and whose ancestors are as far as I know 'Japanese'. The idea discussed here can be easily abused by political intensions; 'You see, we are not the only bad ones. They had the reasons to be invaded!' To transcend dichotomized concepts is not to justify violence caused by Imperial Japan's colonial invasion or any kind of violence at all. One important thing we must not forget here is always to keep us humble enough to regret what happened in the past.

How can we overcome such dualistic and simplistic ideas that Koreans and Chinese were/are the victims and Japanese were/are the perpetrators? Do we continue to treat the question as a taboo, or can we ever detach or liberate ourselves from such narrow ideas? In 'Pax Pacifica', all the characters have their own lines, and show their own point of view. Ryunosuke Akutagawa's famous short story, 'Yabu no Naka' (1975), gives us interesting aspects.[10] Literally, the truth is 'in the bush', because depending on who speaks about the event, the fact shows another different face. It can be said that all are truths. Based on this concept, we also can say the same thing about the Pacific War or the Fifteen-Year War. There are as many facts as people who experienced it, and even as people who did not exist at the time.

Difficulties of presenting 'voices' and the potential in drama as an art form

Another important and possibly controversial factor of the play is that the 12 characters can be read as stereotypical representations. How can we illustrate diverse elements of a human being? If the words and lines of the characters only indicate their limited humanity, how can we transcend them? What does the number of characters (excluding the 'Wise Person'), 12, indicate in this play? Does it exclude other possible actors/parties involved, and will it eventually help to simplify the conflict, or, on the other hand, does it try to include other possibilities as well? What is the art of drama to begin with? Drama is an art of fiction where actors represent others trying to understand what they feel and think. A director conducts the whole scenario, and helps actors represent their characters. The sophisticated art of drama is neither to stereotype characters nor to give answers to the audience, but to elicit empathy for the characters.

Gayatri Chakravorty Spivak (1988) cautions that the portrayal of oppressed people can render them even more voiceless. Would our drama project manage to avoid this to happen? We must find a way to escape this vicious circle of using and abusing the voiceless, which leads to silencing them. We must continuously criticize ourselves and not put them in the position where they are even less understood. We must clarify who we are, for whom we are trying to work, how we do it, and what we want from it. Especially when we try to 'represent' the voiceless people in the play, we need to realize that we have the voice, and this fact may lead us to oppress the voiceless even though we want equality or solidarity with them. Again as Akutagawa's another famous short story, 'Rashomon' (1975), shows, human thoughts and emotions change all the time even in one person, it is impossible to 'summarize' one's standpoint, and one's ideas and being cannot be 'represented' easily. If we do not discuss these contradictions in depth, and even if we would like to have dialogue with all the characters/ parties, the project will fail.

Therefore, I believe we need to recognize that representing the politically oppressed is almost impossible. Nevertheless, a fact that we are faced with is that the conflict situation might turn into a violent outbreak, so we should not give up easily. What can help us transcend this complicated situation? Regarding the current disharmonized East Asia every day, what can be done to change this situation for the better and eventually to discover the root of the conflict clearly and then transform this conflict by peaceful means? In order to truly understand what happened, what people failed to do, and what they want for their future, a traditional history textbook is not sufficient. It might become much easier if we use some kind of tools such as music, dance, literature, or drama, since they may create a starting engine for our purpose of the project, and may speak to all people of different generations in different areas. Moreover, fortunately, art forms bring participants a lot of fun, leading, it is hoped, toward the positive attitude of dialogue. Art can be an instrument to reveal voices of people, and helps to bind people. For mutual understanding, healing and closure, we need to at least humbly try to hear as many 'voices' as possible, the voices of people in different times and different positions, while we try to be careful with the contradictions mentioned in the paragraph above.

Our drama project, 'Ho'o pono pono: Pax Pacifica', is an alternative way to start dialogue among people in the region. In the WPF workshop, we have asked participants to select the characters that they cannot empathize with and to read their lines. The purpose of this was at least to break through the walls you are stuck with. The drama form gives us time and space for dialogue, not debate. As explained earlier, the drama represents the bigger picture of the conflict in the region. It sheds light on many different conflicts altogether at once. This form of art is very effective because we can challenge anything with art/fiction, as in creativity we are freed from time and space. This brings all the actors onto the same stage at the same time, and enables the audience and actors to understand each other. It is hoped they stop blaming, and start using empathy, non-violence and creativity.

Conclusion: The drama theatre, a 'peace-space'

It is necessary to overcome the ingrained habits of dichotomizing conflicts, stereotyping parties involved, and silencing the voiceless. Creating 'peace-spaces' or 'theatre' opens up the possibility for new phase of dialogue. This art form transcends time and space, encouraging workshop participants or theatre-goers to actively search for dialogue rather than debating to decide the winners and losers. While some may find 'Ho'o Pono Pono: Pax Pacifica' too optimistic and utopian, it is clear that the people who attend the workshops are either mildly interested or highly motivated to work towards finding viable and peaceful means of reconciliation. It is encouraging to see such interest, and their concern helps us to work together even harder.

I still have a lot of questions; to what extent and what kind of responsibility do people who were not involved with the violence have? Did baby victims have a responsibility for being killed at war? Am I who was not born then responsible for what happened before and during the war, and after? I believe I still have indirect responsibility for what my ancestors committed. Do I have to apologize, for whom, and to whom? In addition, how and when can we judge the apology is enough, and the sincerity behind it exists? Is there any way to measure this?

Peace is an ability to transform a conflict as Galtung defines it, and I would add that peace also means a space and time for dialogue. In order to achieve reconciliation in the region, we need to work by peaceful means. There is no ultimate cure, and we need to combine various different creative ideas, but the times are perilous and we cannot afford the luxury of cynicism. We need the vision to pursue this work, otherwise nothing will change. By pursuing the drama project and cherishing its process, I would like to have deep dialogues with people who are, at whatever level, involved with the issue. People who co-exist in the same region need to challenge together, and as there are so many unresolved conflicts, big and small, all over the world, world citizens simply need to work together in the same world community. From such a perspective, we eventually extend actors who appear in the script. Although currently the actors are limited to people in Japan, China, Korea and the US, we understand it as just a mere beginning.[11]

Notes

1 The drama script discussed in this chapter is included as an Epilogue to Galtung's book (2005, pp. 129–42). For more on Johan Galtung and the TRANSCEND International Network, please see www.transcend.org.
2 Refer to *Toransendo Kenkyu* [*Transcend Studies*], 2005, *3*, 1, edited by TRANSCEND-Japan, for the Japanese version, and 2006, *3*, 2 for the Korean version. For TRANSCEND-Japan, please visit www.transcendjapan.org.
3 Edited by Kyoko Okumoto (originally from Galtung's *Pax Pacifica*, 2005, pp. 129–30).
4 TRANSCEND-Japan, 'How Should We Transcend the Framework of Perpetratorhood and Victimhood: For Reconciliation and Peace Creation in East Asia', in the session titled 'Traumas and Reconciliation' at the International Conference Commemorating the 60th anniversary of the Jeju April Third

Uprising: Reconciliation Beyond Memory, 5 April 2008, hosted and organized by the Jeju 4/3 Research Institute.

5 See www.yasukuni.or.jp for more information announced by the Yasukuni Shrine itself, but be aware that they only focus on their propaganda and do not show their 'problems'.

6 However, we must discuss carefully how to establish the East Asia Community through peaceful means for peaceful purposes. The third act of the drama script illustrates an ideal EAC from a TRANSCEND point of view.

7 Kyoko Okumoto, Katsuhiko Nakano and Akifumi Fujita from TRANSCEND-Japan participated in the World Peace Forum in Vancouver and gave a 3-hour workshop session on 25 June at the University of British Columbia. The title of the session was 'Ho'o Pono Pono: Pax Pacifica' and it was categorized as 'Workshop B: Reconciliation and Peace in North-Eastern Asia' by the WPF organization, as part of the Asia Regional Conference.

8 Of course, nobody can deny that Imperial Japan was the 'perpetrator' in the Korean peninsula and other Asian regions. Current Japan with its past as Imperial Japan has failed to reconcile with the others, and still is burdened with its crimes. Since I believe that it is arrogant of Japan to say to its neighbours, 'Let's reconcile!', Japan as a country and the people of Japan should first regret what they have done and humbly apologize with all their heart, then the victims will probably generously say, 'OK, I forgive you'. I hear my Korean and Chinese friends say many times that they are ready to forgive.

9 While he was alive and active, Saburo Ienaga repeatedly emphasized the importance of recognizing 'the unintended crime' or 'crime of omission' and of doing something about it (e.g. see Ienaga 1985). As a person who lived before and during the Pacific War, he admits that he overlooked what was going on at the time, without having recognized that this would have led to something violent towards others. He even condemns himself as a 'war criminal in a negative sense', who failed to work responsibly to prevent war. He blames himself and promises that he would not repeat the same crime, and would challenge with a brave spirit, which he believes is the responsibility of citizens. My feelings echo his ideas, and I imagine that if I do nothing to prevent future wars in our time right now at the beginning of the twenty-first century – in other words, if I do not work hard to do my best to create peace in this society I live in now – I will eventually come to regret what I have not done, my 'act of omission', when things get worse regarding violence of any sort.

10 Akira Kurosawa's famous film, *Rashomon* (1950), has its origins in Akutagawa's 'Yabu no Naka' (1975) and not 'Rashomon'.

11 Please contact the author at okumoto@wilmina.ac.jp for more information about this drama project. Most of the information and articles are written in Japanese, but still the ideas of the project should be shared with anyone in any region of the world. Perhaps it is possible to apply the method to any conflict and try a similar project for reconciliation in the region concerned.

References

Akutagawa, Ryunosuke (1975) 'Rashomon', in *Gendai Nihon no Meisaku* [*Modern Japan Masterpieces*], *19*, pp. 3–16, Tokyo: Obunsha. (Original work published 1915)

Akutagawa, Ryunosuke (1975) 'Yabu no Naka', in *Gendai Nihon no Meisaku* [*Modern Japan Masterpieces*], *19*, pp. 217–34, Tokyo: Obunsha. (Original work published 1915)

Galtung, Johan (2005) *Pax Pacifica: Terrorism, the Pacific Hemisphere, Globalisation and Peace Studies*, London: Pluto Press.

Ienaga, Saburo (1985) *Senso Sekinin* [*War Responsibility*], Tokyo: Iwanami Shoten.

Spivak, Gayatri Chakravorty (1988) 'Can the Subaltern Speak?', in Cary Nelson and Lawrence Grossberg (eds), *Marxism and the Interpretation of Culture*, pp. 271–313, Urbana: University of Illinois Press.

17 Drama and well-being

Narrative theory and the use of interactive theatre in raising mental health awareness

John Somers

Introduction

I deal first with a number of theoretical, dramaturgical and practical issues that impinge on the kind of practice I am discussing in this chapter. I hope that this section will inform the reader of the philosophical context in which the work is set. I then show, through an interactive theatre case study, how this is applied in practice.

Drama's therapeutic role

Some claim that all dramatic experience is therapeutic. It is axiomatic that workshop leaders, teachers and educational and community theatre companies generally expect that some change for the better will take place as a result of their work. At the very least, there is an expectation of 'doing good'. More specifically, certain drama activities aim at achieving potentially complex psychological and emotional shifts – the work of dramatherapists and psychodramatists, for example. We can show the therapeutic scale of drama in the following continuum:

Psychodrama

Dramatherapy ——————————————— Performance Theatre

On the left there is explicit therapeutic intent. Theatre on the right of this continuum exists variously as entertainment, mental chewing gum, polemic, propaganda, as a mouthpiece for dominant stories and as an alternative, counter story.

The area in between, especially on the left of the continuum, is inhabited by a great range of drama activity that has explicit or implicit aims to change. Many of these changes could be seen as therapeutic. One such area is applied drama in which I am involved.

Applied drama

Applied drama can be defined simply as 'The use of dramatic activity to achieve, often premeditated, change in a given societal circumstance'. Applied drama, therefore, is developed with a particular aim in mind – it has a job to do. I use the term 'applied drama' rather than 'applied theatre' as, although the case study discussed in this chapter plainly uses theatre elements, much of my other work is not performance based. Thus the more generic term 'drama' avoids its unwarranted association (particularly in the lay mind) with theatre spaces and performance. The parallel in another art form would be the generic term 'dance' rather than using any of the multiple sub-sections of that art form.

Applied drama requires practitioners who are skilled in drama and theatre, and who have relevant knowledge, skills and awareness in areas such as psychology, pedagogy and sociology.

The working process can be typified as follows:

- Research into the context in which the drama intervention will take place;
- An understanding of the humans who inhabit it;
- The definition of aims;
- The construction of a dramatic experience that is structured to provide optimum conditions for participant change;
- The delivery of that experience;
- Evaluation of the outcomes to judge the effectiveness of the intervention.

All of this may be – and often is – created with and by the target group. Applied drama has the maximum potential for therapeutic affect, as it is custom-made for each individual set of circumstances and constitutes a collaboration between facilitator and participants, director and actors, children and teachers.

Narrative theory

Our world and our sense of our place in it are only accessible through story. We live in the instant and anything that has passed, or is in the future, can only be represented through story. We are surrounded by stories. Large proportions of education use story as the vehicle for learning – most obviously in literature and drama, but also, for example, in history (which, by definition deals with that which has passed) and geography (to inform us of the places and cultures that, even in our modern, mobile society, we may never visit). To be denied story is to deny ourselves a past or a future, the ability to reflect or surmise. The distancing effect of story gives us a perspective on events as we model them outside the immediacy of their happening. The plight of the Alzheimer's sufferer gives us an example of the limitations of not being able to access stories.

Specificity

Effective drama is always specific in the circumstances it portrays. It thrives on the detail of human circumstance and this helps participants identify with the people and their issues. It is difficult to gain any proper engagement with an issue if it is only subject to generalities. If we are asked, for example, 'What do you think or feel about hunger?' the response might be 'It depends. Are the people involved so hungry and without support that they are in danger of dying – through crop failure, for instance in an isolated area of the globe without social services, or did they simply miss lunch because of an oversight, and will eat heartily that evening?' Drama allows us to create that human and contextual detail, to avoid generalisations, and this is the secret of its ability to engage people.

Validation

One of the crucial roles for applied drama work is to create a sense of validation of people's experiences. Many people who have defective well-being are embarrassed at their condition and do not wish to share the issues they are experiencing with those they feel may not understand. There can be something quite positive in witnessing the story created by a group of drama workers who have taken the trouble to capture aspects of a life circumstance of audience members. For this to be effective, the latter need to feel that the storyline and the characters within it reflect the verities of their own experience.

Morally implicated audience

Most European theatre still takes place in a darkened auditorium with an illuminated stage. This suggests a strict demarcation between performers and audience, with the latter usually expected not to speak or interact openly with the stage action. The rituals associated with this form of theatre are well understood and usually adhered to. The nature of interactive theatre is different in that it expects and supports audience members' engagement with the story and its characters. Consequently, the distinction between the audience and performance spaces intentionally is blurred and is not demarcated by light or physical barriers. The audience often will come to the performance with a prior knowledge of aspects of the story and some of its characters, together with hypotheses about what is going on in their lives. This technique involves the use of personal and official artefacts and written documents that orientate audience members to the story through hypotheses that are generated by two questions: 'Who are the people in this story?' and 'What's happening to them?' I term this resource a 'compound stimulus'.

Authenticity

The representation will fail in its objectives if it is judged by its target audience as unauthentic. The interactive theatre programme 'The Living at Hurford' dealt with the struggle of small family farms to stay in business following the foot and mouth disease outbreak in the UK in 2002. Written by me, it was performed by community actors in a barn on a farm that had experienced the disease. When a farmer came up to me immediately after the programme ended, poked me in the chest and said 'I don't know what you know about farming boy, but how you wrote it is how it is,' I felt that the long period of research, which included talking with farmers, had produced something that he felt represented his world. Another said after another performance 'That's my life you put up there tonight.' Unless the target audience feels that the story captures its lived reality, the power of the medium to engender change and establish validation will be weakened.

Attitude change

Research shows that applied drama and theatre involvement is one of the most effective ways of altering attitudes and behaviour (Fox 1997, p. 27). A meta-analysis of existing, published research by James Catterall (2002), for example, found that: 'Drama helps with understanding social relationships, complex issues and emotions; improves concentrated thought and story comprehension.'

Research I did in the 1980s based in 35 schools across the UK showed that students positively changed their attitudes to disability as a result of experiencing a series of structured drama lessons (see Somers 1996). I believe that the ability of dramatic experiences to achieve this is based in its provision of authentic fictions, rooted in the detail of human circumstance.

Targeting

Unlike the usual theatre experience in which there is generally no way of ensuring the homogeneity of audience members, applied drama practitioners usually know the composition of the target audience/workshop participants. This enables its practitioners to create a dramatic experience that is most likely to engage those involved. This does not preclude variety within the target participants; in a recent project on stress in the veterinary profession, for example, audience members included student vets from each of the five study years, veterinary surgeon researchers, practising and retired vets, counsellors, therapists and those engaged in the governance of the profession. What they all shared was a knowledge – or in the case of the students, a growing awareness – of the profession and the stresses it may generate in its members.

Intertextuality

Drama's power to change attitudes is rooted in the notion of intertextuality, the dynamic relationship of stories. In this case it is the interpenetration of the performed story with the story that forms the personal identity of the individual. David Novitz (1997) posits that we create the story of our self-identity through a constant process of selection and editing of the events that occur in our lives. Significant events and stories have the ability to create modifications to our perceived identity. A dramatic experience can do this too, but only if it connects strongly with 'who we are'. Although I hold that this can be achieved in workshop conditions, in the space left to me in this chapter, I have chosen to focus on interactive theatre.

How is an interactive theatre programme researched, developed, delivered and evaluated?

To achieve an authentic performed story that is significant for the target audience, it is necessary for those making it to understand as fully as possible the issues involved. A period of research on the topic, plus experimentation with the dramatic form that will carry the story, are essential. It is crucial that those working on the programme have ready access to individuals who have expert knowledge of the topic – through experience and/or training. This advisory group can ensure that what is being created possesses the necessary qualities of authenticity.

The programme[1] can be developed from a script that has been created through research, or through a devising process. The latter can be open and free, but given time constraints and the need to set some productive limitations, I usually provide a 'spine' comprising a scenario, snatches of dialogue and an overall feel of the dramatic form. Whatever the development process, it is essential that the actors are deeply involved in researching the topic. Typically, I start my rehearsal/development process with two or three weeks of pooling the outcomes of research undertaken by the actors. In this way they come to understand and gain ownership of the project.

The first stage of the programme's delivery often involves the orientation of the audience to the issues and story through the use of a device I call a 'compound stimulus'. Simply, this is 'compound' in that it comprises several items, and a 'stimulus' in that it encourages story making. Much of this work involves an intimacy that can only properly be achieved by limiting the audience to around 40 in number. This optimises the opportunities for audience members to become involved in the storyline, the characters and the issues affecting them. It also makes all of the interactive work manageable. Unlike the well-made play, in which the audience meets the characters, identifies or 'feels' the problem, sees the characters wrestling with the problem before a dénouement, interactive theatre often stops its performed story at the crisis point. A facilitator[2] then intervenes and invites audience members to understand better the problems the characters are experiencing, and to suggest ways in which they can move the story on in productive ways. I now describe one project of this nature.

'On the edge'

The 'job' here for applied drama was threefold. To:

1   raise awareness of mental illness and specifically to increase knowledge and understanding of psychosis;
2   contribute towards reducing the stigma and discrimination surrounding mental illness;
3   raise awareness of available help and improve help-seeking behaviour.

The preparatory research was conducted over a period of 6-months and involved the guidance of a highly committed advisory group, comprising those with personal experience of mental health issues, mental health professionals, an arts therapist and representatives of mental health charities and carers. This group also advised on the whole development process and attended and fed back on early performances. The programme was developed by Year 3 undergraduate students in the Department of Drama, University of Exeter during the first semester of the 2003/04 academic year as part of a module on Applied Drama. This group toured the programme to post-16 audiences in schools, colleges and universities and to conferences for mental health professionals. Subsequently the programme was taken on by *Exstream*, the theatre company of which I am Artistic Director. The project received funding of £148,000 from The Wellcome Trust and other funders and was toured nationally.[3] It won the Southern Region Department of Health Award for innovative practice and the National Institute of Mental Health England, National Positive Practice Award. A full and independent research report was produced on this programme's effectiveness in meeting its aims.

Prior to the start of the module and during the final stages of my pre-module meetings with the advisory group, I wrote a scenario and suggested scene structure, together with extracts of dialogue. This was discussed with the advisory group and, after modifications, was deemed authentic. This formed the starting point for the students to begin the devising process to develop the complete performance element. Group members divided all of the other tasks between them, including preparation of the compound stimulus, data projected visual images, sound effects, music, publicity and the follow-up pack.

The storyline

The compound stimulus contained 14 items. It was enclosed in a shoe box. Those working with the post-16 group had been asked to explore the content and meaning of the box in the week before *Exstream* visited.

Items included: a letter from a school expressing disappointment at Terry Gardner's falling work standards in his AS Level studies; a photograph of a middle-teens girl, another of an older woman, and a third of a mid-teens boy with a male friend; a sports trophy for a regional event with an engraved dedication plate to Terry Gardner, a birthday card to Terry from his grandmother; a bottle of TCP[4] and cotton wool; a letter from British Olympic sprinter, Darren Campbell's agent urging Terry to keep up his training routine; a personal note from a girl; a congratulations card from 'Mum and Dad' to Terry to celebrate his good GCSE examination results at 16.

As outlined above, the compound stimulus was used by the teacher/ lecturer in the week before *Exstream* visited. Before using it, the teacher announced that the box was part of a fictional story that would be performed by the theatre company next week. Participants were told that it was found under a boy's bed. Each object was extracted in turn by individual participants and its significance explored in relation to the other artefacts. This process was scheduled to last 30 minutes and at its end, the participants gained an incomplete but intriguing insight into the lives of the characters.

The performance element ran for 50 minutes.[5] It traced the progress of Terry Gardner from being a happy boy, successful both academically and in his athletics, to the point where he experiences a first episode of psychosis. The contents of the compound stimulus were embedded in the performance element and the shoe box could be seen under his bed.

Briefly, the factors at play were his father's coaching of Terry's athletic abilities and his refusal to acknowledge that Terry had a problem; Terry's gradual slipping into a psychotic state (the TCP, which his grandmother, recently dead, used to dab on his grazes, has become a magic liquid for Terry, who anoints himself with it); Terry's mother's inability to tend to her son properly because of not wishing to alienate her husband; Terry's schoolmates' denigration of him – they use terms such as 'psycho' and 'nutter' to describe his increasingly erratic behaviour; the growing bewilderment of his loyal girlfriend, Sonia, who has the greatest insight into Terry's changing state and the motivation to help Terry, but does not know how to; the inability of the school to understand what was happening to Terry; Terry's phone calls to his dead grandmother.

The performance element ended at a crisis point when Terry is seeing bacteria inhabiting his bedroom, thinks the picture of Darren Campbell is glowing and pulsating and, in an attempt to protect her, shouts at and bundles Sonia out of his bedroom. She meets Terry's mother on the landing and they hold each other as his mother finally faces up to the problem.

The facilitator (for the 6-month tour, this role was taken by a psychiatric nurse who was seconded by the Devon Partnership NHS Trust) stepped in and asked audience members to discuss with their neighbour what they thought was going on with Terry and those around him. They were then invited to select characters to whom they wanted to talk (hotseat) in order to understand better the chosen characters' feelings and motivations. What followed differed depending on the audience group. Sometimes audience members split into groups to work with an actor to discuss one of the character's responses within the story. At other times, audiences were asked to decide on a scene that would move the story on positively and that the actors played out. Most often, audience members were invited to give advice to the characters on how they could improve the situation.

To provide some kind of closure, in the last 10 minutes of the 2-hour period, the facilitator presented, with slides, the possible routes to recovery that Terry might take. Each venue was given a sophisticated follow-up pack, 'Back From the Edge', which could be used at varying levels of time commitment and complexity to follow up and deepen the audience's understanding.[6] The person who had booked the programme contracted to use the follow-up pack in the week following *Exstream*'s visit. Early Intervention (EI) workers[7] were informed of the performances and it was expected that their attendance would create enduring links between them and the personnel at each venue.

The research/evaluation[8]

I believe it necessary to evaluate programmes' outcomes in relation to their aims. Such an evaluation can be as simple as a post-programme questionnaire, or involve much more complex qualitative and quantitative research tools. 'On the Edge' was subject to the latter, including a 6-month follow-up interview with selected participants.

Key findings[9]

1 The data showed increased student awareness and knowledge of psychosis following completion of the programme. Students, teachers and mental health professionals regarded the subject as important and almost all respondents believed that the programme effectively raised awareness of psychosis.
2 The programme challenges stigma in a variety of different ways.
3 Students appear to be better equipped to seek help after participating in the programme.
4 *On the Edge* is perceived as a high-quality Interactive Theatre programme by many students, teachers and mental health professionals. The major strengths of the programme are its realism, its capacity to

involve the audience and the sense of safety that it gives to exploring mental ill health issues.

5 The programme deals briefly with the complex and controversial issues surrounding street drugs and understanding the psychotic experience. The small amount of feedback commenting on these two issues suggested that the overall educational message is clear and focused.

6 The programme format of the shoe box and the 2-hour session worked well because it encouraged participants to become involved in the characters' lives and because it presented the information in ways that accommodated different learning styles. The play was regarded as the most memorable part of the programme and received substantial support as an interesting and powerful way of portraying the issues.

7 Not all schools found time for the third part of the programme despite 'contracting in' to provide this educational support.

8 The education pack 'Back from the Edge' had a mixed reception; some teachers were enthusiastic while others felt that the information was not easy to access. Lack of available time to read and reflect on the materials contributed to this reaction.

Conclusion

This was a complex project that set itself ambitious goals. The research outcomes show that many of these were achieved and there is strong evidence that this interactive theatre programme is an effective way of dealing with a very sensitive topic. During the tour, 12 audience members presented themselves to the psychiatric nurse or to the local EI workers to seek help. It is likely that many other consultations took place subsequent to the company's visits, facilitated by information provided to each audience member at the end of the 2-hour visit.

I claim that applied drama of this nature is an essential element in supporting well-being, especially through its ability to deliver powerful and authentic portrayals of issues that are difficult to root in discussion that directly uses participants' experience as illustrative material.

Notes

1 I use the term 'programme' because the terms 'production', 'play', performance or 'show' do not adequately capture the range of theatrical, artistic, sociological and pedagogic structures that such work entails. I refer to the performed story (just one of the elements) as 'the performance element'.

2 A facilitator acts as a bridge between the audience and the story. They can signal and support ways in which audience members interact with the characters.

3 The company undertook a national tour between October 2004 and March 2005, performing to 123 audiences, of which 79 were in 54 schools, colleges and universities where the target audience age was between 14 and 22. Forty-four were performances for teachers and mental health professionals where the programme

was used as a part of continuing professional development (CPD) and or as a conference presentation to support the new Early Intervention (EI) in Psychosis services that were being introduced in England at the time.

4 TCP is an antiseptic lotion commonly used in households for minor wounds.

5 Excluding the compound stimulus and the follow-up, the whole programme required 2 hours.

6 This was prepared by Dr Glenn Roberts, the consultant psychiatrist who assisted with the development of the programme. The pack was subsequently adopted by the National Institute for Mental Health in England (NIMHE) for national use.

7 EI workers have been appointed across England. Swedish research shows that the sooner intervention takes place, the more rapid the recovery of the patient.

8 The research used both quantitative and qualitative methods:
- Pre- and post-performance questionnaires for students at schools, colleges and universities (from 29 institutions; not all completed both parts of this research).
- Evaluation forms from those attending non-student performances ($N = 474$).
- Interviews with students, teachers and those attending non-student performances (72 interviews with 133 students, teachers and mental health professionals).
- Cast research diaries that recorded the number and gender balance of people in the audience, the type of questions asked in the hotseating, and any striking or unusual occurrences during the 2-hour session.

9 The key findings have been extracted in abbreviated form from the Executive Summary contained in the final evaluation report produced by Dr Rowena Passy (principal researcher and author) and Dr Jos Dawe. The full report is available from the author.

References

Catterall, J. (2002) *Critical Links: Learning in the Arts and Student Academic and Social Development*, Washington, DC: Arts Education Partnership.

Fox, Kate (1997) *Taskforce on Underage Alcohol Misuse*, London: The Portman Group.

Novitz, D. (1997) 'Art, Narrative and Human Nature', in L. Hinchman and S. Hinchman (eds), *Memory, Identity, Community*, New York: State University of New York.

Somers, J. (1996) 'The Nature of Learning in Drama in Education', in J Somers (ed.), *Drama and Theatre in Education: Contemporary Research*, pp. 107–20, North York, Canada: Captus Press.

18 'The Theatre of Attachment'™

Dramatherapy with adoptive and foster families

Joan Moore

All the world's a stage and all the men and women merely players.
(*As you like it*, Shakespeare, 1599)

This chapter considers the dramatic components of dramatherapy in work with adoptive and long-term foster families, whose children suffered extensive neglect and abuse in their family of origin. Blaming themselves for past rejection, they repeat patterns of interaction from their early years, when they learned to withdraw or become excessively demanding to ensure survival. This dramatherapeutic approach addresses specific attachment needs through sensory experience that invites children to explore new ways of being.

By incorporating embodiment play, projective materials and role, dramatherapy can be viewed as a holistic intervention to meet children's developmental needs. Sensory materials (cloth, clay, etc.) assist participants to experience through the body, material that may otherwise be blocked by the higher 'thinking' cortex. In this 'theatre of attachment' model, parents and children are seen together. Early mother–infant interactions are replicated using the 'mirror' of the interactive audience. Parents take part in plays devised from the child's history while children show their participating 'audience' how life was for them. This shared emotional experience brings about improved mutuality.

Throughout history, theatre has projected issues of attachment and identity that illustrate the universality of emotion as the essence of humanity. Themes such as trickery and betrayal, abandonment, chaos and destruction, power, identity and confusion, prevalent in the children's stories mirror those arising in Greek tragedies, legends, folk tales and particularly, in Shakespeare's plays. Consider Iago's jealous rage toward his rival in *Othello*; Lear's desperation for his daughters to prove their affection for him; Juliet's choosing to confide in her Nurse rather than mother, yet betrayed by both; and Rosalind's thrill in disguising herself as a male, exploring new freedom on her escape to the Forest of Arden.

Plays require performance, definitions of which incorporate varying views as to whether performance is a process or the result of a process. For instance, Goffman (1959) defines it as an activity that serves to influence others, while Schechner (2006, p. 12) describes performance of art, rituals or ordinary life as 'restored behaviours', that are reflexive and symbolic, for which people train and rehearse, thus can be repeated and transformed in order that:

> 'meaning emerges through 'reliving' the original experience and given appropriate aesthetic form so the individual understands better not only themselves but the time and cultural conditions that compose their general experience of reality'.
>
> (Schechner 2006, p. 18)

Here, play is *performance* when carried out publicly, *performative* when it is more private (Schechner 2006, p. 92). When we enact one another's social dramas, through awareness of original settings, we gain new perspectives. Since, in life history work, we benefit from the presence of others to assist our understanding I am drawn to Turner's etymology of the word 'performance', from the old French, 'parfournir' meaning 'the proper finale of an experience' (Turner, 1982, p. 13) and not to do with 'form'. This interpretation permits 'performance' to be more private, valuable for participants confronting intense pain and shame in the process of discovering their true strengths.

Value and purpose of life story work using drama

Most of us take for granted hearing stories from our childhoods. Yet, for many in foster and adoptive care, such stories have been lost. These children need to understand why they were taken from their family of origin and require their substitute parents to understand and validate their experience. Siegel (1999) described the brain as an 'anticipation machine'. In dramatic play, we rehearse for the future. Practice improves movement, speech, and confidence. Resolution of anticipated problems is planned. Dramatising the 'monster' or 'witch' that represents abuse enables mastery over frightening and inhibiting experiences. With support, children explore a variety of ways, including magic, to destroy or banish 'monsters' or 'witches', such as slaying them with (pretend) weapons, ripping a painting of the 'monster' or bashing its mask until it has no further power to intrude. For traumatised children who inevitably find trust exceptionally difficult, play is the natural way to facilitate communication. Therefore inclusion of adoptive parents in the process helps them develop bonds with their children.

Children need help to find a balance between the extreme manifestations of attachment behaviours described by Howe (2005) and Crittendon and Claussen (2003). Through the senses, we bypass the 'blocking' mechanisms of the higher 'reasoning' cortex, directly accessing the emotional centre of the brain where pre-verbal (implicit) memory is stored. 'Avoidant' children are encouraged to explore expanded horizons, learn alternative responses so as to relate to others' feelings. 'Ambivalent' children may address anxieties concerning separation and reunion. Moreno, the father of psychodrama, famously advised 'Roles don't emerge from the self, but the self may emerge from role' (Landy 2001, p. 30). Safe holding, occurring in fictional context, allows fearful children to discover how different their early life might have been if born to these new parents who are encouraged to exhibit pleasure from being with them 'I love to see you smile like that . . . the colours in your painting are so beautiful.'

For these children who missed the experience of being held in infancy, 'mirroring' serves to replicate early mother–child interactions, that *'attachment dance'* (Winnicott 1971; Hughes 1998) in which attentive mothers amplify their baby's affect and soothe, using touch, holding and voice. In drama, reflection and exaggeration of affect show children what you notice about them, to increase their self-awareness. Klein (1975) identified a process of 'splitting', the projection by baby of all that is 'good' or 'bad' onto mother. Those who never satisfactorily separated from mother may find it hard to manage more than one relationship simultaneously and may persistently 'blame' one (substitute) parent while 'courting' the other. Naming feelings assist connection between physical and mental states, through expressing them in the body. The earliest stage of role play occurs at 12–18 months when children begin to 'talk for teddy' (Jennings 1998). In drama, using puppets as 'transitional objects' (Winnicott 1971) we explore our feelings towards each other.

Many of these children missed their earliest lesson in 'cause and effect' when, from the secure infant's perspective 'I drop the toy, mummy gives it back to me (each time) therefore I am lovable, worthy of attention.' By 'stepping into another's shoes' we witness the impact of actions from and on our audience, so examine the possibility of change, while learning about ourselves. Following extensive loss often experienced as rejection, children come to expect disruption and feeling let down. In drama we rehearse beginnings and endings of relationships, and explore their value, to build broader, more balanced perspectives.

Improvisation is a vehicle towards increased self-knowledge – a means to notice and explore feelings, including those we most resent when we see them reflected in others. Our feelings often show us who we really are and offer new insights into what we are capable of! The 'me but not me' is something of a 'double whammy'. The part I am acting is *not* the 'real me' yet is inevitably revealing the 'real me' because I am contributing parts of myself to that *role*, for instance my voice and interpretation of that role. Taking roles invites practice at ways of being that may seem foreign to our usual nature, yet contributes to greater balance and harmony. Stock fears of appearing foolish or incompetent 'once identified can be given names and over time, held in check or transmutated' (Johnson 2006, p. 273). The desire for control eventually lessens, replaced by a curious, creative attitude of embarking on a journey with, rather than for, an audience.

It is valuable to have fun, and children are far more easily engaged through play. Often children will make fun in such a way that parents fear their child is not taking the situation seriously enough – they prevaricate or make excuses to disappear. However given the sensitive, traumatic content likely to be addressed, it is imperative that children are allowed to manage it in their own way. Making jokes is a useful way to dispel tension, prior to acknowledging the power of past memories to affect our feelings and the pain they have caused us. When ready to address their strong feelings I find children generally engage without resort to mockery. By then they have entered a new level of consciousness.

Parents have said they experience this work as emotionally intense and demanding. In child-led drama, they struggle to know what to say and when. Inevitably, they start out concerned about their children being given freedom to take control of the play. Yet in the course of exploring these very dilemmas, the vast majority reach heightened self-awareness, enabling greater mutuality with their child who respects power granted within safe boundaries. Children know the difference between play and reality as Lahad (2000, p. 12) observed:

> they know they can turn a chair into a horse and fight a battle. They know if the horse is galloping or stopping, eating or hungry. But when a parent enters a room and suggests that the horse is trotting or asks if we shall give it some food, the child will rather quickly respond, 'Oh Daddy, it's just a chair!'

When seeing their parents being flexible and playful, far from jeopardising the parents' authority, the child experiences empathy, powerfully countering the self-blame suffered by children such as Tom who was used to believing he was bad:

Tom's story

In a drama about pirates, Tom's character, the *Pirate*, 'killed' everyone, *sharks*, *whales*, all others except himself. The *Pirate* felt powerful, stating he didn't need *anyone*. As a fellow (almost dead) *pirate*, I reflected my sadness at his being all alone, wondering how he would cope if he cut his knee. Who could cook him nice dinners, or play with him, if everyone was dead? Together, we agreed to create a magic spell to bring back his '*friend*'. In the final scene, the *Pirate* hid, declaring he was buried '*too deep*', that he smelled '*too bad*' to come out. Eventually, he allowed rescue. A ceremonial *barbecue* celebrated his safe return.

Preparation for role

At the start, there may be no plot, or story, yet we can all take on a role, create a character. Landy (2001) proposes that each role may have a 'counter role', an antagonist to the protagonist. We need a 'villain' so the 'hero' can display his heroism. Some of the roles we play are conscious, some may be unconscious until we draw them out or have them drawn from us. Attachment disordered children find it difficult to seek help when they need it. Working with school-excluded children, Sue Jennings (2007) found these children unable to take on a fictional role, but inhabiting 'every-day' roles such as 'clown', 'rescuer' and so on. I have observed that when children practise role situations that are 'complementary' such as 'doctor and patient' as well as 'opposite', such as 'angel and devil', they begin to recognise when help is needed, say, to catch a 'burglar' or assist at an 'operation'. We can explore the role by interviewing the character as if on TV. As we try out the pose this character may assume, we feel the change in our body. A *soldier*, for example, may stand very erectly, a *villain* creep and hide, while a *sick person* might fold inwards. It is feeling this physical change that helps us realise and project feelings. Others' reactions to the role we project further inform us how to continue. We may compare our fictional role to real life.

Therapeutic process

Relationships are secured through improved mutual understanding that results from sharing the child's life history. Re-enactment can be in or out of metaphor. In the family home where the child is familiar with his surroundings, power is more equally shared. Weekly records of the story or play the child has created maintain links and continuity while enhancing children's self-esteem.

Carly, age 12 and Sophie, age 10, had been in their adoptive placement for 4 years, following a complex history of domestic violence, abuse and neglect. Their experience in their birth family had differed in that Carly had been cared for by her maternal grandfather, while Sophie had been her mother's favoured child and remained with her prior to foster care. When their grandfather died from a heart attack, 6-year-old Carly found his body. She returned to her mother's care but never recovered her clothing and possessions. Carly's anger and resentment towards her mother remained unresolved. Their mother died while they were in foster care, leaving no opportunity to say 'goodbye'.

The adoptive parents had experienced strict parenting in childhood. In adult life, the adoptive mother had multiple health problems affecting her employability. The side effects of medication further impacted on her mobility and self-esteem. The father supported and deferred to his wife on most decisions, which left her feeling that she was caring for three children.

These rather orthodox parents had been shocked and shamed by their children's behaviour. They felt criticised by their religious friends and teachers at the children's school.

Carly, a popular girl with 'street cred' was experienced as intimidating by teachers and, at times, her adoptive mother from whom she'd begun to steal money and items of make-up. Sophie, by contrast was a more reclusive 'see-saw' child who found it hard to make and keep friends. Sophie would throw herself at her parents as if desperate for affection, yet make divisive, upsetting remarks to them. My intervention was for ten sessions, four of which involved the whole family.

The focus being on the life history, both girls created dramas that reflected their particular experience. In the 'Course of True Love' (fourth session), Sophie cast the therapist as a *customer*, herself as *cashier*. Her adoptive mother took the part of *Gwen* while the therapist became *Annabelle*. Sophie also became the *police officer* and *baby* of Gwen (Mum) after she marries *Albert* (therapist).

The Course of True Love. . .

The cashier called Gwen took over the till. Gwen's old friend, Annabelle came into the shop. 'Hiya!' said Annabelle who talked non-stop while the cashier served someone else. The other shop assistant noticed Annabelle slip a couple of things down her front. She told the cashier, who pointed to a sign saying 'all goods must be paid for', stating as it was company policy she would have to call the police. Annabelle denied it, but the shop assistant ran the CCTV tape that showed her in action. Annabelle said 'How could you! After all the years we've known each other!' Gwen replied 'Yes but it's been going on a long time hasn't it?' 'What do you mean?' demanded Annabelle. 'Ever since you fancied that Billy Tibbles! That's when it started!' said Gwen 'There's been things goin' missing a long time!'

The police took them both to the police station. Gwen and Annabelle started fighting, thumping and kicking. The policeman split them up and locked Annabelle in the cells to calm things down. Annabelle hammered on the door and swore at them. 'If you don't be quiet you'll lose your shop and your kids!' warned the policeman. He interviewed Annabelle and realised she had picked one dodgy man after another so had no one reliable to help her bring up the kids. The policeman said 'We have a new scheme. We will find you a man. You don't have to marry him, because we'll pay him!' Annabelle agreed to her kids going into care. She didn't want anyone telling her how to parent!

Then he realised Gwen hadn't chosen her men wisely either. Gwen agreed to let the police find her a partner so she was allowed to keep one of her five children. She chose Albert. 'He sounds nice!' she said. Albert and Gwen got on brilliantly. They fell in love and had a baby, called Sophie. They held Sophie in their arms and doted on her. 'Isn't she absolutely gorgeous!' they say, admiring everything about her. Baby Sophie adored her parents too.

One day the police officer returned. 'Sorry, this arrangement has to end now!' Shocked, Albert asked 'Why?' 'The money's run out!' the officer explained apologetically. Albert looked at Gwen and told the police officer. 'I love her! I'm not leaving her now! It wouldn't be fair on her or the baby!' 'OK' said the policeman. 'As you've made good progress, Gwen, you can have your shop back'. 'Good! I'll stay home and look after the kids' said Albert. 'No way! You can work at the supermarket and share the childcare same as me!' said Gwen. 'OK' said Albert. And they lived happily ever after. . .

The play developed into a story of rivalry between two women who had made unfortunate choices. Enactment brought back some very emotive memories for Sophie of attempts to help her birth mother and of how resistant she had been to support – she had always been angry with everyone. But Sophie still missed her, mourning the fact that: 'I never got to say "Goodbye" to her – no one helped me with my feelings about that.'

Watching the play helped Sophie recognise her birth mother had choices, which meant Sophie, too, could choose to address problems or continue to 'fester'. Previously, Sophie had often taken weeks before she'd felt motivated to rectify matters after an argument. Now she began to 'sort it out' within an hour or so. Seeking and accepting help is a key attribute of secure attachment (Howe 2005).

On hearing her history, Carly worried she might be like her birth mother. She stole more items of money and cosmetics from home, was repeatedly in trouble at school, excluded a day or two and ran away twice. Caught between childhood and adolescence, Carly had become stuck in her attitude towards parental authority, persistently jeering at them, fearing she herself was 'stupid'. A story about a donkey that suffered mockery, but now felt accepted and useful, served to help Carly recognise that our attitudes stem from the way we are treated.

A play was devised to explore parental authority and its purpose.

Carly accepted the role of *Queen*, while her adoptive mother played the wayward teenage *Princess*, *Prissie*. The therapist took the role of the *Princess's friend*, *Essie*, who enticed *Prissie* to stay out late to meet some 'men'. *Prissie* was attired in clothes deemed too 'tarty' to be suitable for a *Princess*. The *Queen* was (advised) to set a time for her daughter to come home (if she decided to allow her out). At first, in role as *Queen*, Carly had declared she didn't mind what the *Princess* wore to go out, or care what time she got home. She resisted using parental authority to curb the *Princess's* freedom. We could have asked Carly at what age she might agree restrictions were necessary. However the therapist felt it would be more useful for her to explore this for herself, using the privacy of fiction. Interestingly, when in the drama, £20 went missing from the *Queen's purse*, the Queen began to assert her authority, phoning *Essie's mother* to see where the girls were! The enactment led Carly to acknowledge the importance of negotiating privileges, ideally in advance. However this was still only the fifth session. Difficulties continued at home and school. Carly had dropped out of dancing, a favourite activity, at which she was skilled, declaring she hated the teacher. In a drama set in *dance school*, we explored how she could assertively address bullying. Sophie, too, struggled with feelings of grief and poor self-esteem.

To help them understand the sequence of past events the therapist wrote a play that illustrated their history. Parents joined in enactment, with dolls representing the children. The therapist acted as *birth mother* while parents shared other roles such as those who tried to help. Carly took charge of the music to introduce each scene, while Sophie filmed the action on her mobile phone.

The play, *Shut up* started with a scene in the school playground between birth mother, *Laura*, age 11, and friend. *Laura* described the fire that ended her parents' relationship, angry at her mother: 'I'm just glad that stupid cow is out of my life! I don't care if I never see her again! She never stops telling me to shut up!' Three years later, Laura meets the girls' father. When Sophie was born, the *doctor* warned *Laura* she risked her health by continuing to have children. Upset, she responded: 'What do you know? Bet you ain't got kids!' The *police*, already worried by rows and house fires, heard *Laura* had strangled her oldest son. *Laura's* new partner, *Alan*, was aghast at the plan to send Carly away. Angrily, he asks 'Just what is your problem? The kid isn't difficult!' *Laura* responds: 'Shut up! I've just too much to cope with that's all'. Alan's pleas, 'you can't turn your child out', were to no avail. *Granddad* collected Carly and arranged to visit *Laura*. Months later, *Laura's brother* told *Laura* of her father's death and Carly, 6, discovering his body. *Laura* cried 'Oh God! I can't believe it. And all Carly's stuff is at his place too! She'll blame me for it, I know!' Two years on, the *social worker* removed the children after one was scalded. *Laura* screamed: 'Why does everyone keep having a go at me? Where's the help when you need it, eh? You're good enough at criticising but all the times I ask for a bit of money to help me out, I get nothing!'

We performed this play twice. Carly and Sophie found the play both amusing and movingly, sad. Carly now saw how events had conspired so no longer felt to blame. She recognised her parents had made wrong choices, albeit limited by their circumstances. Sophie suddenly realised the man who had taken her little brother from the foster home had actually been her father, of whom she'd no previous memory or mental image. The play acted as a container, a microcosm of time, repetition of which served to anaesthetise the girls against their most painful memories, evidenced by Carly's progressively smoother narration, on second reading. Afterwards, the therapist returned in role as *Laura* to answer their questions, explain why she had neglected them, made unwise decisions and let them down, and gave Carly and Sophie 'permission' to love their adoptive parents who described to the girls how different their life could have been if they had been born to them and made plans for having far more fun in the future.

Both parents demonstrated strong commitment to helping the girls through this difficult process. Taking part in this play enabled them to experience how hard the birth mother's life had been and to feel more closely bonded to the girls. Recognising Carly's need for more attention, Mum began daily make-up sessions, to guide her. The incidents of pilfering ceased and Carly began to negotiate her privileges. Sophie needed practice at trying out various roles to help her manage relationships. When there were disagreements, parents playfully experimented with role reversal, addressing their children as if they were the parents, which helped to prevent escalation to problematic proportions.

Just as adoptive parents experience the child's trauma, we see that children can be drawn into their new family's rituals, enabling development of new identities. Turner quotes Van Gennep on the qualities of being in a state of change, observing 'the rules for togetherness are known and shared' (Turner 1982, p. 42).

Conclusion

New perspectives are gained by children and parents through sharing roles in enactment, both in and out of metaphor. Re-enacting their history leads children to rebuild their identity as heroic survivors rather than mere victims of horrid adversity. Having fun increases family enjoyment, facilitating greater self-respect and mutual closeness. The consistently low re-referral rate of these families indicates the success of this approach. That many children benefit seems to evidence the plasticity of their brains (Glaser 2000; Balbirnie and Glaser 2001), demonstrating capacity for 'rewiring' with previously traumatic memory appearing to shift to the realms of ordinary memory in the higher cortex.

Provided parents' attachment patterns are not overly insecure, child-led play and drama enable those struggling with complex children to develop their relationship in a manner that helps their children feel safer to attach.

Bibliography

Ainsworth, M. (1978) *Patterns of Attachment: A Psychological Study of the Strange Situation*, Mahwah, NJ: Lawrence Erlbaum Associates, Inc.

Balbirnie, R. and Glaser, D. (2001) 'Early Experience, Attachment and the Brain', in *Fragile, Handle with Care: Child Abuse Review*, pp. 76–88.

Crittenden, P. and Claussen, A.H. (eds) (2003) *The Organisation of Attachment Relationships: Maturation, Culture and Context*, Cambridge: Cambridge University Press.

Gerhardt, S. (2004) *Why Love Matters: How Love Shapes a Baby's Brain*, Hove: Brunner Routledge.

Glaser, D. (2000) 'Child Abuse and Neglect and the Brain – A Review', *Journal of Child Psychology and Psychiatry*, *41*, 1: 97–116.

Goffman, E. (1959) *The Presentation of Self in Everyday Life*, New York: DoubleDay.

Howe, D. (2005) *Child Abuse and Neglect: Attachment, Development and Intervention*, Basingstoke: Palgrave Macmillan.

Hughes, D. (1998) *Building the Bonds of Attachment: Awakening Love in Deeply Troubled Children*, Northvale, NJ: Jason Aronson, Inc.

Jennings, S. (1998) *Dramatherapy, Theatre and Practice*, London: Jessica Kingsley Publishers.

Jennings, S. (2007) *Project Report – Playtherapy with Excluded Children*, Romania: Rowan Studio.

Johnson, C. (2006) *The Improvisation Game: Discovering the Secrets of Spontaneous Performance*, London: Nick Hern Books.

Klein, M. (1975) *Envy and Gratitude and Other Works: 1946–1963*, London: Hogarth Press.

Lahad, M. (2000) *Creative Supervision: The Use of Expressive Arts Methods in Supervision and Self-supervision*, London: Jessica Kingsley Publishers.

Landy, R. (2001) *New Essays in Dramatherapy: Unfinished Business*, Springfield, IL: Charles C. Thomas.

Schechner, R. (2006) *Performance Studies: An Introduction*, 2nd edn, London: Routledge.

Siegel, D. (1999) *The Developing Mind: Towards a Neurobiology of Interpersonal Experience*, New York/London: Guilford Press.

Sunderland, M. (2007) *Proceedings of Conference on the Impact of Trauma on the Developing Brain*, Bedford, March 2007.

Turner, V. (1982) *From Ritual to Theatre: The Human Seriousness of Play*, New York: PAJ Publications.

Winnicott, D. (1971) *Playing and Reality*, London: Tavistock Publications.

19 The 'puppet' that felt a breeze of its own energy

Applied social theatre in the field of sexuality in Moldova[1]

Lilia Raileanu

In*(spiration)*troduction

In August 2002, a training workshop, 'Psychosocial Animation for HIV/ AIDS Prevention', introduced the method of social theatre to the Republic of Moldova for the very first time. Thirty civil society members took part in the training, facilitated by Guglielmo Schininà, author of Chapter 3 in this book.

After training, I was one of the practitioners inspired by this method and eager to apply it immediately. Working, at that time, mainly in the field of human rights and mental health with lesbian, gay, bisexual, and trans-gender people, (LGBT), I decided to use it in that field.

This chapter aims at describing the experience of practical application of social theatre involving a socially excluded community, in this case the LGBT community, rather than bringing theoretical arguments, although it does highlight certain hypotheses and tries to analyse them. The practice was applied in an inclusive setting addressing sexuality issues and involving participants with various sexual orientations and identities.

Shrugging shoulders when hearing the name of this country: Republic of Moldova

The Republic of Moldova, (part of the Union of Soviet Socialist Republics in the past), is a small country in South-Eastern Europe, neighbouring with Ukraine and Romania. In 1991 it became an independent state. In terms of ethnic structure, it is populated by Moldovans (part of them identify themselves as Romanians), followed by Ukrainians, Russians, and other ethnic groups, (the Gagauz, Bulgarians, Jews, Byelorussians, Germans, etc.). The Republic of Moldova has a population of 4 million people covering an area of 33843.5 km^2 (Republic of Moldova, official website, n.d.). The most widely spoken languages are Romanian (officially recognised as 'Moldavian') and Russian. Chisinau is the capital of the country. The main problems Moldovans face are poverty, migration, trafficking in human beings, corruption, and discrimination.

A 'puppet' community: The situation of the LGBT community in the Republic of Moldova

Until 1995, homosexual relations were classified as illegal. The issue of homosexuality is still treated and perceived by some mental health specialists and academics as a disorder or perversion. In the research 'Evaluation of LGBT Mental Health Policy in Moldova' (GenderDoc-M, 2006, p. 20) it is mentioned that 50 per cent of the respondents and mental health professionals considered homosexuality as being a disease or a behavioural disorder. However, an encouraging fact is that 76 per cent of the respondents within the same study mentioned that they are willing to pursue further training on the issue of LGBT. Also, it is important to mention that the official position of the Ministry of Health follows the one of the World Health Organization, which removed homosexuality from the list of mental disorders in 1990.

In terms of freedom of expression, for three years in a row Chisinau City Hall refused to give permission to organise public gatherings as part of the Gay Pride festivals that are organised every year (Amnesty International, 2008, n.d.). In 2008, again, just a day before the public gathering as part of the Gay Pride festival, City Hall banned it (Marandici, 2008, p. 3). The activity of religious organisations that condemn social inclusion of the LGBT community has intensified. Consequently, given the described situation, the most common problems faced by the LGBT community are discrimination, domestic and public violence, and a lack of friendly health, consultancy, cultural and entertainment services.

Energy for the 'puppets': Developing social theatre in the Republic of Moldova

After the first training workshop in the field of social theatre, the most motivated practitioners participated in a 2-year project, 'Youth Against Social Exclusion in the Republic of Moldova',[2] within which the participants benefited from several workshops in the field of social theatre in Italy and Moldova, while monitored by trainers, among them Guglielmo Schininà, who supervised the project described in this chapter.

Several initiatives were implemented within this project, including in the field of sexuality. Other fields of social theatre applications were: youth and migration of their parents, rural youth, boarding school children and street children. The initiatives were directed towards the initiation of a dialogue concerning the problems of these target groups and participation in finding solutions.

Today, other training workshops and applied activities have been carried out as well. The project 'The Power of Dialogue' (2005–06) was carried out by 'Formaat', an organization from the Netherlands, by means of which two other workshops in the field of participatory drama, facilitated by Luc

Opdebeeck (Formaat, the Netherlands) and Adrian Jackson (Cardboard citizens, UK) were offered to practitioners.

A 'staged taboo' on everyone's lips: The context of the practical activity

In April–May 2003, after the first training workshop on social theatre, I facilitated workshops aimed at creating a forum theatre on 'Discrimination and Homosexuality'.[3] The format of a forum theatre was chosen because it corresponded to the competences obtained following training.

It should be mentioned that for many participants of homosexual and bisexual orientation, appearing on stage in the forum theatre during the second Gay Pride festival in Moldova was a huge risk, as most of them had not come out to their families, closest friends or colleagues, and they risked becoming victims of homophobia as a result. Some of them were going through the experience of domestic or other types of violence. That is why the actors' situation was characterised by fear and risk on the one hand, and by the wish to diminish inner pressure, to make a change, to express the oppression and its effects on them on the other hand. One of the noticeable features was the spirit of solidarity within the group.

After the forum theatre during the Gay Pride festival, the members of the group took the initiative to continue the workshops.

A project involving also the LGBT community (including some of the participants at the forum theatre) was developed by carrying out a number of workshops on 'Sexuality', from which young people of different sexual orientations and identities could benefit.

The group comprised 14 persons of different sexual orientations and identities, aged between 19 and 30, both students and professionals, and Romanian and Russian language speakers. The workshops were carried out once a week, mainly on Saturdays, and lasted for 4–5 hours. They went on for 8 months, except for holidays. In all, approximately 30 workshops have been carried out.

The entire project comprised the following steps:

1   Creative workshops.[4]
2   Social communication preparation.[5]
3   Social communication.
4   Activity evaluation.

Workshop objectives were discussed with the participants. Thus, as approved by the group, the following objectives were pursued: to create a safe place for exchange of experience on the issues of sexuality between persons of different sexual orientations; team building; development of participants' personality; and participation in developing solutions for social change. During the activities the objectives were constantly re-evaluated.

The creative workshops were structured in sections as follows:

- Sexuality and cultural aspects (cinema, theatre, music, poetry, etc.);
- Sexuality and body;
- Sexuality and individual memory;
- Sexuality and fantasy;
- Sexuality and reality.

Within this process, the approach described in Claudio Bernardi's chapter from this book was used, namely the one from the social theatre pattern as a complex circle (Schininà, 2004; Bernardi, 2004; see Chapter 5, this volume).

From an 'apparent personal apathy' to an 'apparent social apathy': Individual and group dynamics

Activity dynamics started with creating a safe place for participants by means of individual knowledge and expressive activities, after which the group was built; individual expression, exchange of experience and the meaning search on each of the above-mentioned issues followed; problems and assets for each of them were identified; the last step focused on finding solutions and resources at the macro-social level. Techniques of social theatre, theatre of the oppressed, art-therapy and psychodrama were used.

Regarding the beginning of the creative workshops, several participants expressed verbally and non-verbally different communication barriers, including fear of expression, loneliness, limited social network, non-acceptance by the others.[6] 'The fear of expression' was one of the most visible elements. 'Inner pressure and negative self-perception' on the one hand and 'presence of motivation and power to change' on the other hand were present. At the same time, aspirations towards changes, a wish to understand their own experiences, and eagerness to know and create were expressed. As individual dynamics ran as a continuous thread through our activity, we illustrate this section with comments by a participant.

> I found people just like me, with many problems and searching for their inner selves. I felt I was not alone in my own darkness. A new life began for me, a new communication, and a different way of thinking. I reconsidered all my life values and arranged them in an original way for myself.
>
> (Woman, age 24)

After several workshops (approximately in the middle of the process) we could outline the following group profile: there are still communication barriers, as a result of 'inertia of fear of expression', going from apathy to anxiety, of the manifestation of inner conflicts, and the appearance of insights. The participants called the workshops 'a safe place for expression and communication, realisation of important moments, self-knowledge and knowledge of others'. Elements of positive self-perception were present.

> Playing the role of a puppet, I suddenly felt a gleam of energy, which made me believe I can have more of it and I can come to more through my own initiative.

Related to the end of the process, before the social communication step, participants' comments included 'solidarity with others', 'new friends, thus an extension of the social network', 'an increase in self-confidence', 'ability to solve problems', 'perception of problems as a resource', 'development of creativity', 'development of creative thinking', 'and finding out new things'.

> I discovered a new potential in me, unknown before. I found out what it means to be creative, unusual and that my problems can become a source of power for me. I made new friends and I'm sure we have a lot in common and we have all built a new world for us. It is beyond limits, restrictions, regularities, and the ordinary. It was the most beautiful experience of my life and I feel lucky I took part in it!!!

As you can see, the tendency towards social change is contained in the last comments by the participant. For the purposes of social communication, the group chose to organise an exhibition and produce a play showing emotions, feelings, pain, aspirations, and negative and positive experiences.

About ten workshops of dramaturgy work were organised.

Within the dramaturgy workshops, the participants selected individually and then together with the group, the most important and significant scenes they would like to present to the public. The scenes had a metaphorical, abstract, rather than narrative style. Each scene had its own logical context among other scenes. The message of the play shows on the one hand the pain and internalised oppression of the people looking for their identity (the non-acceptance and 'taboos'), and on the other hand it shows the path taken in looking for 'The Loved One' who would understand and accept. Also, the play is showing the 'ideal', the desired images that embody actors' aspirations and express the joy of being together with the person they love.

The end! The paradox

It was not easy for the participants to decide whether they wanted to present their work in public or not, and what form that would take. At the beginning of the chapter it is mentioned that the forum theatre on homosexuality raised issues that the participants were very enthusiastic to perform and debate with the public, despite the risks they were undertaking. However, this time, after a long journey covering their personal development, it took days of reflection to decide to perform in front of the public, and finally to perform without using the forum. They were also aware of the fact that the scenes, which were abstract and metaphoric, had to be adapted, so they become clearer for the audience to understand. At first glance, one could say that this shows evidence of a social apathy or passivity, or resistance to change. Before accepting these assumptions, let's look at some circumstances and a hypothesis.

In the first instance, in the forum theatre during the Gay Pride festival, when the wish for change was combined with fear and risk, it may be assumed that people were participating because of the desire to get free from being closed in, from living behind masks, and from lying about their identity. It was an expressed desire for coming out. Also, the workshops process was from the beginning directed towards implementing a certain method, forum theatre, while in the later process we did not have that purpose. In the second instance, regarding the present application, when the need for safety, understanding, acceptance, communication and personal expression were met, the social commitment became less important at that particular moment, or, better to say there was a larger social change commitment, as what happened in the workshop space was also social.

The workshop period was very intensive as energy, commitment and emotions were involved within it. It might be that the participants needed time to integrate the important personal and social outcomes into their lives. Two years later, in 2006, when a new initiative coordinated by me started using legislative theatre to promote the anti-discrimination law in Moldova, some of the previous participants were actively involved. Legislation is about people and some of them were ready.

As mentioned earlier, the dramaturgy was focused mostly on internal oppression, and the performance shows the results of oppression, and, to a lesser extent, the actual relationship between the oppressors and the oppressed. A reason for this was that the training was mostly based on personal development, rather than on social change, because that was what the participants requested for their needs. However, from the point of view of long-term goals and taking into consideration the context, the described project can also be called an action for social change.

Notes

1 I want to thank Guglielmo Schininà, Italy, social theatre expert, for inspiration, training and supervision within the creative workshops; Sara Risi, Italy; European volunteer, Dorina Verdes, stage director, for her support in planning and carrying out sessions; Tatiana Baciu, Dr in Psychology for supervision; Valentina Olarescu, Associate Professor, Dr in Psychology, for consultancy in art therapy methods application; the participants at the workshops for cooperation and inspiration; and the Charity Centre for Refugees.

2 The project was implemented by the Italian Consortium of Solidarity and the National Youth Council of the Republic of Moldova (NYCM), financed by the European Commission.

3 All the initiatives and projects mentioned in the chapter involving the LGBT community were implemented in partnership with 'GenderDoc-M'.
4 By 'Creative workshops' we mean all the workshops until the 'Social communication' phase.
5 By 'Social communication' we mean the activities aimed to be performed outside of the Creative workshop space involving another auditorium or spectators.
6 These interpretations were based on the creative outcomes of the participants: drawings, written texts, non-verbal expressions in the form of body-sculptures and theatrical scenes.

References:

Amnesty International Website (n.d.) 'Moldova', in *Amnesty International Report 2008*, retrieved October 2008 from http://thereport.amnesty.org/eng/regions/europe-and-central-asia/moldova

Bernardi, C. (2004) *Il Teatro Sociale*, Rome: Carocci.

GenderDoc-M, Credo and CBS-Axa (2006) *Evaluation of LGBT Mental Health Policy in Moldova*, Chisinau: GenderDoc-M.

Marandici, I. (2008) 'Moldovan Society Divided over the Soviet Past, Human Rights and Moral Values', *Political and Security Statewatch: Monthly Analytical Bulletin on Moldova Issued by IDIS 'Viitorul'*, 5, 12, available at: www.eurasianhome.org/File/PSS_no.5_May_2008.pdf

Republic of Moldova Official Website (n.d.) Retrieved October 2008 from www.moldova.md

Schininà, G. (2004) 'Faraway, So Close. Psychosocial and Theatre Activities with Serbian Refugees', *The Drama Review*, *48*, 3: 33–50.

20 Where professional actors are too 'good'

The RAP (respect and protect) project

David Evans, Sandy Akerman and John Tripp

Background

With the highest teenage conception rates in Europe and incidences of sexually transmitted infections (STIs) soaring, experts agree that the UK has the worst adolescent sexual health in Europe (UNICEF 2001; Office for National Statistics 2002; Ellis and Grey 2004). The greater their social and education disadvantage, the more vulnerable are young people to poor sexual health. Sub-groups of the most at-risk youngsters are readily identifiable and yet to date there are few, if any, interventions in the UK that have broken the trans-generational cycle of deprivation and social exclusion.

In mainstream educational settings with a less vulnerable population the Apause team (Added Power And Understanding in Sex Education) at the Department of Child Health – Peninsula Medical School, Universities of Exeter and Plymouth had already achieved rare success in Sex and Relationships Education (SRE) (Mellanby *et al.* 1995). Within this context Apause received a government grant from the Teenage Pregnancy Unit in 1999 to investigate extending SRE provision to more vulnerable groups. A salient part of the Apause programme uses peer educators to facilitate the practising of relationship skills through role play (Evans *et al.* 1998), and Apause was commissioned to develop a parallel peer programme for pre-16s outside mainstream education.

Social Cognitive Theory (SCT) (Bandura 1986) provides the theoretical framework for Apause programme development. A promising study by David Evans (Evans *et al.* 1998) suggested there were important reasons to believe that a peer-led, drama-based approach could prove a powerful vehicle to facilitate learning through the social influences implicit in SCT. Experts were appointed to the research team to cross-reference with the Apause theory base practices from applied drama, dramatherapy and participatory learning approaches (Welbourn 1995). Our rationale was that our clients, who were already disaffected by formal and instructional pedagogies, would find the consensual, play-based, experiential and fictional structures offered by the drama-based and participatory methods more engaging.

What follows is an abbreviated account of the key practical challenges, theoretical considerations, novel solutions and an emergent framework for evaluation.

Key players

For the purposes of clarification, our *peer-educators* are young people around 1 to 5 years older than the *learners* who are aged between 14 and 16. The learners are placed in educational settings but outside mainstream schools. Such institutions, often referred to as 'units', include Pupil Referral Units (PRU) – separate institutions not attached to any mainstream schools, Pupil Inclusion Units (PIU), – attached to schools but usually peripherally situated, and finally, Mother and Baby Units for girls who are pregnant or in their first year as parents. Whenever the term *learner* is mentioned, the reader should assume that that person is encountering the programme within their institution or 'unit'.

The research was directed by Dr John Tripp with a stable supervisory group including Dr Sue Jennings and Dr Alice Wellbourne, and a more fluid group of senior facilitators including Fiona Macbeth and Sandy Akerman. David Evans was a member of the supervisory group for the first year but then became the lead researcher.

Challenges

With the funding brief to work using a peer-education approach, the team concluded that the only credible peer-educators would be those whose life experiences were similar to the learners in the units – the peer-educators themselves having had personal experience of social exclusion and/or a seriously disrupted education. The corollary to social disadvantage is that peers face multiple personal challenges, including drug problems, exclusion from school, domestic violence, abuse and re-ordered families, teenage pregnancy and parenthood and criminality. Every team of peer educators also has at least one member who had good performing arts skills. This person, usually a little older and more mature, has experienced similar personal challenges, but their presence within the team has the positive effect of role modelling creative and authentic responses within a framework of acceptable behaviour. This relationship in turn is further developed within the units.

The RAP project thus involves two vulnerable groups of young people. Peer-educators and learners alike experience chronic instability in their life circumstances with frequent traumatic episodes. Social disadvantage and unpredictable lifestyles create dilemmas and challenges for the young people, which inevitably impact on their ability to engage in learning experiences. What they have learned about relationships is often through inadequate role models, with behaviours generally judged to be antisocial and dysfunctional being perceived as both normal and socially viable. While on the one hand exhibiting a desire to be empowered to make alternative choices, the young people are sceptical that there could be a reality preferable to the one to which they have become accustomed. Although there is no typical unit, characteristic of most of them is an atmosphere of carefully monitored and contained emotional volatility that can occasionally overspill into outbursts and acts of violence. One peer-educator reported, on first entering a unit, having to dodge a flying snooker cue.

As a base-line requirement the project needed an explicit framework within which each young person, peer-educator or learner, could contribute and collaborate with the expectation that they would be respected and enjoy an atmosphere of safety and trust. Irrespective of any predefined programme outcomes, all participants should find the experience intrinsically rewarding and generative of a personalised learning experience. The director stipulated that because the funding was to develop a public health intervention, the 'product' should be accurately described to achieve programme fidelity and replicability.

Project development

The project evolves in two distinct locations with two phases of activity. The *developmental phase* when the programme is devised and rehearsed, occurs away from the units, while the *facilitation phase* happens within the units. At no point has one phase been dropped or given precedence over the other for more than a few weeks.

The learning environment

With routines common to both, the *developmental* and *facilitation phases* are structured to generate a consistent affective learning environment. In this respect we found the 'Ritual–Risk' and 'Embodiment, Projection, Role', frameworks offered by Sue Jennings to be mainstays in constructing the affective landscape of the experience (Jennings 1999). In any group encounter, participants (peer-educators and learners) always have a *social orientation* stage in which low-key socialising takes place, typically this can involve making coffee, smoking (off the premises), checking out music on MP3 players and I Pods and catching up on the past week's events. *Space definition and preparation* involves re-arranging furniture, covering or removing any potentially distracting objects (TV, Hi Fi, computers, pool table) and putting the correct number of chairs in a 'circle'. This signals to less 'keyed-in' participants that something is about to commence and by the time the senior facilitator(s) are seated there is a 'drift' towards participants taking their seat and forming a much more regular circle. Next is a more formalised *introduction stage*, which might recap on names and any practical business or change of circumstances that might materially impact on the session. This is deliberately brief and leads into the *warm-up stage*. This 'selective inattention' followed by more formal engagement is analogous to Schechner's notion of the integral audience (Schechner 2003: 211), but may also be observed in term of Jennings' (1999) ritual–risk transition.

The warm-up is usually a game, although through previous experience the facilitators had learned to call it an 'exercise'. This is usually circle-based and starts by making final adjustments to the arrangement of chairs. Predominantly these are variations of transition games where players exchange places by crossing the space. Exercises gain in complexity incrementally, with participants taking it in turns to offer elaborations and new games. It is within this stage that other exercises, with a more physical emphasis, are introduced. This element of the workshop comprises the 'Embodiment' phase of Jennings' (1999) Embodiment, Projection, Role (EPR) developmental model and, ideally, contains physical metaphors and motifs that are to be revisited in the 'Projection' and 'Role' phases of the workshop. For example a mirror exercise (Embodiment) is an introductory metaphor for negotiating stopping points in the progression of sexual intimacy, which is then re-visited as a floor puppet exercise (Projection), which is in turn reiterated through spoken dialogue and role-play (Role). Both development and facilitation sessions, if sensitively stage managed, have the feeling of moving 'smoothly through the gears' with participants agreeing to start off in the relatively safe and ritualised embodiment phase, moving through to the more challenging cognitions involved in a projection activity and finally into the much riskier phase of committing to a role-play. Closure, again, is highly formalised with a 'de-roling' and reflective final phase. Thus the ritual–risk–ritual cycle is completed.

Conditions of engagement

While different individuals bring different dynamics to the space, overall the research team has concluded that a certain consistency and continuity are required. The team identified three conditions that needed to be met and were all regularly achieved: (1) an ethos of calm respectfulness and consensus must be established and maintained; (2) a 'safe' sense of attentiveness and playfulness needs to be continually engendered; and (3) perhaps most critically, there must be respect for individual privacy and an understanding that learning is not dependent on individuals making personal disclosures. The fictional 'I am not being myself' contract of a theatre space facilitates this third condition and allows all participants to engage without feeling coerced into putting their personal behaviour and private circumstances up for public scrutiny. Ethically this is important because none of the senior facilitators are therapists and the programme is not a therapeutic intervention. This respect for individual privacy has proved critical to achieving role and group functionality. On those few occasions where individuals have manoeuvred the work to focus on an exclusively personal agenda, other participants have expressed disaffection and withdrawn their cooperation. In one salutary incident the ethos of the workshop broke down as one peer-educator accused others of not taking their story seriously and deliberately acting badly.

This condition of privacy creates the paradox of researchers instigating challenging situations to which peer-educators contribute insights through role-play, directing and scripting while simultaneously maintaining that characters and circumstances are fictional. A successful method is to draw a large mask on a flip-chat and invest the mask with some essential character attributes and role functions. A peer-educator is then invited to ritual-istically mime removing the mask from the paper and place it on their face. Because the attributes of the mask are jointly agreed using contributions from all group members, the actor playing the mask is accountable to the group having neither licence to recreate highly autobiographical material nor the burden of feeling the characteristics of the mask are their personal responsibility. The psychological structure of the masks varies in com-plexity, but even at their simplest they always contain two oppositional drives dubbed 'Wants' and 'Worries'. This was derived from Boal's *domin-ant will* and *counter will* (Boal 1992: 51) and refined by David Evans (Evans *et al.* 1998) in his work on negotiating sexual intimacy. In effect it means that no character enters a role-play with a single aim, rather whatever the character's dominant motivation for a scene may be it is always counter-balanced by some other, often cautionary or overriding consideration. For example a protagonist might want to take the physical side of a sexual relationship to a greater degree of intimacy and is prepared to be proactive, but is also concerned that applying too much pressure could result in a break-up and ending the relationship completely. In constructing the scenarios and the consequent lines of interrogation we were influenced by Landy's model of 'role', 'counter-role' and 'guide' (Landy 1999). Very early on in our exploratory improvisation, the researchers were struck by the highly confrontational and oppositional form the scenes took. Seemingly innocuous negotiations quickly escalated into two extreme and intractable positions from which the actors found it difficult to manoeuvre and find solutions. The repetitive exploration of such scenes tended to back the young people into stereotypical responses that reflected too much their own personal struggles, risking destructive and violent outcomes. Hence while 'roles' and 'counter-roles' emerged quickly, finding solutions by way of a 'guide' needed greater resourcefulness. Often the only guidance they were able to relate to was their sense of danger and running out of control; in these instances the general consensus was that the characters simply needed to keep safe by getting away from the situation or looking for ways of avoiding the confrontation. By carefully examining the situations it was also possible to suggest that the characters might not be as isolated as they had initially felt, and the presence of other characters who might have a mediating influence could be invoked. Hence a friend, carer, teacher or health worker would be introduced as a highly significant third party.

Peer-educators as actors and facilitators

A feature of using peer-educators as facilitators is that they are not just professional actors with a role to play, but they, like the learners, are struggling with many of the themes encountered in the intervention. It is precisely because they are like the learners and continue to struggle with similar issues that the learners are prepared to listen to them and learn with them. It is also why 'distancing techniques' are essential to both protect peers and learners yet allow playing of very sensitive and threatening situations. Peer-educators strive to achieve a subtle balance of exercising their influence as peers while maintaining the fiction of dramatic action as the dominant learning medium. Other role functions are achieved by successful peer-educators. For example even when they are not formally in role as actors playing characters, they are still in role as facilitators. Peers purposefully stimulate discussion through questions, helping learners to construct meanings while refraining from being doctrinaire about their personal beliefs. Thus the facilitation in the units becomes a complex set of agreements whereby the peer-educators may own up to their own struggles if they feel it helps the learners, while having to remind themselves and the learners that the dramatic presentations, characters and stories of the intervention are fictional.

Additionally, peers organise group-based activities, make best use of available space, are sensitive to levels of involvement and judge when to move on to the next stage of a session. Even when they are 'passive' and just having a smoke or a cup of coffee with the learners, peer-educators must apply certain disciplines that prevent their 'casual' interactions from undermining the themes, behaviours and relationship values constructed during the more formal activities. Thus it is essential that the peer-educators offer positive role models, and while they acknowledge that there is much common ground between both groups, the peers are trained to focus on building a currency around such desired outcomes as improved self-beliefs and interactional skills.

The 'scripted performance workshop'

The broad format of each session and the narrative structure unifying the series of ten or so visits to the units are enshrined as a series of 'scripts'. Evolution of the RAP scripts is a methodical and iterative process involving careful video records of developmental workshops, transcriptions of recordings into scenarios, testing both in rehearsal and in the facilitation phases and then reworking as necessary. As each script 'matures' with use it becomes an increasingly information rich documentation of the whole

RAP ethos, including both the performative and facilitative experience. Typically a script for one session contains many, if not all, of the following components:

- explicit explanation of theoretical principles and learning outcomes;
- practical tips on the most effective management of the space, materials, learning exercises and human resources;
- dramatic vignettes of evolving characters and relationships;
- explanatory texts to be read aloud, from which legal and health information, programme values, lines of questioning, and a range of solutions may be extracted.

The relationship between the participants and the scripts remains somewhat uncharted territory. It is quite common to make an assessment of a client group and decide to customise the experience by drawing on scenarios from different sessions and reassemble them into a unique chronology. Probably more consistent than the content of the scripts is the adherence to the three conditions of engagement described above.

Despite the fact that most of our peer-educators struggle with dyslexia or a reading difficulty, several very practical benefits of a script-based programme have emerged.

The peer-educators do not need to undertake the onerous task of memorising the scenes in order to perform. The process of reading aloud from the script (no matter how much of a struggle) is a powerful reminder to peers and learners alike of the fictional nature of the experience. In fact the physical presence of the script in the hands of the actors is sometimes described as a 'shield' or 'mask' from behind which the peer-educators can feel safe enough to deliver their role. This reduces embarrassment and enables both the peers and learners to talk about the characters as though they were separate entities from the persons present in the room. Conversely there have been times when over-zealous acting has produced such an emotive and partisan response that the learners have been unable to engage in any critical analysis of the characters and situation. Indeed, Bandura (1977) posits that such high levels of emotional arousal are undermining of self-efficacy, arguing that low levels of arousal while coping with a challenging situation engender a sense of assuredness and efficacy.

Having established the symbolic nature of the language and characters within the scripts, it makes for a much easier transition to get the learners to pick up a piece of scripted text and read it themselves. From the perspective of SCT, the prior modelling by respected peer-educators of reading from a script adds valuable social currency and appeal to the task of a learner working from a script themselves. Thus engagement with a role and participating in a shared group experience is much more readily achieved through the intermediate and projective phase of a script reading than through a full blown commitment to an improvised role. The metaphor of a script as a code for behaviour and life choices is particularly powerful when participants feel enabled to interpret, make judgements and re-write existing scripts or develop their own codes. Hence understanding the workshop script as a mutable code and this being analogous to one's personal life codes over which one has authorship is a theoretical cornerstone of the RAP project and maps directly on to Bandura's (1997) *self-efficacy belief.*

The role of scene manager

The workshops are primarily facilitated by a peer-educator who plays the role of *scene manager*. The credibility of the sessions relies on the strength and flexibility of this young person. The scene manager needs to understand and maintain the ethos of the programme. It is essential also that the other peers respect and respond well to their scene manager, trusting that he or she will enable them to do their job and give them space to participate in the discussions. The craft of the scene manager, while ultimately remaining the unique construction of that particular peer-educator, is also guided by the script. Critical lines of questioning, points of information and strategies developed by scene managers from previous sessions are recorded in the format of dialogue and stage directions.

Integration of 'floor puppets' and other resources and activities

None of these activities are 'stand alone' experiences, rather they grow out of the episodic narrative of the characters' relationships. Thus *emotion masks* (commissioned photocopiable black and white cartoons) are linked to warm-up exercises, interpretation of characters' feelings and more detailed analyses of characters' own interpretations and responses. The mask, then, is built in to the interpretative pedagogy of the work with participants becoming increasingly adept at finding appropriate vocabularies to describe characters' emotions and cognitions.

The use of floor puppets was originally developed by David Evans for mainstream classrooms to investigate negotiations of sexual intimacy. This highly stylised form of presentation makes very specific demands as moveable hands and mouths are manoeuvred around two black silhouettes representing the bodies of the couple. The social reality that young people engage in negotiations of sexual intimacy with the use of few if any words is reflected in the silent gestures of the puppets. Without exception each peer expressed anything from anxiety to contempt at the thought of presenting puppets to other young people. In early rehearsals it was necessary to remind the peers that this was a research programme and that their job was to 'try it out'. The peers playing the characters of Sam and Chris are trained to prepare the floor puppets slowly and sensitively on the floor while the scene manager begins reading the script. Within seconds the atmosphere in the room changes completely as everyone is drawn into the early sexual negotiation between the young couple. The use of *hotseating* initiated by questions from the scene manager with further questions from the learners allows unspoken thoughts, motives and feelings of the characters to be revealed.

Other, including commercially produced, resources are also successfully built into the stories of the various relationship. These include condoms and demonstration applicators, 'drunk simulation goggles', anatomical diagrams, 'Top Trump' cards for drugs, and a board game for tracing the spread of STIs.

Evaluation

The iterative cycle of programme development and delivery identifies the intervention within the action research tradition (Hart and Bond 1995) and all stakeholders are given opportunities to provide feedback through semi-structured interviews. Teachers, learning assistants and carers have been almost unanimously positive in their appraisal of the programme. Interviews with learners again demonstrate that the experience is greatly valued. Peer-educators themselves, by no means the most financially stable, healthy and socially integrated individuals, are perhaps the greatest testimony to the transformative processes in which they are engaged. Because of our sustained contact with them over months and even years, the research team have been able to track such positive outcomes as successfully returning to full-time education, keeping out of criminal activity and drugs, acceptance on and completion of degree courses, entering and staying in full-time and part-time work, more rewarding friendships and sexual relationships and successful parenting.

Our programme theory has allowed us to develop a set of observational criteria based on a guided mastery model (Bandura 1997: 329), which enables the team to monitor immediate impacts and stepwise gains in learners' attitudes, interactional competencies and intentions towards more pro-social behaviours and rewarding relationships. (See Appendix).

The future

We look to more visionary interagency support, trust funds and research grants to advance this development programme to a position where it may have some quantifiable impacts on public health.

References

Bandura, A. (1977) 'Self Efficacy: Towards a Unifying Theory of Behavioural Change', *Psychological Review, 84*, 191–215.

Bandura, A. (1986) *Social Foundations of Thought and Action: A Social Cognitive Theory*, Englewood Cliffs, NJ: Prentice Hall.

Bandura, A. (1997) *Self Efficacy: The Exercise of Control*, New York: Freeman.

Boal, A. (1992) *Games for Actors and Non-actors*, London: Routledge.

Ellis, S. and Grey, A. (2004) *NHS Health Development Agency*, available at: hda-online.org.uk

Evans, D., Rees, J., Okagbue, O. and Tripp, J. (1998) 'Negotiating Sexual Intimacy: APAUSE Develops an Approach Using a Peer-led, Theatre-for-development Model in the Classroom', *Health Education*, 9, 6: 220–9.

Hart, E. and Bond, M. (1995) *Action Research for Health and Social Care: A Guide to Practice*, Buckingham: Open University Press.

Jennings, S. (1999) *Introduction to Developmental Play Therapy*, London: Jessica Kingsley Publishers.

Mellanby, A.R., Phelps, F.A., Crichton, N.J. and Tripp, J.H. (1995) 'School Sex Education: An Experimental Programme with Educational and Medical Benefit', *British Medical Journal, 311*: 414–17.

Office for National Statistics (2002) www.statistics.gov.uk/

Landy, R. (1999) 'Role Model of Dramatherapy in Supervision', in E. Tselikas-Portmann (ed.), *Supervision and Dramatherapy* London: Jessica Kingsley Publishers.

Schechner, R. (2003) *Performance Theory*, London: Routledge Classics.

UNICEF (2001) *A League Table of Teenage Births in Rich Nations*, available at: www.unicef-icdc.org

Welbourn, A. (1995) *STEPPING STONES: A Training Package on HIV/AIDS, Communications and Relationships Skills*, London: ActionAid Hamlyn House.

Appendix

The RAP project: building perceived self-efficacy through peer-led guided mastery using a drama-based intervention

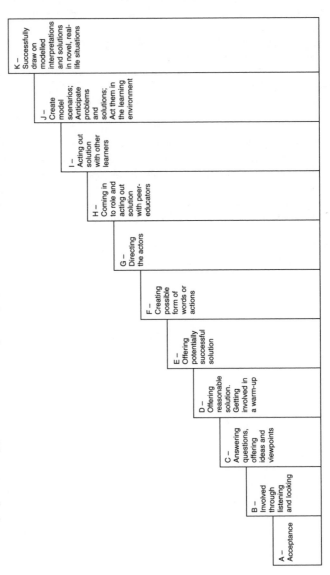

Figure 20.4.1 The RAP project

Epilogue
Talking to actors

Roger Grainger

Actors and social belonging: at first sight one would not readily associate them. Logically speaking, people who devote their own lives to taking on other people's roles might not be expected to possess a developed sense of having their own social role to play within society. From this strictly logical point of view, they have chosen to be spectators, not actors, firmly locating themselves in the audience rather than on-stage.

And this has been their social role, sometimes as court jesters or National Theatre Players, sometimes as strolling vagabonds and street-corner buskers; always stationed on the outside looking in, or within some imaginary inside of their own, being looked at by *real* insiders for purposes of pleasure – the insiders' pleasure, that is. Just as their skills depend on distance, so their lives are lived at a distance. They reflect society in on itself in a way that society finds liberating, casting them well and truly on the outside where they can be safely 'distanced' if the truth they embody becomes unacceptable ('Lights, Lights, give me some light . . .').

Logically speaking, considering they either exclude themselves or are excluded – or both – it is strange that their symbiotic existence does not depress them so much that they embrace a more conformist attitude to life. Why do they go on being actors? What is it about the job that attracts them so much that they cling to the identity even when they actually have not acted for months, or even years?

The answer is actually quite straightforward. It has to do with a certain discovery that actors make about the relationship they enjoy with their fellow human beings when they encounter them in a way that is both distanced and immediate: distanced for mutual safety and immediate for sharing. Actors find the social belonging they crave in a game – a very serious game – that they and the audience undertake to play together. In accepting the role, the audience receives the life offered it *in role*: an imaginary personage, but a living person.

The quality of this relationship, intermittent though it is (and dependent on being in a play and having an audience) goes a long way towards atoning for the alienation undergone by a 'rogue and vagabond', a phrase frequently used by actors to express the way they experience their role vis-à-vis society. In theatre, the overcoming of the psychological inhibition of intimacy through imaginative catharsis (Grainger and Duggan, 1997) and the removal of barriers erected by social categorisation, actors and audiences, 'insiders' and 'outsiders' provides a blessed release of interpersonal tensions. For actors in particular it is a licence to belong.

Looked at like this, acting possesses a paradoxical logic that depends on accepting that human psychological defensiveness masks a longing for personal encounters, and imaginary 'worlds' mediate human truth about reality. I asked actors to tell me how they themselves saw their job. What does it do for them? What do they really think it does for society as a whole? Or is it simply a form of entertainment? As an actor myself, I had strong views that I wanted to put to the test without disclosing what they were, so I tried not to ask leading questions. In the end I limited myself to a single question: What is real acting? I said that I realised that there are many kinds of acting, but is there a fundamental 'acting experience' that they could focus on? I asked 30 actors and received 25 replies, almost all of which throw light on the social awareness of the person who wrote the letter.

1   Acting itself is a social event. As a personal experience, it depends on the presence of other people. An actor rehearsing by herself imagines other people she is playing to; not merely other characters in the drama being rehearsed, but an invisible audience, one necessarily implied by the action of inhabiting a dramatic role:

> Having an audience is essential. If you haven't got one you have to invent one. This is no effort, because they are really present waiting, as part of the story you're acting. It's much better if they're real people of course, but the people you play to when you're working on the part by yourself are really *paying attention*. From that point of view they're ideal – but the crackle of actual popcorn is better, all the same.

Actors, it seems, never play to themselves; there is always someone else in the audience; and not just one person, however receptive:

> Going on stage is like diving into a swimming bath: there needs to be a reasonable depth of water to buoy you up. Audiences share their presence with the actors – their reality makes the actor more real, so that he or she can share the role being played in a more personal way.

At this point the actor concerned lost his nerve, adding 'Does that make sense?' Well, yes it does; but it gives a one-sided impression of what happens. Actors empower the audience as well as being empowered by them. Just as one audience member may assume the role of a hundred, so a solitary actor is divided up to touch a number of individual lives in the most personal way:

> It seems to me that playing to an audience of say 1000 people I am playing to different characters, different backgrounds, different hopes and dreams – and yet there are moments when all these differences seem to vanish. And you become one with your audience, one with the author, one with your fellow actors and one with yourself.

Another actor took up this theme of theatre as reaching *out* and *across*:

> The stage is a place where the invisible can appear. Theatre is not simply realism. It is something exciting and magical, like the 'Theatre de complicite' – an extension of story-telling which is necessary for human beings, which enriches our souls, changing our perspectives so that we can see into other people's lives.

2   Societies speak the language of relationships, which are personal. Human society has to do this if it is to remain human. It is also true that societies function in ways that individuals and groups find depersonalising and reductive of human freedom. The wider agencies involved in structuring societies can crush and distort the expression of personal feeling, when they do not drive it underground altogether – a fact that Bertolt Brecht devoted his life to exposing in theatrical form. Brecht's 'alienation effect' uses theatre to draw attention to ways of organising life that end up by reducing it through exploiting our emotional vulnerability. ('Provisional structures must be erected, and there is the danger that they may become permanent' – Brecht, 1949).

In theatre we are given an opportunity to stand back and recognise plays as plays, structure as structure, and ourselves as fellow victims of its seductiveness, so that we are released into a more aware way of being human. Theatre audiences, says Iris Murdoch, 'Are alienated so as to produce their own drama by participation' (1992: 6). This seems to be the case with actors as well as audiences. The actors I contacted reveal their devotion to the play as *itself*; as a play, that is, something it is their job to use their skill to 'get across'.

> Acting is about the portrayal of human nature – finding truths within ourselves as actors and so illuminating comparable truths of the characters that we are to play.

> Technique is used to communicate the inner life of a play's characters, so that an actor's skill is to use your imagination to take up

someone else's identity. We develop the ability to share the character with the audience.

You should never add more to a character than the author intended. In a farce, for example, the audience wants you to make people *laugh*; timing of a line, tone of voice, way of moving, are there for the sake of laughter. The 'truth' of farce is human hilarity.

For actors, then, truth tends to mean what Carl Rogers called 'congruence', the absence of their own hidden agendas. Thus Hamlet instructs the Players 'Let not your clowns speak more than is set down' (Act III sc. 2). The actor who uses his or her part as a personal or professional showcase is particularly deplored. A Shakespearian actor urges:

If what you are doing is funny, don't be funny doing it.

At another level, an actor's truth consists in their willingness to put their entire personality at the service of the play:

The best acting has the actor using his own truth – physical, vocal and temperamental; his humanity and human experience; his sensitivity; his humour (if possible!) and his constantly honed craftsmanship – to tell an audience, economically, passionately but humbly, with lucidity and flexibility, what *he* [sic] considers to be the truth of what the author *of this particular script* wanted to tell about *this particular character* in *this particular context.*

3   Theatre presents relationships that enable social awareness to develop.

The quality of shared experience and imagination gives birth to a powerful awareness of the meaning of being human and the significance of being alive, which reaches out beyond the theatre and into the world.

It is impossible to talk about real acting without saying what real theatre is, too. Real theatre is effective within life. You take a special journey to a sacred space – it radically alters your attitude to life, affecting your underlying perspective on things. It develops you spiritually, by bringing your spiritually into contact with life. A play can do this.

The actors with whom I was in contact return again and again to the same underlying idea: to communicate without imposing your own personality or invading someone else's space. To do this requires self-control and devotion to the task of sharing, which itself means not simply giving, but giving and receiving. Theatre and acting are about the interchange of the experience of being human.

> For theatre to take place there should be a real experience of taking part in something *shared*. This doesn't necessarily mean making things easier, more straightforward, because the urge to share means the urge to overcome barriers in the way of sharing. 'Suspending disbelief' doesn't, or shouldn't, come all that easily, or we wouldn't have to stress the fact that it involves an act of *willingness*.

> Actors and audiences do not simply drift off into a world of make-believe, a blessed release from reality. The intention is to use imagination to being home truth.

Several actors make this point about theatrical realism, underlining the hands-on nature of theatre's social role. Actors, they say, play *with* life not *at* it:

> 'Real' is not 'realism', but the reality of human truth. The best acting is still the least; hard to achieve, sometimes too hard to acknowledge: but we've all seen it, infrequently – but its rarity makes us want to see it all the more.

Actors react to what is happening in the world of the shared story, using their own reality to work alongside that of the audience:

> Listen and look, re-act: never, never, strive.

The actor who wrote the above calls the state of mind involved 'being true'. She speaks of actors as 'messengers', and of the way they can let their own egos muscle in between themselves and the audience, thus inhibiting the sense of community on which theatre depends, and in which it lives. She says this from the background of three decades of experience in stage, television and film. After so many years of being immersed in the machinery of show business, she speaks mainly about truthful encounter.

A recurrent theme of these letters is the sense of human solidarity, the basic awareness of belonging to the human race that draws actors into sharing their personhood with the audience. As another actor says:

> Something operates between people to create life – a need for encounter.

Here then is the counterbalance to the notion of the actor's role as a means of avoidance, a way of assuming an alternative self, for this is role used as a means of encounter with other selves – a way out of isolation for all concerned. Here the driving force is not fear of involvement but desire for relationship, with role as intermediary.

One way of saying this is that, as human beings, understanding of life escapes us because we are immersed in what we ourselves are trying to grasp; at the same time, however, when we stand back from it in order to understand it, we distance ourselves from any personal, experiential, reality it can hold for us. In his *Tractatus Logico-Philosophicus* (1922) Wittgenstein posits two ways of construing the world we perceive: on the one hand it involves but escapes us, and on the other we escape it in order to involve it in a limited way, as something we can manage to *describe*. Theatre, however, gives us permission to belong in a world shaped to give it meaning yet fully habitable, immediately recognisable, because of the authenticity of the ideas it embodies and the emotions it arouses in us. It involves us in a wholeness that although artificial (it is bound to be this) is able to convince us. It has always been my own conviction, ever since I have been in theatre myself, that it exists in order to heal wounds inflicted by life:

> Because it combines structure (character, plot and presentation) and freedom (through suspension of extra-dramatic reality), therapeutic drama is experienced as liberating by people oppressed by a restricted sense of themselves as independent persons – as in depression – or by the lack of an integrated self-image, as in schizoid awareness.
>
> (Grainger, 1990)

Nowadays I would go further, and claim that all theatre has this effect, not only that which is self-consciously 'therapeutic'. Plays affect the way we think and feel about one another at the deepest levels of our awareness and in the most ordinary way, when we find ourselves affected by the kind of involvement with another person that Aristotle calls 'catharsis' – the emotionally purging effect of allowing ourselves to be drawn into situations that do not at first sight concern us, only to discover that in fact they do. This is the principal on which theatre functions, and it gives plays the power to unlock feelings that have been kept waiting too long for an opportunity to be released and shared, once the fictional framework has been established.

Obviously we are not dealing with individuals on their own here, but with persons in relation to other persons; with society, in fact:

> Acting is not only psychoformative, but also socioformative. The wound it heals is ruptured human betweenness, the privatisation of relationship which turns us in on ourselves at the expense of our fellows.

When we set out on this journey we do so together. In a memorable phrase, an actor talks of 'stepping off the edge of the world and suddenly finding yourself flying'. The message of theatre is that you do not actually fly alone. All the same, this existential collusion is not obvious. Actors still tend to talk about themselves as if theatre were a kind of talent competition (although very few of the ones who answered did this). Audiences persist in thinking of the event that changed their way of looking at, and feeling about, life as if it were less important than almost anything they normally do in the course of living; after all, it's not as if theatre was real, they say. However, it is on such unreal realities that society depends for its existence.

From the actor's own point of view, acting is intensely real, the most real thing in life. None of the actors with whom I was in touch suggested that what they had devoted their working lives to was a job like any other, simply a way of trying to make a living. On the other hand, nobody actually spoke in terms of 'serving society' or 'benefiting the community'. Their membership is less clear-cut than this, their relationship with the rest of the world more ambiguous. The fact is that in order to belong within society, there is no need to feel that you do; as an actor, your social function is better served by participant observation than by unquestioning acceptance of social norms. Actors are extremely aware of having a particular kind of job, one that requires a special way of looking at life and the world in order to be properly performed. Being an actor needs a special talent for impersonation, but this is by no means all it calls for. Acting is seen here by its own practitioners as a value to be honoured, rather than simply a talent to be nurtured (Grainger, 2006). This is revealed in their willingness to 'trust the medium', surrendering to the life that comes from, and through, the play when it is performed, rather than relying on their own efforts to control or dominate the performance. (As the actor previously quoted put it, 'Never Strive!')

I don't possess it, it's something given to me.

I suppose I'm really in it for the surprises, the times when it works; and there's no way of telling when that may happen.

It always seemed to happen at the same point, about five minutes into the play. Suddenly things came together so we all knew what it was about. We couldn't explain what it was that we suddenly knew, we just knew it (describing 'Krapp's Last Tape, a solo performance').

Sometimes if you stop trying so hard the play takes over, if you find the courage to let it. It's as though you're all playing together in a different world altogether.

> When you think about it, it's something to do with letting the action be itself, not planning it as you do in ordinary reality.

This then may be what actors mean when they talk about the 'special reality' of acting: something real enough to take over from their own efforts and *run the show*, a medium for values that influence and affect life; an imitation that is sincere enough to be seen 'beyond' and not merely 'through', the purpose of which is not to deceive but to illustrate – as Plato uses 'Stories which are deliberately cast as myths, and must not be taken as anything else.' With Plato, Iris Murdoch says, 'The idea of truth plays a crucial role' – as it very obviously does for some of these actors – 'and reality emerges as the object of truthful vision' (1992: 39). In theatre truth is by means of illusion rather than in spite of it.

Theatre then is the unreal reality that brings home to us our common humanity. I had suspected it, and now I have independent evidence. Theatre provides us with a vehicle for the active acknowledgement of our social identity. There are of course other such vehicles; liturgy, for example, gives religious people opportunities to encounter God and one another, and God *in* one another, and this too depends on a dramatic reversal couched in story form, a healing of wounds and a reconciliation of opposites. Wherever person relates to person there is human society, because there can be no social belonging without the meeting of individual experience; these things are obvious.

They are also vague, and only take on any kind of definition when they are acknowledged by independent witnesses and thus become social truth – albeit of an anecdotal and 'unscientific' kind; the kind we associate with works of art that gain their special quality of authenticity through the recognisability of the truth they express rather than through any quantifiable properties they may possess. As a paradigm of human relationship, theatre typifies this approach, as it points beyond itself, away from the contrived world it presents to the truth it represents. As for the actors themselves, we ought perhaps to reconsider the assumption from which we started out. If actors are alienated, or alienate themselves, from society, it is so they will be in a position to communicate a particular intensity of social experience. Does this mean that they function outside an imitation of the truth? If so, why do they, as individuals, lay such emphasis on the integrity of their calling – its truthfulness?

Acknowledgements

I would like to acknowledge the valuable help given to me by the following: Joss Ackland, George Baker, David Beasley, Ann Beach, Ken Campbell, John Clegg, Stephanie Cole, Delia Corrie, Vernon Dobtcheff, Robert Fyffe, Doreen Grainger, Roger Hammond, Ewan Hooper, Glenda Jackson,

Gerald James, Barbara Jefford, Alec McGowan, Stephen Moore, Brian Murphy, Jeffry Wickham, Brian Wilde.

References

Brecht, B. (1994) 'Courage Modell', in P. Thompson and G. Sacks (eds), *The Cambridge Companion to Brecht*, Cambridge: Cambridge University Press. (Original work published 1949)

Grainger, R. (1990) *Drama and Healing*, London: Jessica Kingsley Publishers.

Grainger, R. (2006) *Healing Theatre: How Plays Change Lives*, Victoria, BC: Trafford.

Grainger, R. and Duggan, M. (1997) *Imagination, Identification and Catharsis in Theatre and Therapy*, London: Jessica Kinglsey Publishers.

Murdoch, I. (1992) *Metaphysics as a Guide to Morals*, London: Chatto & Windus.

Wittgenstein, L. (1990) *Tractatus Logico-Philosophicus*, London: Routledge. (Original work published 1922)

Index